What Is Curriculum Theory?
Second Edition

D0067097

This primer for teachers (prospective and practicing) asks readers to question the historical present and their relation to it, and in so doing, to construct their own understandings of what it means to teach, to study, to become "educated" in the present moment.

Curriculum theory is the scholarly effort—inspired by theory in the humanities, arts, and interpretive social sciences—to understand the curriculum, defined here as "complicated conversation." Rather than the formulation of objectives to be evaluated by (especially standardized) tests, curriculum is communication informed by academic knowledge, and it is characterized by educational experience. Pinar recasts school reform as school *deform* in which educational institutions devolve into cram schools preparing for standardized exams, and traces the history of this catastrophe starting in the 1950s.

Changes in the Second Edition:

- Introduces Pinar's formulation of *allegories-of-the-present*—a concept in which subjectivity, history, and society become articulated through the teacher's participation in the complicated conversation that is the curriculum.
- Features a new chapter on Weimar Germany (as an allegory-of-the-present).
- Includes new chapters on the future, and on the promises and risks of technology.

Provocative, compelling, and comprehensive, the Second Edition of *What Is Curriculum Theory?* is indispensable for scholars and students in the fields of curriculum studies, teacher education, educational policy, and the foundations of education.

William F. Pinar is Professor and Canada Research Chair at the University of British Columbia, Vancouver, Canada.

STUDIES IN CURRICULUM THEORY
William F. Pinar, Series Editor

For additional information on titles in the Studies in Curriculum Theory series visit
www.routledge.com/education

What Is Curriculum Theory?

Second Edition

William F. Pinar
University of British Columbia

Routledge
Taylor & Francis Group

NEW YORK AND LONDON

Second edition published 2012
by Routledge
711 Third Avenue, New York, NY 10017

Simultaneously published in the UK
by Routledge
2 Park Square, Milton Park, Abingdon, Oxon OX14 4RN

Routledge is an imprint of the Taylor & Francis Group, an informa business

First edition published by LEA 2004

Library of Congress Cataloging in Publication Data
Pinar, William.
    What is curriculum theory? / William F. Pinar. — 2nd ed.
    p. cm. — (Studies in curriculum theory)
    Includes bibliographical references and index.
    1. Education—Curricula—United States. 2. Education—Political aspects—United States. I. Title.
    LB1570.P552 2011
    375.0001—dc22
                        2011004381

ISBN: 978-0-415-80410-3 (hbk)
ISBN: 978-0-415-80411-0 (pbk)
ISBN: 978-0-203-83603-3 (ebk)

Typeset in Sabon and Gill Sans
by EvS Communication Networx, Inc.

Printed and bound in the United States of America on acid-free paper
by Edwards Brothers, Inc.

SUSTAINABLE FORESTRY INITIATIVE
Certified Fiber Sourcing
www.sfiprogram.org

For Bill and Donna

Contents

Preface

We are entering, I suspect, upon a time of troubles.
—Tony Judt (2010, March 25, 15)

"It is not just the terrorists, the bankers, and the climate that are going to wreak havoc with our sense of security and stability," Judt (2010, March 25, 15) explains; "identities" will become more "mean" and "tight", as the "indigent" and the "uprooted" press against the "ever-rising walls of gated communities from Delhi to Dallas." Many of us, I suspect, share Judt's sense of dread. In a subsequent essay, Judt (2010, April 29, 18) points to the economic provocations of our current insecurity and instability, namely the replacement of the production of goods and services by "financial transactions." Reflecting this fundamental shift in the structure of the U.S. economy is the devastating deterioration of the nation's infrastructure, a sharp decline in intergenerational mobility (and a corresponding increase in intergenerational conflict: Watson 2007, 492 n. 4), and the acceleration in economic inequality. After thirty years of income redistribution from the middle to the upper classes, now the top 1 percent of Americans owns 34 percent of the nation's private net worth, and the top 10 percent controls more than 70 percent (Kristof 2010, A31). Quite aside from its immorality, such inequality makes no economic sense (Reich 2010, A19).

All of this is deeply "corrosive," Judt (2010, April 29, 19) understood, as "it rots societies from within." Since 1970, he reminds, the American dream has changed: no longer is it social democracy but getting rich, and quickly. Across a series of topics, we are now thinking "economistically" (2010, April 29, 19). Succinctly summarizing the decades since the election of Richard Nixon in 1968, he writes: "We have substituted endless commerce for public purpose" (2010, May 13, 21). Nowhere is that substitution more obvious than in American public education, where schools have been converted from educational institutions to businesses, in their latest incarnations as cram schools. "It's a terrible time for American teachers," as one journalist acknowledges, "almost every school district is facing monster budget cuts, and a number of politicians have tried to make them the villain in the story" (Collins 2010, A17). It is likewise a terrible time for America's schoolchildren, pressed not to discover and cultivate their talents or understand the world they inhabit. Schoolchildren enrolled in today's cram schools are pressed to do one thing: produce higher scores on high-stakes standardized exams.

Standardized testing used to be confined to college-entrance examinations like the Scholastic Aptitude Test (SAT). These standardized tests have long claimed they are "objective" assessments of aptitude rather than reflections of actual achievement. It is not obvious how they can claim to be "objective" given that many students take the tests twice. Many students are aided by tutors and coaches, giving them an edge over those who can't afford extra help and those who don't want it. Test preparation, Andrew Hacker (2009, 39) reports, is a *$1 billion* business, led by the Kaplan company, owned by *The Washington Post*, and the Princeton Review (not affiliated with the university). Test preparation makes no effort to enlarge students' vocabulary or improve their understanding of, say, algebra. Test preparation classes focus on the test's formatting, instructing students to decode how multiple-choice questions are posed and teaching them how to guess the answers test-makers want. Are these the "cognitive skills" necessary for America's ascendancy in the 21st century? They were during the Weimar Republic, the parliamentary democracy of Germany between World Wars I and II. From his study of Weimar white-collar office workers, the perceptive Weimar journalist Siegfried Kracauer (1995, 113) concluded: "Having been emptied of all substance, these classes are now no longer subject to anything other than the binding neutrality of contentless thought." Such "contentless thought" is precisely what standardized testing requires.

Several colleges and universities now accept what school reformers refuse to accept: that standardized tests are one and not even the most important indicator of academic achievement. Several colleges and universities have made entrance exams "optional," thereby acknowledging that "standardized tests are incomplete scorecards on how a student will fare in college; *they favor families who can afford test prep*, while minority students tend not to do well" (O'Shaughnessy 2009, 1, emphasis added). Some cite the marketing motives in, not the wisdom of, these institutions' decisions (2009, 1). But cynicism over the self-interest of these admission policy changes sidesteps the issue. Standardized testing reproduces social and economic inequality. It substitutes "contentless thought" for academic knowledge and critical thinking. Stripped of subjectivity and social purpose, standardized testing breeds cynicism, and not only among teachers.

"The last time," Judt (2010, April 29, 17) recalls, that "young people expressed comparable frustration at the emptiness of their lives and the dispiriting purposelessness of their world was in the 1920s." Then Judt backs up, likening our present moment to the decade before the 1920s, specifically to 1914, when, he notes, few predicted the "utter collapse of their world and the economic and political catastrophes that followed" (2010, April 29, 17). I am not predicting the utter collapse of our world, but I do share Judt's dread of the future as a period of "insecurity," insecurity that is simultaneously economic, political, psychological, and geophysical. Such pervasive insecurity breeds distrust, Judt points out, and distrust corrodes the basic bonds that structure social democracies. The very institution that represents "we-the-people"—the government—is ridiculed by a noisy minority who recasts it as the greatest threat to our liberty. "Welcome," Mark Lilla (2010, 53) warns, "to the politics of the libertarian mob."

"A new strain of populism," Lilla (2010, 53) explains, "is metastasizing before our eyes." While it may be new, this populism—it was very much a factor in the 2010 U.S. midterm elections, just past—is, Lilla suggests, continuous with the same libertarian tendencies that have accented American political history for the last half-century. "Anarchistic" like the 1960s, "selfish" like the 1980s, and incorporating both, today's populism is, Lilla (2010, 53) asserts, "estranged, aimless, and juvenile." What is "new" is that contemporary version is personified by the "petulant" who claim to need no help from anyone, especially not from their own representative government. It is alarm over this "threat," Lilla (2010, 53) concludes, that could bring Americans "into the streets." If government is a threat to liberty, why do "we-the-people" encourage its invasive incursions in the nation's schools? Could it be that schools are exactly where "we-the-people" want liberty eliminated?

This primer for teachers—prospective and practicing—asks students to question this present moment and their relation to it. In so doing, I am asking us to reconstruct our understanding of what it means to teach, to study, to become "educated" in the present moment. As part of the one-hundred-year-old scholarly effort to understand the curriculum, curriculum theory can help with such a project. Rather than the formulation of objectives, the implementation of which is to be evaluated by (especially standardized) tests, curriculum is understood in this text as complicated conversation, as communication informed by academic knowledge. Curriculum is characterized by educational experience, not test scores. So understood, school reform is decoded as school *deform* in which educational institutions devolve into cram schools focused on preparing students for standardized exams. I locate the genesis of this catastrophe in the 1950s, when gendered anxieties over the Cold War and racialized anxieties over Supreme-Court mandated school desegregation emphasized public education as "feminized" and as "black," requiring (in white male politicians' minds) regulation, that is, "reform." Soon supplemented with TV images of millions of students protesting racial injustice and the Vietnam War, schools were forced first from being laboratories for democratization to opportunities for social and economic mobility, then to sites wherein the political "excesses" of democracy could be contained and redirected economically. The Kennedy administration's national curriculum reform (undertaken in reaction to the 1957 Sputnik satellite launching and animated by liberal concerns for equality of opportunity) was quickly co-opted by conservatives (beginning with Richard Nixon's election in 1968) in their ongoing efforts to re-establish "law and order" in the service of capital accumulation.

This symbolic status of the school in the American popular imagination—as gendered, racialized, as requiring "reform"—renders it vulnerable to such projective identification, as parents send their offspring from home to schools, extending the privacy of the former into the public character of the latter. Evidently easy in this extension of family life into public life is the splitting off of the disclaimed parent, the one who fails to adequately influence his or her child's formation as a person and specifically as a successful person. It is as if the teacher is to somehow take up the slack. As the split-off, disavowed "bad parent," the fantasized "teacher" becomes vulnerable to scapegoating and demonization. In the First Edition (Pinar 2004), I forefronted the American South, and especially its racial history, to contextualize in general terms the bipartisan demonization of teachers that drives school deform. In this edition, I feature the Weimar Republic to accent the Bush–Obama education era as one of intensifying political polarization and economic destabilization, an era in which no child is to be left behind in a race to nowhere.

Also new in this Second Edition are the chapters on the future, focused on various information technologies. These promise not only democratization and the facilitation of learning, but subjective disintegration as well. I provide reports of research showing just such effects. Also new in this edition is my movement from autobiography to allegory, concepts in which subjectivity, history, and society become personified in the teacher's participation in the complicated conversation that is the curriculum. Etymologically, "allegory" means to "speak publicly in an assembly." Its ancient Greek antecedents forefront its communicative character. *Speech that is at once concrete and abstract, allegory is—like autobiography—a specific narrative that hints at a more general significance.* Moving from autobiography to allegory, I ask teachers to self-consciously incorporate the past into the present, threaded through one's subjectivity. As an ethical, political, always intellectual undertaking, such an understanding of the curriculum, I suggest, enables *educational experience.*

Organization of the Book

In the Introduction I define curriculum theory, contextualizing it historically, starting with the 1950s but emphasizing the present moment. And
what a moment the present is. Unemployment remains painfully, obsti-
nately high, as do the deficits of the federal government. Several states
approach insolvency, as do many municipalities. Political compromise is
decoded as "caving in" and political polarization promises to intensify.
During the November 2010 elections, one candidate denied allegations
that she was a witch while another admitted he doubted the value of
school desegregation (Applebome 2010, A16). That campaign may now
be "history" but the new "populist" presence promises—I am writing
this during December 2010—gridlock in the U.S. Congress. That present, and its history, I confront in chapter 1.

As valuable and timeless are the lessons that African American autobiography teaches us (summarized in the First Edition: 2004, 40–48),
in this largely revised chapter 2 I teach a similar if differently directed
lesson. Still acknowledging the social sources of subjectivity and subjectivity's centrality in social protest (as in African American autobiography), in this Second Edition it is subjectivity's significance to the
complicated conversation that is the school curriculum that commands
my attention. Here I focus on threading one's subjectivity—simultaneously socially structured and historically informed—through academic
knowledge to communicate with others. What we education professors
used to call "subject matter" becomes a double entendre, as the school
subjects serve as the media of formation for the human subject. Indeed,
it is through academic knowledge, I am suggesting, that we find our way
into the world.

The key curriculum question—*what knowledge is of most worth?*—is
animated by ethics, history, and politics. As such, it is an ongoing question, as the immediacy of the historical moment, the particularity of
place, and the singularity of one's own individuality become articulated
through the subject matter—history, poetry, science, technology—one
studies and teaches. Expressing one's subjectivity through academic
knowledge is how one links the lived curriculum with the planned one,
how one demonstrates to students that scholarship can speak to them,
how in fact scholarship can enable them to speak. No empty abstraction
invoked to enforce compliance now for the sake of a time yet to come,
the future is here and now. Finding the future in an era of pervasive presentism and instrumentalism is not obvious, however. In fact, the future
will not be found in front of us at all, but in back of us. Reactivating the
past reconstructs the present so we can find the future. In chapter 2 I
discuss one concept that can enable us to do so: allegory.

In chapters 3 and 4, through short, indeed impressionistic, histories of the Weimar Republic and U.S. Cold War politics, I illustrate allegory as a curricular concept, a concept that connects autobiography with history. Studying the Weimar Republic is fascinating in itself, as the scholarship I summarize in chapter 3 shows. Here, however, interwar Germany functions as a cautionary tale for the United States today. Like Faulkner's rendering of the Battle of Gettysburg, "maybe this time" (quoted in Pinar 2004, 242) things will turn out differently. Maybe this time democracy won't be defeated. "If we are able to see the parallels between what they did and what we are on the verge of doing," Kaja Silverman (2009, 11) suggests, "we will not only prevent a new catastrophe from occurring but also change the 'character' of the past." I wish I shared Silverman's confidence. Whatever our fate, we must act *as if* we can prevent the new catastrophe.

The fissures of the present moment in America aggravate public anxiety, anxiety that is (in part) redirected as school reform. How could that happen? How can one thing—public anxiety—become another: school reform? As Freud's colleague Ernst Simmel ([1918], in Kaes, Jay, and Dimendberg 1995, 8) knew: "Whatever in a person's experience that is too powerful for his conscious mind to grasp and work through, filters down to the unconscious levels of his psyche. There it lies like a mine, waiting to explode the entire psychic structure." While subjective and social processes are not always analogous, here the juxtaposition is appropriately suggestive, as public anxiety over the Cold War, over 1960s racial and gender politics, over youth revolt, did become (in part) refocused as school reform. From the outset, as I show in chapter 4, the motives were multiple, rendering school reform both convoluted and malleable, readily appropriated by those whose political convictions were quite contrary to the liberal Democrats who first undertook it. From redressing military and scientific setbacks (symbolized by Sputnik) to correcting economic errors, school reform has never been about itself. Now its fervor intensifies as political polarization and economic instability threaten the very survival of the nation.

Juxtapositions can be subtle or crude and everywhere in between. If they are too subtle, distinctions fade; if they are too crude, distinctions are all that we can see. I am too close to this material to decide, but I think the allegories I have chosen—the Weimar Republic and the Cold War—are simultaneously subtle and crude. Subtle and crude also characterize the sources of my study, as I draw from both sophisticated scholarship and newspapers. The former enabled me to take "the long view," while the latter kept me focused on the events close at hand, dating the material. I wanted the material to be dated, as I am arguing for the school curriculum to be temporally attuned and subjectively situated.

Such multi-faceted juxtapositioning helps us enact the curriculum as a complicated conversation.

From the past in the present I focus on the future in chapter 5. Focusing on the future risks effacing the past and obscuring the present. I insist on sharp distinctions among past, present, and future in order to contradict the presentism of our time. In the First Edition I focused on those futuristic discourses that extolled the promise of the new information technologies: their democratizing consequences, their evidently unlimited potential in classrooms, their unprecedented facilitation of communication across borders. Today the future doesn't look so bright. Despite their conveniences, computers cannot perform for us or our students the intellectually and psychologically demanding labor of academic study. Nor, clearly, does the Internet ensure democracy: with its increasing commercialization it is not obvious that its consequences will be democratic at all (Chun 2006, 67). Of course, as James Carey (1992, 193) notes, "no matter what form of government we live under in the future, it will be called democracy." By dispersing subjectivity into sensory immediacy, the new information technologies may be destroying that coherence of subjectivity prerequisite to democratic citizenry. In contrast to the *consumer*, the *citizen* is capable of juxtaposing the private and the public, holding these separate, often dissonant domains together in creative tension, sometimes sacrificing the former for the sake of the latter. The infamous "death" of the "subject" (e.g. the individual person)—proclaimed by various "poststructuralist" theories (see, for instance, Cusset 2008, 280)—collapses the public into the private, as distinctions blur between humanity and its technological prostheses. It has already happened once before—in Weimar Germany—as chapter 6 reminds.

In chapter 7 I return to the present, reminding us of the meaning of curriculum as complicated conversation, contrasting the concept with classroom discourse (although it includes that) and contemporary calls for curricular standardization through testing. To educate the public means individually reinvigorating the academic curriculum, not instituting a uniform national curriculum as Diane Ravitch recommends. What is required is the reactivation of subjectivity in teaching, of private passion in public service, teachers confirmed not as facilitators of learning but as individuated communicants in a complicated conversation that is the curriculum informed by academic knowledge, subjectivity, and the historical moment. As welcome as her repudiation of "accountability" is, Ravitch reinscribes the delusion that schools can be the Archimedean lever by means of which history can be corrected and society transformed. Like university professors, public school educators can teach only if they are free to teach according to their professional intellectual judgment. Without such academic freedom, there is no freedom or teaching at all.

In the final chapter I summarize, hoping to find a way to a future we cannot now see before us. This challenge is not the equivalent of activating the Global Positioning System (GPS) in our cars. But we educators can stay focused, despite the nonsense around us, directed by our own ethical convictions, informed as these are by study and academic knowledge. So focused, and according to our professional commitments and personal circumstances, we can teach. It might make a political difference if we agree to work individually together, but that collective project I leave to our representative bodies. I am thinking of the American Association of University Professors (AAUP), the American Federation of Teachers (AFT), and the National Educational Association (NEA), but other professional bodies might well join in an inter-organizational effort to save what is left of public education in America. That means restoring the centrality of *study* (not teaching or learning) in education. It means valuing teachers for what they know, not just what they can "do," especially when such "behavior" reduces to numbers on meaningless exams. As you now appreciate, "what is curriculum theory?" is quite the question.

Acknowledgments

I wish to express my gratitude to my dear friend and colleague Bill Doll. I have known Bill since 1976, first in upstate New York, then in Louisiana, now here. Among the many gifts he has given me, Bill (who turned 80 in January 2011) brought to my attention (over twenty years ago) Richard Rorty's concept of "conversation." I thank you for your unfailing and ongoing generosity and friendship, Bill. I also thank Donna Trueit, Bill's wife and my friend. Among her gifts to me was Michael Oakeshott's book on conversation. Jeff and I are so grateful that we live nearby! This Second Edition is dedicated to you.—WP

List of Abbreviations

DDP *Deutsche Demokratische Partei*; Germany Democratic Party
DNVP *Deutschnationale Volkspartei*; German National People's Party
KPD *Kommunistische Partei Deutschlands*; Communist Party of Germany
MSPD *Mehrheitssozialdemokratische Partei Deutschlands*; Majority Social Democratic Party of Germany
NSDAP *Nationalsozialistische Deutsche Arbeiterpartei*; National Socialist German Workers' Party (Nazi Party)
SPD *Sozialdemokratische Partei Deutschlands*; Social Democratic Party of Germany
USPD Independent Social Democratic Party of Germany

Introduction

Distracted by the pursuit of wealth, we increasingly ask our schools to turn out useful profit-makers rather than thoughtful citizens.
—Martha C. Nussbaum (2010, 141–142)

Because my academic discipline is education, my work as a scholar and theoretician is structured pedagogically. As a classroom teacher, I present what has been written on the subject I am trying to teach, invite your comments and questions, and in the process try to contribute to the conversation. As a teacher, I am not trying to implement "objectives" or be "effective," to make an "impact," something better left to tanks or think tanks. As a teacher, my commitment is to informing students about the subject they are studying—in this instance, curriculum theory—while helping them to understand it. As I can't hear your questions and comments, I will do this by restating the subject in as many different terms as I can, illustrating them. I will, then, teach curriculum theory by enacting it textually. Instead of making an argument "about" curriculum, I participate in—by reconstructing—an ongoing conversation dedicated to understanding curriculum. Rather than devising an "airtight" argument, I deliberately cut "holes" in the curriculum-as-plan (Aoki 2005 [1986/1991], 159) to enable students to breathe, thereby creating space and encouraging voices (Miller 1990, 2005). Sometimes polemical, this primer for prospective and practicing teachers asks students to question the historical present and their relation to it, and in so doing, to reconstruct their own understandings of what it means to be "educated."

What is curriculum theory? Informed by theory in the humanities, arts, and interpretative social sciences, curriculum theory is the scholarly effort to understand the curriculum, conceived here as "complicated conversation." In the service of educating the public, curriculum is characterized by spirited and informed communication. This latter term is usefully defined by James Carey (1992, 23) as "a symbolic process whereby reality is produced, maintained, repaired, and transformed." Through the study of the school subjects, individual human subjects come to form, in society, at particular historical moments, with specific and changing cultural significance. Because the curriculum is that complicated conversation between teachers and students over the past and its meaning for the present as well as what both portend for the future, curriculum theory is focused on *educational experience*. Through the study of academic knowledge we articulate our experience in the world so that we may understand what is at stake in what we read and say in schools and in other educational settings (Sandlin, Schultz, and Burdick 2010). The curriculum is our key conveyance *into* the world.

My curriculum-as-plan anticipates the curriculum-as-lived (Aoki 2005 [1986/1991], 160) by juxtaposing glimpses of the world as academic knowledge that I structure as a screenplay. While hardly scripted, this screenplay (this book) constitutes a complicated conversation concerning *what knowledge is of most worth*, given the course I am offering you. To provide my answer to the question—What Is Curriculum Theory?—I thread my subjective experience through academic knowledge, thereby reconstructing both and inviting you to do the same. Through academic and self-study we reconstruct ourselves and the world we inhabit. It is the screenplay, as Post-World War II Italian poet, novelist, essayist, and filmmaker Pier Paolo Pasolini (2005 [1972], 192) pointed out, that expresses *"a will of the form to become another."* Through self-reflexive academic study subjectivity becomes reconstructed as social democracy. Private passion becomes public service.

In its commitment to the systematic study of educational experience, curriculum theory is necessarily critical of contemporary school reform. Indeed, "educational experience" seems precisely what politicians do not want, as they insist on standardized test scores, the so-called "bottom line." By linking the curriculum to student performance on standardized examinations, politicians have, in effect, taken control of what is to be taught: the curriculum. Examination-driven curricula demote teachers to technicians in service to the state, the same accomplishment the right wing enjoyed in Germany eighty years ago. The cultivation of self-reflexive, interdisciplinary erudition and intellectuality disappears. Rationalized as "accountability," political socialization—the cultural reinscription of authoritarianism—replaces education.

Because both Democrats and Republicans have supported school reform, it can appear that it has been neither "liberal" nor "conservative." I have always insisted (including throughout the First Edition) that since its appropriation by Richard Nixon—in his 1968 call for schools to go "Back to the Basics"—school reform has been "right-wing," but "authoritarian" may prove a more clarifying descriptor, as the concept is detached from (if still often associated with) political ideology. Authoritarianism has "traditionally" been defined as a "tendency to submit to authority," but Marc J. Hetherington and Jonathan D. Weiler (2009, 33) insist the phenomenon is "much more complicated" than that simple definition specifies.

In their largely empirical study, Hetherington and Weiler (2009, 34) report that those who "score high' in authoritarianism demonstrate a "greater need for order" while expressing "less tolerance for confusion or ambiguity." They exhibit a "propensity to rely on established authorities to provide that order" (2009, 34). A series of statistical correlations follow: those scoring high in authoritarianism also tend to believe in "biblical inerrancy" (2009, 35), "negative racial stereotypes" (2009, 38), "traditional parenting practices" as in "spare the rod, spoil the child" (2009, 2), aggressive foreign policy (2009, 84), gender stereotypes, including anti-gay attitudes (2009, 93). "White evangelicals" are more authoritarian than other religious groups, and southerners are more authoritarian than are non-southerners (2009, 60).

"Authoritarianism runs deep among some racial minorities," Hetherington and Weiler (2009, 6) point out, as well as among "lower education and lower income whites," and these are "traditional Democratic constituencies, though, importantly decreasingly so, for lower education whites." Add to these facts an ongoing authoritarian repudiation of the 1960s—with its associations of Cold War dangers, racial integration and civil rights protests, as well as anti-Vietnam War violence, political democratization and cultural revolution—and is it any surprise there was bipartisan support for *No Child Left Behind* and *Race to the Top*? What "liberals" have, in general, failed to realize is that the authoritarianism associated with school "reform" threatens the democratization of American society, as John Dewey appreciated ninety years ago. As will I (especially in chapter 4), Hetherington and Weiler reference Richard Hofstadter's *Anti-Intellectualism in American Life*:

> Dewey's anxiety about adult authority stemmed from his desire to avoid something with which we are still trying with much difficulty to avoid—the inculcation of conformist habits in the child. If there was anything he did *not* want, it was to breed conformist character.
> (Hofstadter 1955, 382; quoted in Hetherington and Weiler 2009, 49)

For Dewey, according to Hofstadter (and as Hetherington and Weiler [2009, 49] point out), what is at stake is nothing less than democracy itself, as democracy becomes an impossibility in the face of mass conformist education characterized by, in Hofstadter's words, an "authoritarian" pedagogy. *Converting public schools into cram schools institutionalizes just such authoritarianism; in doing so, school reform threatens social democracy in America.*

The present historical moment is, then, for public school teachers and for those of us who work with teachers, an ongoing calamity. The school has been deformed into a business, plundered by profiteers; the education professoriate is discredited as they are directed to "align" teacher education to politicians' agendas. As the great curriculum theorist Dwayne E. Huebner (1999, 231) recognized more than thirty years ago, many educators are lost, submerged in present circumstances, unable to imagine the future. This submergence in the present is not unique to educators; the legendary historian and public intellectual Christopher Lasch observed that Americans generally have become "presentistic," so self-involved in surviving the present that, for us: "To live for the moment is the prevailing passion—to live for yourself, not for our predecessors or posterity" (Lasch 1978, 5).

While Lasch's (1978) portrait of what he termed "the culture of narcissism" seems sometimes overdrawn (as was his caricature of progressive education in that book, as I note in chapter 8), it is, in my judgment, largely accurate. "The intense subjectivity of modern work, exemplified even more clearly in the office than in the factory," Lasch (1978, 102) observed, "causes men and women to doubt the reality of the external world and to imprison themselves ... in a shell of protective irony." Exhausted by an unrelenting daily psychological intensity and an acute, even physical, sense of threat, many retreat from a public sphere that no longer seems safe, let alone supportive or worthy of their emotional investment. But in the apparent safety of private life, many discover no solace there either. "On the contrary," Lasch (1978, 27) notes, "private life takes on the very qualities of the anarchic social order from which it supposed to provide a refuge."

With no place left to hide, many retreat into—and, Lasch argues, become lost in—themselves. The psychoanalytic term for this personality disturbance is *narcissism*, not to be confused with being egotistical or selfish (see Lasch 1984, 18). Recoiling from meaningful engagement in the world, the privatized self atrophies—Lasch (1984) uses the term *minimal* to denote that contraction of the self narcissism necessitates—and becomes unable to distinguish between self and other, let alone participate meaningfully in the public sphere. The past and future disappear in an individualistic obsession with psychic survival in the present. As Lasch (1978, xvi) suggests: "The narcissist has no interest in the future because, in part, he has so little interest in the past."

Because the public sphere—in teachers' case, the classroom—has become so toxic for so many, not a few have retreated into the (apparent) safety of their own subjectivities. But in so doing, teachers abdicate their professional authority and ethical responsibility for the curriculum they teach. Teachers have been *forced* to abdicate this authority by the bureaucratic protocols that presumably hold them "accountable," but which, in fact, render them unable to teach. (Instead, teachers are supposed to "manage learning.") As a field, curriculum studies—in the past too often a support system for the school bureaucracy—was complicit with this presentistic capitulation to the "reform" *du jour*. As the distinguished curriculum historian Herbert Kliebard (1970) made clear, the ahistorical and atheoretical character of curriculum studies disables teachers from understanding the history of their present circumstances.

My work in curriculum theory has emphasized the significance of subjectivity to education. That significance is not as a solipsistic retreat from the public sphere. As Lasch (1978, 9) points out, subjectivity can be no refuge in an era when "[t]he possibility of genuine privacy recedes." The significance of subjectivity is that it is inseparable from the social; it is only when we—together and in solitude—reconstruct the relation between the two that we can begin to restore our "shattered faith in the regeneration of life" (Lasch 1978, 207) and cultivate the "moral discipline ... indispensable to the task of building a new order" (Lasch 1978, 235–236). Our curricular challenge is simultaneously subjective and social.

"Confronted with an apparently implacable and unmanageable environment," Lasch (1984, 58) suggests, "people have turned to self-management ... a technology of the self." The method of *currere*—the infinitive form of curriculum—is no such technology. A sketch of subjectivity-structured temporality (reactivating the past, contemplating the future, in so doing complicating the present), this method is no defensive effort at psychic survival, but one of subjective and social risk, the achievement of selfhood and society in an age yet to come. To undertake this project of social and subjective reconstruction, we must remember the past and imagine the future, however unpleasant each domain may prove to be. Not only intellectually but in our character structure, we must become "temporal," living simultaneously in the past, present, and future. In the method I have devised, returning to the past (the "regressive") and imagining the future (the "progressive") must be understood (the "analytic") for the self to become "expanded" (in contrast to being made "minimal" in Lasch's schema) and complicated, then, finally, mobilized (in the "synthetical" moment). Informed by academic study, such a temporally differentiated sequence of ourselves as individuals might enable us to understand the problem that is the present.

The first step is to acknowledge the ongoing calamity that is school deform. School deform—in which educators have no formal control over the curriculum, the very organizational and intellectual center of schooling—has several markers, prominent among them "accountability," an apparently commonsensical idea that makes teachers, rather than students, responsible for students' educational accomplishment. But the simple timeless fact is that education is an opportunity offered;

no one—not parents, not teachers—can guarantee that students will take advantage of it. *Of course* teachers must make, in every way on every day, every ethical effort to ensure students do act on the opportunities offered them in schools, but, as parents know, even authoritarian coercion does not ensure that children will realize what is at stake in the decisions they make. This is an inconvenient truth politicians refuse to acknowledge.

In part I, I review the historical markers of this absurd situation, focusing, in chapter 1, on the early 20th-century remaking of the school as a business, a scheme in which teachers first became factory workers, children the raw material, and the curriculum the assembly line producing saleable products. During the last decades of the 20th century teachers were "promoted" from the assembly line to the corporate office where they were to serve as "managers of student learning." "Never have corporate values reigned in the United States so supremely as they do today," Daniel Noah Moses (1999, 89) rightly observed, "when an overarching corporate metaphor has invaded all aspects of American society, including academia." In the new century teachers have been demoted, now domestic, not public, servants, hired to force kids to cram for standardized exams. Demonized, teachers have no rights, only obligations.

In chapter 2, I review the method of *currere*, a method focused on self-understanding through academic study. Our profession is profoundly, proudly, necessarily subjective. What becomes clarified is that our subjective engagement with what we study converts to the conversational forms through which education occurs. By banishing subjectivity, by scripting curriculum and linking students' study to standardized test scores, politicians end the complicated conversation that is the curriculum, replacing it with political socialization for political submissiveness. To teach autobiographically, I suggest, is not to introduce personal matters into classroom discussion, although these can on occasion be appropriate. To teach autobiographically in this Weimar time is to thread one's subjectivity through subject matter, converting private passion into public service attuned to the historical moment. Such autobiographical labor takes allegorical forms, knowledge that is simultaneously specific and general.

At the intersection of subjectivity and history, allegory requires the symbolization of subjective experience. Allegory contradicts the collapse of symbolization that (as we see in chapter 5) cyberspace encourages, as online speech becomes condensed, rendered staccato in an immediacy that spreads like an oil slick. Allegory opts out. It starts in solitude, itself not an obvious move to make, as the crowd comes with you. Only after that room of one's own becomes quiet enough to hear oneself think, then one can initiate conversation, first with oneself, then with others, others who are also occupants of rooms of their own. In complicated conversation we discover that we are subjectively structured like allegory itself, simultaneously literal and symbolic creatures, utterly and uniquely ourselves and a member of the species, informed by those who have preceded us, those in our midst now, and those yet to come. How might one structure this temporally structured study in curricular form? In the first edition, written in rushed fashion during the U.S. presidential campaign of 2004, the American South served as my allegory-of-the-present. In chapter 3, I offer a different, again timely allegory: Weimar Germany. The differences between "then-and-there" and "here-and-now" are multiple and sharp, but the echoes are sometimes loud, even unnerving.

While studying Weimar Germany allegorizes the present historical moment in general terms—political polarization, economic destabilization, scapegoating, and demonization—studying the United States of the 1950s and 1960s sets the stage for the present movement in particular terms, e.g. schools as symbolic sites. To help us understand this fact, I invoke the psychoanalytic notion of "deferred action" (*Nachträaglichkeit*), a term Freud employed to explain how the experience of trauma gets deferred—and, I would add, displaced—into other subjective and social spheres, where it is often no longer readily recognizable. In chapter 4, I argue that the "trauma" that was the Cold War in the 1950s and the 1954 Supreme Court decision to desegregate the public schools—coupled with the visibility of students in 1960s civil rights and anti-Vietnam protests—was "displaced and deferred" onto public schools. In the aftermath of these events, public education became racialized and gendered in the American popular imagination, in need of containment and correction. (You will see, in chapter 3, efforts at "correctional education" during Weimar.) We can understand the authoritarianism of school deform only if we understand that the school is the displaced and deferred site of misogyny and racism. School is the place where the "excesses" of democracy are contained, this through controlling the curriculum by installing test preparation as its only *raison d'être*.

In acknowledging that racism and misogyny have been "deferred and displaced" into public education, I am not suggesting that they have been *absorbed* there. Despite the 2008 election of an African American President, racism and misogyny remain pervasive in the United States today, evident in the peculiar intensity of the defamation of the President's character. White racism in America remains corrosive and endemic, especially (but hardly only) in the South, still the political epicenter of U.S. presidential politics (Black and Black 1992). Nor am I arguing that the subjugation of public school teachers is *only* racialized and gendered. It is classed as well. In contrast to elite professions such as medicine and law, public school teaching has long been associated with the lower middle class, and not only in salary. Public school teaching has historically required a shorter and less rigorous credentialing period. Moreover, many teachers have been—in the popular imagination if not always in fact—the first members of their families to complete higher education. (One hundred years ago, public school teaching rarely required a college degree.) The political problems of public education are, in part, class-based, but they are straightforwardly so. There is little that is deferred and displaced about the class-based character of the political subjugation of the teaching profession.

Certainly teachers' present political subjugation—its peculiar intensity and irrationality—cannot be grasped by class analysis alone. While class conflict in the United States has produced strong political reaction, it has not tended to produce the vicious contempt teachers and *their* teachers—the education professoriate—have encountered. To grasp this "overdetermined" reaction, one must invoke models of racial prejudice and misogyny, wherein complex and convoluted psychological structures and processes intensify emotion well beyond rhyme or reason. We must move to the sphere of psychopathology to grasp the history of U.S. school deform.

We glimpse this phenomenon of deferral and displacement in chapter 4 where, relying on the scholarship of Robert L. Griswold, we study the gendered character of the Kennedy administration's educational response to the Cold War, specifically its embrace of physical fitness in 1960 and 1961. This was the same period during which the national curriculum reform movement was launched. The national curriculum reform movement was dedicated to aligning the secondary school subjects with the academic disciplines as they existed at the university and, in so doing, establishing academic "rigor" in the schools. To accomplish this curricular alignment, the control of curriculum had to be taken from teachers. The continuing legacies of Cold War curriculum politics structure the absurd situation in which teachers find themselves today. Starting then, teachers began to lose all control over the curriculum, including the means by which students' study of it is assessed.

While 1960s curriculum reform was gendered, it was profoundly racialized as well. It was 1954 when the Supreme Court ruled that public schools must be desegregated, but in the South this did not occur until the late 1960s and early 1970s, under the presidential administration of Richard Nixon. (Desegregation has never occurred in the North, as primarily white suburban school districts continued to ring primarily black urban ones.) As schools became racial battlegrounds and the pretext for white flight, and as college students fought to desegregate other public spaces (perhaps most famously lunch counters and public transportation), racial anxiety only intensified among many whites, an anxiety right-wing Republican presidential candidate Barry Goldwater exploited in his 1964 campaign against Democratic President Lyndon B. Johnson. It is the same white racism Alabama Governor George Wallace tried to exploit in his 1968 and 1972 presidential campaigns. While this pervasive and intensifying white anxiety—not limited to but especially intense in the South—was focused upon the public schools, it echoed through the culture at large, as broader issues of racial justice and, indeed, of the American identity itself (was this still, or even primarily, a European nation?) were stimulated by the desegregation of the nation's schools. Public education—in the North especially in the urban centers, in the South everywhere—became racialized.

No doubt contributing to the racialization of public education in the American popular imagination was the very visible and aggressive roles played by (especially university) students in the civil rights movements of the late 1950s and the 1960s. To illustrate students' participation in the civil rights movement, we glimpse the civil rights activism of the Student Nonviolent Coordinating Committee (SNCC), including the Committee's establishment of "freedom schools." These schools and the student activism they reflected and expressed were located in the Deep South, the epicenter of the segregated nation's racial crisis.

From this regressive moment—reactivating the past in the present—I move to the progressive moment, in which we focus on futuristic conceptions of education as primarily technological. In this future screens—especially, computer screens—are everywhere, prosthetic extensions of our bodies, dispersing our subjectivities outward, far from our concrete everyday communities into abstract cyberspace and a "global village." In this prosthetic extension of the everyday ego we took ourselves to be, the self seems to evaporate. Subjectivity itself mutates, and the "self" autobiography purports to identify and express distends into hypertextual personae, ever-changing cyborg identities (Bryson 2004). In today's politics of public miseducation, the computer becomes the latest technological fantasy of educational "utopia," a futuristic fantasy of "teacher-proof" curriculum.

After considering the future in the present during the progressive moment, we turn to the analytic moment. There we face the facts, namely the profoundly anti-intellectual conditions of our professional labor. These are conditions both internal and external to the schools. Due to the anti-intellectualism of American culture generally, and due to the deferral and displacement of racism and misogyny onto public education more specifically, the school curriculum can only be eviscerated intellectually. We cannot defy this destruction of public education until we face as well its internalized consequences, prominent among them a pervasive and crippling—very much internalized—anti-intellectualism. Accompanying frank and ongoing self-criticism must be the reinvigoration of our commitment to engage in "complicated conversation" with our academic subjects, our students, and ourselves. Such complicated conversation requires the academic—intellectual—freedom to devise the courses we teach, the means by which we teach them, and the means by which we assess students' study of them. We must fight for that freedom as individual teachers in specific classrooms and as a profession through our representative bodies: the AAUP, the AFT, and the NEA.

After these moments of reflection and self-understanding that the analytic phase provides, in the synthetic moment (chapter 8), we reconstruct ourselves, both as individuals and as a profession. After the "evaporation" of the ego that regression to the past and contemplation of the future invites, we return to the present, mobilizing ourselves—as individuals, as a profession—for public service, educating the public. Public education structures self-formation and social reconstruction while, in it its present deformation, its destruction blocks both.

The democratic project of educating the public is the service of an "ethically and politically self-conscious understanding of society" (LaCapra 2004, 196). At first broadly vocationalized, now justified only economistically (disguised by the veneer of social concern), the education of the public has devolved into "business." As James Carey (1992, 105) has rued: "Economic man became the whole man, the only man." In our time publicly funded education is being sold to businesses in the name of privatization, rationalized in the names of competitiveness, efficiency, accountability. "The logics of the marketplace offer our salvation," Peter Taubman (2009, 58) points out, and "so does accounting. The analogy between investing in education and seeing dividends and investing in the market and making or losing money reduces education to cash." No longer does academic study provide the opportunity to understand what is at stake in being alive, at this moment, in this country, on an endangered planet.

Teachers can express intransigence to this fascist regime by expressing loyalty to the profession, by refusing to teach to the test, by insisting that students engage with ideas and facts critically and with passion through solitary study and classroom deliberation. "Simply stated," Frank H. T. Rhodes (2001, B8) understands, "faculty members must recapture the curriculum." Without reclaiming academic—intellectual—freedom teachers cannot teach. They may "instruct" or "facilitate" but they cannot teach. Without intellectual freedom, education ends; students are indoctrinated, forced to learn what the profiteers (e.g. test-makers) declare to be important. In Texas, political indoctrination occurs openly, self-righteously (see Brick 2010, A17). Everywhere else it occurs covertly through standardized tests, which eliminate all academic content irrelevant to them. Having left no child behind, we are now paying them (Hernandez 2008, September 25, 1) to run in a race to nowhere. That last phrase is also the title of a film directed by Vicki Abeles in honor of her teenaged daughter who suffered stress-induced illness thanks to school deform (Cox 2010, A2).

To the extent our circumstances and preferences permit, we can refuse to participate in the sadistic stupidity that is school deform. Intransigent, we teachers can quietly continue to teach, intellectually engaging our students in academically informed conversation concerning the key concepts and concerns of past and present. Engaging in such complicated conversation constitutes a curriculum in which academic knowledge, subjectivity, and society become reciprocally reconstructed. It is such reconstruction, such educational experience, that is the promise of education for our private-and-public lives as Americans. It is to this promise curriculum theory testifies. If we persist in our cause—the very cause of democracy, dependent as democracy is upon educating the public— someday the nation's educational institutions will no longer be cram schools, no longer academic businesses plundered by profiteers, but sites of public education, opportunities for individual creativity, erudition, and interdisciplinary intellectuality. Someday—if we remember the past, contemplate the future, analyze, then mobilize in, the present—we can teach with the dignity and respect the profession deserves. For you, let this someday be today.

Part I

The Problem That Is the Present

Chapter 1

School Deform

1 The Race to Nowhere

> All too often, however, in the history of the United States, the schoolteacher has been in no position to serve as a model for an introduction to the intellectual life.
>
> —Richard Hofstadter (1962, 310)

While a consequence of the American preoccupations with business and religion (as Richard Hofstadter [1962] has documented), the closure of complicated conversation in the current regime of power can also be traced to American pragmatism as well. John Dewey's pragmatist predecessor—William James—was, David Simpson (2002, 98) reminds us, "consequence oriented," concerned with the "practical cash value" of experience. The significance of experience—of thought, action, and event—becomes its effect on a particular situation. As Simpson (2002, 98–99) notes, James' "faith in instrumentalism" provided a "green light" for applied social science with its emphasis upon measuring outcomes quantitatively.

From the inception of the nation, Americans have been obsessed with "the practical cash value" not only of experience, but of practically everything. While situated in early-20th-century Europe, the statement of Robert Musil's character Ulrich (to Agathe) in the novel *A Man Without Qualities* speaks to those cultural and historical conditions in America in which the common school became first a factory, then a corporation, now a cram school, but always a business:

> Our age drips with practical energy anyway. It's stopped caring for ideas, it only wants action. This frightful energy springs solely from the fact that people have nothing to do. Inwardly, I mean. ... It's so easy to have the energy to act and so difficult to find a meaning for action! There are very few people who understand that nowadays. That's why the men of action look like men playing ninepins,

knocking down those nine lumps of wood with the gestures of a Napoleon. It wouldn't even surprise me if they ended up by assaulting one another, frantic at the towering incomprehensibility of the fact that all their actions will not suffice.

(Musil 1995 [1979], 87)

Economic avarice, political posturing, and the worldwide threat of terrorism marks our era as entirely continuous with Musil's. While hardly confined to the cram school, the subjectively emptied-out authoritarian demand for "action" is chillingly conspicuous today.

Such "action" accents contemporary school deform, the $4.3 billion dollar *Race to the Top*. The appointment of the Secretary of Education—a friend of Barack Obama's brother-in-law—evidently derived from "action," specifically from playing pickup basketball in Chicago, where Michelle Obama's brother Craig Robinson played pickup with Arne Duncan. Robinson introduced Duncan—the former superintendent of the Chicago public schools—to the Obamas (Zeleny 2009). Duncan became a family friend, and now heads up the agency determined to destroy public education in America.

To design and manage the assault on public schools Duncan chose Joanne S. Weiss, a partner and chief operating officer of the NewSchools Venture Fund. Weiss is an "education entrepreneur," Diane Ravitch (2010, 218) points out; Weiss had previously led several education businesses that sold products and services to schools and colleges. The administration dangled $4.3 billion before financially struggling states, threatening to exclude any that limited the number of charter schools (2010, 218). *Race to the Top* also provided funds, Ravitch (2010, 183) notes, for states to build data systems that would link student test scores to individual teachers, rationalizing merit pay schemes linking teacher salaries to increased students' test scores.

That ought to get some action, right? "We're getting more changes in 18 months in education than in the previous decade," boasted Duncan (quoted in Gabriel 2010, September 2, A18). He exclaimed: "I'm ecstatic. This has been the third rail of education, and the fact that you're now seeing half the nation decide that it's the right thing to do is a game-changer" (quoted in Lewin, 2010, July 21, A3). The crude mixed metaphor discloses a sports mentality supplemented with self-righteous satisfaction. Does the Obama administration's conversion of education from self-formation through academic study and the democratization of civic life to a "race" reflect, finally, an enthusiasm for sports? If so, this would not be the first time. As you will see, just such a conflation between thought and action, mind and body, occurred during the Kennedy administration and the first wave of school reform (see chapter 4, section V).

As the "race" metaphor implies, someone playing the game must lose. Jonathan Zimmerman (2010, 29) points out that under *No Child Left Behind*—which *Race to the Top* intensifies—it has been primarily poor students who have been victimized by the government's insistence on standardized tests as the only measure of educational achievement. Threatened with closure under both the Bush and Obama administrations, schools "tailor their curriculums as precisely as possible to the tests, even providing minute-by-minute scripts for the teachers" (Zimmerman 2010, 29). Despite widespread protests of this practice—including a partial fast by legendary school critic Jonathan Kozol in 2007 to protest against the "vicious damage being done to inner city children" by NCLB (quoted in Zimmerman 2010, 30)—school deform zealots continue their authoritarian insistence on stripping intellectual content from the curriculum, replacing ideas and knowledge with "cognitive skills," vacuous context-free puzzles that presumably transfer to any (job) setting. Rather than studying, say, climate change or the history of the civil rights struggle, students in the second grade should be able to "read two-syllable words with long vowels," while fifth-graders should be able to "add and subtract fractions with different denominators" (Lewin, 2010, A3). Such "skills" instantiate historical amnesia, political passivity, and cultural standardization.

The continuity between *No Child Left Behind* and *Race to the Top* discourages those who expected sharper ideological differences between the Bush and Obama administrations. In certain areas—financial regulation, health care reform, consumer protection—there are significant differences. In military matters there is less difference—the phased withdrawal of U.S. troops from Iraq and Afghanistan proceeds slowly—and in educational matters not at all. Such continuity in educational policy has been the case for decades. Diane Ravitch (2010, 16) asserts a sharp distinction between the Reagan years and the George W. Bush years, but the ideological continuity is more striking than the shifting rhetoric (so-called "standards" to "accountability"). As a symbol conveying concerns for the future of the nation, education has been appropriated by authoritarian forces (as noted earlier, both Democrats and Republicans, European and African Americans) determined to stoke the economic engine, instill order in society and discipline in young people by emphasizing "cognitive skills." This decades-long assault on the public schools accelerated during the 1980s when the Reagan administration shifted the nation's political agenda from "social equality" to "economic growth" (Lilla 2010, 54). Democrats too embraced school deform. Ravitch (2010, November 11, 24) notes that attacks on public schools are now the "received wisdom" among "liberal elites," but, as Representative John Kline, Republican of Minnesota, the ranking minority member of the House Labor and Education Committee, admitted, *Race to the Top* "came straight from the traditional Republican playbook" (Gabriel 2010, September 2, A18).

Key to this bipartisan determination to destroy public education in America is the demonization of teachers. Demonization is an old and drearily familiar game. During Weimar Germany, it was Jews who were targeted. While gentle at first—the Kennedy administration simply side-stepped teachers and education professors in 1960s school reform—school deform took demonization more and more seriously as zealots decried "failing schools" and "incompetent teachers." During the Bush administration education professors were added to the list of targets. Both groups of professionals have been silenced in public discussions of the destruction of U.S. public schools. As during the Bush administration's embrace of the Weapons of Mass Destruction (WMD) deception for invading Iraq, many "analysts" simply parrot politicians' crude demonization strategies. They do so even in respected magazines like *Harper's*. "For decades," Amanda Ripley (2010, 64) "reports" (without data), "education researchers blamed kids and their home life for their failure to learn." Reference please? And when did the location of responsibility become *blame*? As Harry Frankfurt (2005, 1) bemoans: "One of the most salient features of our culture is that there is so much bullshit."

Of course students are not to *blame* for failing to learn. On the other hand, do students bear *no* responsibility when they fail to learn? When smokers ignore public health campaigns who is responsible for their "failure to learn"? Is it medical researchers? When born-again Christians sin again who is responsible for their "failure to learn"? No more bullshit: schools do not fail. Like physicians and other professionals, teachers can and do make mistakes. But the inconvenient truth is that it is *students who fail*. Why must one point out such an obvious fact that *everyone* knows? The truth has always been, is now, and shall forever be, that there are students who decline to study. The sad truth is that there are students who are undermined by their families, by their circumstances, by their friends, by themselves. Genetics are always in play, even if educators must act as if they can never be. The truth is that disconnecting the curriculum from students' interests and teachers' intellectual passions ensures the "failure to learn." And it only intensifies the pressure on kids. The "successful" ones learn to reduce learning to test scores; they stop being "students" and become "consumers" of educational "services," pressuring teachers to give them grades they have not earned. Linking learning to test scores encourages drop-outs who can't take the pressure or simply can't be bothered. It encourages schools to expel students whose test scores threaten school "failure" and those bonuses increased scores sometimes bring with them (Ravitch 2010, November 11, 23).

Schools and everyone in them have only become more pressured since Reagan's phony Commission announced that schools had placed

A Nation at Risk. Reading Ripley's misrepresentation of the facts, one would think that—in addition to the conspiracy of education researchers—teachers are to blame for students' failure. Ripley glides by poverty—it "matters enormously" (2010, 64) she concedes—but she does not linger there. It is teachers—not parents, not peers, not themselves—who are "moving poor kids forward" (2010, 64), another simple-minded phrase, as if learning were linear, understanding a straightforward sequence of steps. Of course she means increased test scores, not knowledge of, say, enslavement, segregation, or union-busting. Never mind history or culture, never mind the facts, as Ripley (2010, 63) focuses on "implementation" of this anti-intellectual testing regime, acknowledging that it won't be easy, that it will require realignment of "teacher training, textbooks and testing." Never mind intellectual freedom either.

In our time, totalitarianism still comes with goose-stepping soldiers (as in North Korea) but it is performed in the United States by promoting prejudice and platitudes as "news," as common sense, even in respected magazines. "Great teachers," Ripley (2010, 62) informs us, set "big goals" for their students and, she adds, they constantly check on how they're doing. This basic instructional strategy in stunning in its stupidity: "I do, we do, you do" (quoted in Ripley 2010, 63). What Ripley is describing is autocracy, not pedagogy, a military drill not intellectual engagement. "Knowledge matters," Ripley (2010, 65) reports, "but not in every case." I suppose she means knowledge about education, as she is quick to point out that a master's degree in education is unrelated to "classroom effectiveness," by which she means tests scores, not erudition or intellectual engagement. One wonders what the research shows on the relation between MDivs (masters of divinity degrees, conferred by theology schools) and the moral improvement of parishioners? What does the research tell us about the relation between MBA degrees and economic growth? Most economists and financial advisors did not foresee the 2008 financial crisis coming (certainly my broker didn't), despite economists' insistence that economics is a scientific discipline, capable, by definition, of prediction. Does Ripley report *that* fact? Does Ripley report on the relation between medical school courses and those tens of thousands of deaths caused by medical mistakes each year (Grady 2010, A1)? "Knowledge matters, but not in every case."

Knowledge of the arts and humanities is evidently one of those "cases." Soon after taking office President Obama undertook a campaign to encourage corporations and nonprofit groups to spend money and time in volunteering their efforts to encourage students, especially in middle and high school, to pursue science, technology, engineering, and math (Chang 2009, 1). Never mind that at current rates 650,000 new engineers will have received degrees by 2016, four times the predicted number of openings (Hacker 2009, 38). Never mind that 25 percent of students, according to the U.S. Department of Education, fail to finish high school. For those who do finish their university degrees, many choose fields other than those the President deems key, as the number of degrees conferred in engineering and the physical sciences is actually declining (Hacker 2009, 38). There is nothing new here. During the Weimar Republic, one contributor to *Deutsche Technik* reminded: "In this ruthless world, a nation of poets is defeated, a nation of philosophers hungers, a nation of aesthetes is subject to ridicule. Only a people able to produce arms, weapons, commodities, machines and knowledge is able to survive" (quoted in Herf 1984, 208).

It is, evidently, a "ruthless world" in which the Obama administration operates, as it muscles its anti-intellectual agenda through "state laws … barring the use of student achievement data to evaluate teacher performance" (Dillon 2009, August 17, 1). Both national teachers' unions oppose the use of student testing data to evaluate individual teachers, Dillon (2009, August 17, 1) reports, pointing out that students are often taught by several teachers, making the ascription of test scores to any one teacher problematic to say the least. Teacher unions recommend that teacher evaluations be based on "several measures of performance, not just test scores" (2009, August 17, 1). Student performance is obviously independent of the teacher. Are Yale faculty to be held accountable for George W. Bush? Did Harvard faculty "fail" because Bill Gates did not finish his degree? Teachers offer opportunities; it is students' responsibility to take advantage of them.

Never mind the facts. Arne Duncan has delivered speeches to both teachers' unions, urging them to rethink their positions, especially at a time when "thousands of schools are chronically failing" (Dillon 2009, August 17, 2). Are courts "failing" because the convicted break the law again? Is the government funding studies that link individual physicians with patients, lawyers with clients, economists with investors and pensioners, preachers with the performance of the faithful? Never mind the facts; Duncan is undeterred. "Believe it or not," he (quoted in Dillon 2009, August 17, 2) lamented, "several states, including New York, Wisconsin and California, have laws that create a firewall between students and teacher data. I think that's simply ridiculous." What is "ridiculous" is a secretary of education who demands of teachers what no one demands of physicians, lawyers, economists, or preachers.

II The Less You Know

> Knowledge is no guarantee of good behavior, but ignorance is a virtual guarantee of bad behavior.
>
> —Martha C. Nussbaum (2010, 81)

The former Chancellor of the Washington, D.C. public schools, Michelle Rhee, has been lionized by school deform zealots. Characterizing her as "brash" and "young," a "national symbol of a get-tough management style," former school reformer Diane Ravitch (2010, 172) is less enthusiastic. Ravitch points out that Rhee was committed to making the Washington, D.C. schools the "test case for the theory that schools should operate like the private sector" (2010, 171). Hired by Mayor Adrian Fenty in 2007, Rhee was sure, Ravitch (2010, 171) reminds, that "effective" teachers could "overcome poverty" and any other "disadvantages." For Rhee, "teachers are everything" (quoted in Ravitch 2010, 171). That statement places teachers on a pedestal, but it is clear that Rhee is looking down at—not up to—teachers.

Driven by a "missionary zeal," Rhee proceeded from her "conviction" that students were being "shortchanged" (Dillon 2010, October 14, A19). Teachers, she has slandered, go into teaching for the summer vacations and the health insurance. Rhee opposed tenure because, she alleged, it "hurts children" by making "incompetent instructors" difficult to fire (Dillon 2008, November 13, 1). Oblivious to the centrality of intellectual freedom to teaching, Rhee misconstrues tenure as a self-interested union benefit. "Tenure is the holy grail of teacher unions," Rhee asserts, "but [it] has no educational value for kids; it only benefits adults. If we can put veteran teachers who have tenure in a position where they don't have it, that would help us to radically increase our teacher quality" (quoted in Dillon 2008, November 13, 1). The teachers' union's response also failed to acknowledge tenure's pivotal role in protecting the curriculum. (To his credit, the reporter referenced tenure's historic significance: see Dillon 2008, November 13, 3.)

Rather than confront Rhee's ignorance, the union tried to spread the blame. "Fire all incompetent teachers—that makes a good sound bite," replied George Parker, the president of the Washington D.C. Teachers Union. "But remember that not only teachers are to blame for the problems in this district" (Dillon 2008, November 13, 2). Rather than asserting the centrality of academic—intellectual—freedom to education and tenure's indispensable role in protecting that freedom, Parker cited instead a "chaotic administration" that has failed to attend to problems like truancy and student discipline (Dillon 2008, November 13, 2). Note that Parker appears to accept the assumption that schools are "failing" and that teachers *are* responsible; he is merely extending the noose to others' necks. He even repeats without ridicule the slanderous allegation that teachers are incompetent.

In this dominatrix scenario there is both pleasure and pain. Rhee dangled before teachers a two-tiered salary plan that would pay teachers up to $130,000 a year in salary and bonuses if only they would give up their tenure rights, a totalitarian temptation teachers courageously declined (Dillon 2010, April 7). When seduction fails, there is always domination. In July 2010 Rhee fired 241 teachers, some 5 percent of the Washington, D.C. district's total. All but a few of those dismissed had failed to raise student scores (Lewin 2010, A8). Note that under the logic of school deform, Rhee acted inconsistently, as she herself should have resigned, having failed to force teachers to force students to achieve higher scores on standardized tests. (Rhee did resign after the 2010 election of a new mayor.) Also not accountable—in addition to Rhee—in this chain are students, that is, in their refusal—in some cases their inability—to study. In the demonizing world of school deform, *only* teachers are responsible.

On October 13, 2010, the CBS Evening News reported Rhee's resignation without any acknowledgment of her failure. Two days later *The New York Times* went further. On its editorial page, the newspaper declared that her "departure is a loss for the nation's capital," worrying that "the schools [will] lapse into the Washington tradition of hiring people based on patronage instead of ability—and keeping them on forever no matter how poorly they perform" (Editorial 2010, October 15, A22). Patronage is the power to make appointments on any basis other than merit alone. Why was Rhee hired? Certainly her public school teaching experience didn't recommend her; Ravitch (2010, November 11, 23) reminds that Rhee began her career in Baltimore teaching for Education Alternatives, Inc., one of the first for-profit operations now plundering public budgets. Rhee failed to raise student test scores, yet she was kept on, no matter how poorly she performed. Without experience or expertise or success, hacks are hired to do the bidding of their patrons.

Joel I. Klein presided over the New York City schools for eight years. The "hallmark" of this period has been—no surprise—an "intense" emphasis on standardized tests. Critics warned Klein that test-taking "skills" were replacing "more valuable lessons" in "critical thinking." Those "skills" test preparation presumably inculcates—like "time-allocation techniques" and "multiple-choice shortcuts"—are "poor substitutes" for curriculum-based "understanding" of "key concepts" (quoted phrases in Gootman and Gebeloff 2009, 1–2). Klein countered: "If that's what test prep is about, teaching people to read and understand paragraphs, that's what I think education is about" (quoted in Gootman and Gebeloff 2009, 3). Evidently Klein is clueless that what makes reading valuable is *what* one reads. Just any old paragraph won't do. Literacy is in fact another form of ignorance unless what one reads is significant. Students' interests and teachers' knowledge and judgment converge in determining, in any given situation, what knowledge is of most worth. Decoding decontextualized cognitive puzzles—the typical fare of standardized tests purporting to measure "skills"—mirrors only the intellectually vacuous busywork too many office jobs already require.

Klein resigned in November 2010. "He's leaving us with a legacy of classroom overcrowding ... and our children starved of art, music and science—all replaced with test prep," concluded Leonie Haimson, the head of Class Size Matters (quoted in Otterman 2010, November 10, A24). Even with the sacrifice of academic knowledge that "test prep" enforces, Klein failed to raise test scores, as previously thought. A summer 2010 review found that New York City test scores had been inflated. A correction brought test scores nearly back to their level when Klein's tenure began (Medina 2010, July 29, A21). Despite this deception surrounding test scores (see Medina 2010, October 11) and his failure to raise them, Klein congratulated himself, proclaiming that "people will remember me ... as a man who was committed to changing an educational system that was failing vast numbers of people" (Otterman 2010, November 10, A24). When Klein stepped down, Mayor Michael R. Bloomberg appointed Cathleen P. Black, the chairwoman of the Hearst Magazines, as Klein's successor. Black, 66, has "no educational background," consonant with Bloomberg's preference for executives from the business world (Otterman 2010, November 10, A1). Was not the CEO of Lehman Brothers available?

Accompanying the installation of the business model in education has been, on occasion, the graft and corruption so closely associated with business. In schools, the sums stolen are more modest, of course. Near Houston, for instance, a bonus of $2,850 brought scandal. After an investigation by the Galena Park Independent School District, the principal, the assistant principal, and three teachers resigned in a scandal over test tampering (Gabriel 2010, June 11, A1). Nor are the corrupting demands of high-stakes testing limited to Texas. In Georgia, the state school board authorized the investigation of 191 schools after an analysis of 2009 reading and math tests suggested that educators had erased students' answers and substituted the correct ones (Gabriel 2010, June 11, A3). In another report, as many as *one in five* public elementary and middle schools may have altered test results (Dewan 2010, 1). Investigations in Indiana, Massachusetts, Nevada, Virginia, and elsewhere have also uncovered cheating by educators pressured to raise test scores.

With privatization, profiteering proliferates. Consider the case of Roland G. Fryer, Jr., a Harvard economist. Analogies are not his specialty it appears, as Fryer likens the billion-dollar research investments of pharmaceutical companies in their determination to devise new drugs to the comparative modesty of budgets allocated to scientifically testing educational theories. Are "theories" and "drugs" analogous? As Zimmerman (2010, 30) reminds, there are simply "too many different actors and variables to render reproducible and generalizable knowledge" in education. Add to that methodological insurmountability between the two domains—science and education—a structural incommensurability, as the latter is inevitably informed by ethics, politics, and culture. The Harvard economist is not discouraged, however. Javier C. Hernandez (2008, September 25, 1) reports that Fryer resigned his part-time post as chief equality officer of the New York City public schools in order to lead a $44 million effort called the Educational Innovation Laboratory. The "Lab" will "team" economists and "marketers" determined to "turn around ... struggling schools," specifically in New York, Washington, and Chicago. Given the failure of the "science" of economics to predict the calamitous 2008 financial collapse, might Fryer's efforts be better focused on improving his own "struggling" field?

Economics not only failed to predict the financial collapse, its sophisticated practitioners have acknowledged that the field has also failed to learn what makes for economic growth. (Yet educational researchers are still singled out for failing to know "what works" for "learning.") In 2003, Arnold Harberger, a free-market economist from the University of Chicago, admitted that "there aren't too many policies that we can say with certainty ... affect growth." A year later, a group of distinguished economists (including Paul Krugman and Joseph Stiglitz) signed a joint statement—the Barcelona Development Agenda—that announced, "There is no single set of policies that can be guaranteed to ignite sustained growth." In 2007, the "dean" of economic growth research, Nobel Laureate Robert Solow, allowed: "In real life it is very hard to move the permanent growth rate; and when it happens ... the source can be a bit mysterious even after the fact" (quoted phrases in Easterly 2009, 28). The problem, William Easterly (2009, 28) explains, it not that economists have no explanation of what causes economic growth, it is that "we have too many." Over 145 separate factors have been associated with economic growth, but efforts to make a meaningful pattern of them have failed. Only retrospective, and nationally specific, analyses, seem to yield any understanding of which policies might have had "positive effects" on economic growth (Easterly 2009, 30). Cannot we say the same about schooling? Substitute "learning" for "prosperity" in the following sentence and you see my point. "Perhaps," Easterly (2009, 30) allows, "prosperity [learning] is not after all designed from above; perhaps it emerges from below, from the independent actions of many individuals who figure out their own paths." Indeed.

Given the *trillions* of dollars lost during the 2008 financial panic, given the *tens of thousands of deaths* each year due to medical mistakes, and given the ethically questionable practices of many attorneys, where are politicians' outcries over the "failures" of business, medical, or law schools? Only education schools are targeted, and sometimes in otherwise reputable sources. Lisa Foderaro (2010, A1) begins her "report" by noting: "Not long ago education schools had a virtual monopoly on the teaching profession." Let's stop right there. Would Foderaro have started a report on medical or law schools by asserting that these institutions "not long ago" had exercised a "virtual monopoly" on their professions? One should hope medical schools exercise a "virtual monopoly"! Reports of recent medical school-generated curriculum revisions are intriguing. At New York University, for instance, the "new curriculum" accords medical students "more time" during their third and fourth years to "study popular public health issues like nutrition" and "how disease might affect people differently depending on race, ethnicity, and socioeconomic status" (Hartocollis 2010, September 3, A15). Theoretical considerations join what Dr. Steven B. Abramson, the NYU medical school's vice dean for education, calls an "hands-on" approach, a juxtaposition long favored in teacher education.

Always on the defensive, education schools' efforts to rethink teacher education (see, for instance, Britzman 2003 [1991]; Phelan and Sumsion 2008) are undermined by political intervention and an internally reproduced anti-intellectual behaviorism. Predictably, given school deform zealots' simple-minded assertions of cause (teaching) and effects (test scores)—a general cause–effect relationship that, as we just saw, even economists cannot make—critics target "theory," the one domain of teacher education wherein students study what is at stake in the very idea of the public school in America. Never mind that "theory" in teacher education has always been a small (often besieged) domain in an otherwise avowedly practice-oriented field. But school deform zealots are unconcerned with the truth, despite their demands for empirical data showing the effects of education coursework on teacher "effectiveness" (i.e. student test score improvement). Foderaro (2010, A19) reports that at an appearance at Teachers College, Columbia University—historically a key site for "theory" in teacher education—Secretary of Education Arne Duncan alleged: "Many, if not most, of the nation's 1,450 schools, colleges, and departments of education are doing a mediocre job of preparing teachers for the realities of the twenty-first-century classroom" (quoted in Foderaro 2010, A19). Note that Duncan offers no data. With such evidence-less defamation of character one might expect a libel suit to follow. Worse, this defamation was made at the institution where the significance of the public school for American democracy was importantly elaborated by several legendary figures in American history, among them John Dewey. *There* Duncan presumed to insult those who labor in that important tradition.

An even more stunning instance of ignorance and arrogance (the two so often come together!) comes from David M. Steiner, who has also urged education schools to "reform themselves" (Foderaro 2010, A19). Steiner alleges that schools of education "devote too much class time to abstract notions about 'the role of school in democracy' and 'the view by some that schools exist to perpetuate a social hierarchy'" (quoted in

Foderaro 2010, A19). A former dean of the Graduate School of Education at Hunter College, Steiner sought while there to eliminate theory in favor of the "practical" aspects of teaching, among them making "eye contact," when to use a student's name, when to wait for a more complete answer. Such *teaching by numbers*—Peter Taubman (2009) chronicles the catastrophe that has been New York City school deform in his brilliant book by the same title—is a practical recipe for stupidity. Steiner was lauded for his use of video, a "tool he pioneered," Foderaro (2010, A19) tells us, obviously ignorant of video's long-standing and disappointing history in teacher education. But at Hunter College, Foderaro reports (without one hint of journalistic skepticism), video helped student teachers to see "what works," which for Steiner is "like taking apart a serve in tennis" (quoted in Foderaro 2010, A19).

Aside from the violence of the image, this simplistic reduction of teaching to series of behaviors is the most startling feature of the analogy. What you know is evidently irrelevant. Certainly Steiner is free of theory. And count on no defense of theory from other deans, who could only manage to mumble that Steiner's charge that schools of education are "mired in theory" is, well, "outdated" (Foderaro 2010, A19). Evidently as ahistorical and atheoretical as Steiner is, Susan H. Fuhrman, president of Teachers College, Columbia University, embraced what she called an "explosion of new research" into how children learn (Foderaro 2010, A19). That is, of course, a well-worn card to play; for over one hundred years—certainly since G. Stanley Hall's racialized and gendered theories of adolescence (see Baker 2001, 463, 501; Bederman 1995, 94)—researchers have dangled before the public promises of "discoveries" of "how children learn," always a recoding of the adult determination to get kids to do whatever we want them to. Now we just want them to get a job.

Never mind that for decades U.S. corporations have ruthlessly—treasonously—moved millions of jobs overseas, leaving American workers high and dry, stuck in low-pay "service" jobs, all in order to increase corporate profits, huge amounts of which remain overseas so as to avoid paying U.S. taxes. "Workers have learned to internalize and mask powerlessness," one labor economist (Cowie 2010, A17) concludes, "but the internal frustration and struggle remain." Questions concerning the quality of work life—the "animating" issue forty years ago—are, Jefferson Cowie (2010, A17) continues, no longer asked: "Today the concerns of the working class have less space in our civil imagination than at any time since the Industrial Revolution." Also "losing out in the shuffle," according to David Autor, a labor economist at the Massachusetts Institute of Technology (MIT), are "middle-skill, middle-wage" (entry-level white-collar positions, like office and administrative support work), a trend accelerated by the Great Recession of 2008 (Luo 2010, A12).

Despite U.S. businesses' exploitation of American citizens'—and illegal immigrants'—economic vulnerability, many pin the blame for low economic growth not on business' own anti-patriotic profiteering but—yes, you guessed it—on the schools. To appease influential businessmen—billionaire Bill Gates is now among the most reprehensible as he tirelessly uses his wealth to devalue academic knowledge and insist that test scores are all that matter (Blankinship 2010, A1; Dillon 2009, November 19, 1)—the education of the public has devolved into vocational preparation for participation in the economy. Such miseducation detaches the school curriculum from the academic disciplines and links it to standardized tests so that students can practice solving whatever cognitive puzzles— "so-called performance-based tasks, designed to mirror complex, real-world situations" (Dillon 2010, September 3, A11)—their future jobs may demand of them. Once the American dream had been life, liberty, and the pursuit of happiness. By the end of the last century it had been reduced to owning one's own home. Now that the housing bubble has burst, and high unemployment is, we are told by many economists, the "new normal," what can the American dream be now? Simple survival?

The discrediting of business—as even a model for itself, let alone for education—has not yet reached the charter school industry, however. The qualifications of one founder of a charter school, Zeke M. Vanderhoek, include founding a test prep company. Reading the report one surmises that it was this entrepreneurial expertise that informed his search for faculty, as erudition certainly didn't show up among the prerequisite qualifications. After interviewing 100 of 600 applicants, Vanderhoek chose eight finalists who, he said, exhibited an "engagement factor." Is "the engagement factor" business-talk for being so demanding that students can attend to nothing else but the classroom work required of them? Reminscent of correctional education during the Weimar Republic (see chapter 3, section VIII), Vanderhoek demands that teachers intervene before kids become "troublemakers," insisting that teachers display a "contagious enthusiasm" (quoted passages in Gootman 2009, 3). Never mind his pessimism; never mind likening enthusiasm for education to a disease. Those two qualities could easily morph into "bossy" and "demanding," but these "new-hires" may be willing to be whatever Vanderhoek wants them to be, given the range of responsibilities this businessman demands of them. Vanderhoek's teachers will work longer hours and more days in classrooms with thirty students, approximately six more than the typical New York City fifth-grade class. Additionally, Vanderhoek's teachers will not enjoy the same retirement benefits as members of the city's teacher unions. Finally and most importantly, teachers can be "fired at will" (Gootman 2009, 3).

Recall that in school deform not only charter school teachers can be fired "at will." A Rhode Island school board's decision to fire the entire faculty of a presumably "poorly performing school" was endorsed by President Obama, precipitating controversy nationwide. Teachers condemned the action as an "insult" while "conservatives" praised it as a "watershed moment of school accountability" (Greenhouse and Dillon 2010, 1). The event assumed national significance as hundreds of other school districts must consider similar firings given the regulations of *Race to the Top*. "Teachers were taken aback—and profoundly disappointed," acknowledged Randi Weingarten, president of the American Federation of Teachers (AFT). "Teachers will watch carefully whether Washington, the states and local districts will be partners that help us do our job or whether they'll be scapegoating and demonizing" (Greenhouse and Dillon 2010, 3). While it is significant that Weingarten appreciates that federal policy amounts to simple scapegoating, in another statement she accepts that the school—not the student—is the unit of judgment. "Teachers alone cannot turn around struggling schools," she said, unfortunately incorporating the jargon of the day, "and the administration's plan puts 100 percent of the responsibility on teachers." Dennis Van Roekel, president of the National Education Association (NEA) was also critical of the administration's position, pointing out: "They say they are offering flexibility and an end to micromanaging our schools. But the administration's blueprint mandates to 15,000 districts how they should evaluate and compensate teachers." Weingarten is right to emphasize teachers' liability but mistaken to link it with "struggling schools," implying that schools (as organizational units) could guarantee students' academic achievement. Van Roekel's complaint seems limited to the problem of "micromanaging" (both quoted in Dillon 2010, March 16, 1). Neither of these important representatives of the profession points to the double standard at work, that teachers are demanded to perform miracles parents—even priests—cannot always pull off. And neither representative emphasizes that what teachers offer are opportunities; they do not—cannot, must not try to—control results. Controlling "outcomes" is manipulation and indoctrination, not education.

In the mythology surrounding school reform, the truth is that the celebrated, business-like, emphasis on "outcomes" is in fact optional. Consider the case of Geoffrey Canada, the "magnetic" leader of the Harlem Children's Zone (Otterman 2010, October 13, A18). The Obama administration crafted a grant program to copy Canada's "block-by-block approach" to fight poverty (Otterman 2010, October 13, A18). The British government praised his charter schools as models. A documentary film—*Waiting for Superman*—features him (as well as Michelle Rhee). Like Roland G. Fryer, Jr., Geoffrey Canada lures students to study. Rather than cash or cellphone minutes (Fryer's coin of the realm: Hernandez 2008, September 25, 1), Canada provided trips to the Galapagos Islands or to Disney World. Canada's two charter schools cost around $16,000 per student each year (Otterman 2010, October 13, A18), considerably more than the average. (His organization is reported to have over $200 million in assets and he collects a $400,000 salary: see Ravitch 2010, November 11, 24.) Despite these staggering incentives and the obvious advantages of additional spending, the "outcomes" of Canada's schools are mixed. On the 2010 state tests, Ravitch (2010, November 11, 24) reports, 60 percent of the fourth-grade students in one of his charter schools failed to achieve proficiency in reading; 50 percent failed in the other. And these dismal results despite the fact (that Ravitch also reports) that Mr. Canada *expelled* an entire class of middle schools students when their test scores failed to satisfy his board of trustees.

Obviously "outcomes" are entirely incidental, as we are informed that, despite these results, Geoffrey Canada has attained "superhero status among those who admire him for the breadth of his vision" (Otterman 2010, October 13, A19). "The fact that the impact has not been proven doesn't mean that it doesn't exist, because it is just very, very hard to prove something about an effort as multifaceted and interactive as this is," explained Lisbeth B. Schorr, a senior fellow of the Center for the Study of Social Policy in Washington. "A lot of what you learn comes not just from research, but also from experience" (quoted passages in Otterman 2010, October 13, A19). Public acknowledgment of *that* fact would have saved America's public schools a lot of nonsense over the past four decades.

III "Untimely" Concepts

> To live with courage is a virtue, whatever one may think of the dominant assumptions of one's age.
> —George Grant (2005 [1965], 94)

Since the 1960s—when the leadership of public school curriculum development was assumed by university colleagues in the various academic disciplines—many curriculum specialists have been left working bureaucratically to implement others' materials and content. In the post-Reconceptualization period (Malewski 2009), we have been working to understand how the curriculum-in-place functions, politically, racially, in terms of gender, subjectivity, and "the global village." We have focused on how ideas generated in other fields or discourses—such as phenomenology or postmodernism or aesthetics—might help us understand the curriculum as a multifaceted process, involving not only official policy, prescribed textbooks, standardized examinations, but also the "complicated conversation" of the participants. We have reconceived the curriculum; no longer is it only a noun. It is as well a verb: *currere.*

For those prospective and practicing teachers for whom teacher education has been primarily an introduction to the instructional fields—the teaching of reading or mathematics or science—curriculum theory may come as something of a shock, if only due to its emphasis on "what" one teaches, rather than on "how." Of course, *how* one teaches remains a major preoccupation of curriculum theorists, but not in terms of devising a "technology" of "what works," not as a form of social engineering designed to produce predictable effects (i.e., "learning"), too often quantified as scores on standardized exams. The late-19th-century black feminist (and public school teacher) Anna Julia Cooper was clear on this point:

> We have been so ridden with tests and measurements, so leashed and spurred for percentages and retardations that the machinery has run away with the mass production and quite a way back bumped off the driver. I wonder that a robot has not been invented to make the assignments, give the objective tests, mark the scores and *chloroform all teachers who dared bring original thought to the specific problems and needs of their pupils.*
> (cited in Lemert and Bhan 1998, 235, emphasis added)

Standardized test scores are, finally, meaningless; what remains from education is self-reflexive interdisciplinary intellectuality, the cultivation of "original thought" attentive to others. Erudition and originality have long constituted curriculum theorists' aspiration for public education. Standardized tests foreclose originality, creativity, and independence of mind. Simply stated, curriculum is what the older generation chooses to tell the younger generations (Grumet 1988). The school curriculum communicates what we choose to remember about our past, what we believe about the present, what we hope for the future. Curriculum debates—such as those over multiculturalism and the canon—are also debates over the American national identity.

Because the curriculum is symbolic, its study requires situating curriculum historically, socially, and autobiographically (i.e., in terms of life history and self-formation). Sectors of curriculum scholarship and research include efforts to understand curriculum racially, politically, theologically, autobiographically, and historically, in terms of gender, popular culture, phenomenology, postmodernism, poststructuralism, psychoanalysis, and the arts, all situated locally and in the global village. Traces of this scholarship can be heard throughout this avowedly singular articulation of curriculum theory.

Curriculum theory, then, is a field of scholarly inquiry within the broad academic field of education that endeavors to understand curriculum as educational experience. The curriculum occurs through conversation within and across the school subjects and academic disciplines. While school subject specializations within the field of education (such as the teaching of English or mathematics) tend to focus on teaching strategies within single teaching fields, curriculum theory aspires to understand the overall educational significance of the curriculum, focusing especially upon interdisciplinary themes—such as gender or multiculturalism or sustainability—as well as the relations among the curriculum, the individual, society, and history.

Such an aspiration is undermined by the pervasive anti-intellectualism across American society, accented in petulant populism on the right and institutionalized in the Obama administration's conversion of public schools into cram schools. Because standardized tests measure nothing meaningful, they represent a "perverse" form of accountability (see Rothstein, Jacobsen, and Wilder 2008, 53–54). But even as thoughtful a critic of accountability as Richard Rothstein gets caught in the accountability craze by posing the wrong question. Instead of asking the curriculum question—*what knowledge is of most worth?*—he accepts the primacy of evaluation, asking "what is it, exactly, that young people should achieve" (2008, 141)? By assuming "outcomes" (2008, 73) are key to judging the quality of education, he traps himself in the self-enclosed circuitry of accountability, overlooking the much more fundamental question: what is the intellectual quality of the curriculum? That question positions knowledge and its study as central, not schemes for increasing test scores. The significant consequences of academic study are rarely short term, cannot be quantified, and depend almost entirely on students' circumstances and capacities. Seeing their teachers scapegoated hardly encourages students to exercise their own agency, and that is exactly the "control" (2008, 1) school deform enforces.

"Control" likewise characterized the Bush administration's demands for an educational science of "what works." Taubman (2009, 60) notes the irony, as the Bush administration was not exactly known for its support of science. So why its enthusiasm for an evidence-based science of education? ("Evidence" certainly seemed incidental in its decision to invade Iraq.) Taubman (2009, 60) explains by referencing the Bush administration's "financial interests" in the *Reading First* program, which had claimed an empirically validated approach to reading. Taubman (2009, 60) also points out that the federal funding of so-called scientific research denies "the complexity of emotional life in the classroom and the impact of social, political, and economic forces on students and teaches, not what conservative politicians want to hear." In such anti-intellectual circumstances, theoretical research—such as curriculum theory—becomes a political undertaking, as David M. Steiner's diatribes underscore. Akin to Gilles Deleuze and Félix Guattari's characterization of philosophy, curriculum theory becomes the creation of "untimely" concepts by "acting counter to our time, and thereby acting on our time and, let us hope, for the benefit of a time to come" (Nietzsche 1983a; quoted in Patton 2000, 3).

Banished from the public sphere, curriculum theorists appreciate political powerlessness. (As the great Canadian political economist and communications theorist Harold Innis once acknowledged: "This is the most cruel pang that man can bear—to have much insight and power over nothing" [quoted in Watson 2007, 394].) In the United States, the position of education expert has been discredited by those who have demeaned "the education establishment" as a self-interested "special-interest" lobby that must be constrained in the name of the public interest (Schrag 2007). Even if education professors were acknowledged by the popular media as "must-go-to" experts, the field forecloses such hubris. We understand that *what knowledge is of most worth?* cannot be answered for others; indeed, our aspiration is to forefront the question as an ongoing stimulus to study and complicated conversation. The intellectual labor of curriculum theorizing today can be suggested by invoking Deleuze's conception of theory as a relay of practice, a conception, as Paul Patton points out, that is closer to the idea expressed by Nietzsche's distinction between academic philosophers in uncritical service to the State, and those "true" philosophers who must remain "private thinkers" (see Nietzsche 1983b; Patton 2000, 5).

To remain a private thinker means that one's scholarship, one's thinking, teaching, and writing, are engaged in self-overcoming, the surpassing of the historical, sedimented "self" one has been conditioned and, perhaps, as a teacher, required to be. In working to overcome the "self" conceived by others, one "works from within," from one's interiority, which is a specific configuration of the socius and therefore a public project as well. This apparent paradox—that one's private self is necessarily public—is clarified in Patton's characterization of Jean-Paul Sartre, in many ways the pre-eminent public intellectual of the 20th century in the West. Patton (2000, 5) describes Sartre "as a modern paradigm of the private thinker who spoke and acted on his own behalf rather than as the representative of a political party or social class." Such thinkers "seek to align themselves with the unrepresentable forces that introduce disorder and a dose of permanent revolution into political and social life" (Patton 2000, 6). Such thinkers are private in Nietzsche's sense of self-overcoming while publicly declining to employ their intellectual labor in unquestioning service to the State and in complicity with the political status quo. They work from "within."

Private can imply isolation from historical forces and social movements. Such an implication would be mistaken, as I am underscoring that historical forces and social movements are both the sources of interiority and the provocations of theorizing and teaching. But a certain solitude—a "room of one's own" in Virginia Woolf's famous phrase—is a prerequisite for that "complicated conversation" with oneself without which one disappears onto the social surface, into the maelstrom that is the public world. Without a private life, without an ongoing project of autobiographical understanding, one's intellectual "practice" too often tends toward the miming of what is fashionable or profitable or simply enables us to "get by." A public intellectual who is not also a private person risks the unmediated expression of emotion projected onto the social surface, as interiority not self-reflexively grasped, even reconstructed, can disappear into, and be misrecognized as, "the world." An "organic" intellectual's relation to the "multitude" (Hardt and Negri 2000, 61) necessarily includes one's relationship with one's self, one's self-reflexive reconstruction of one's subjectivity. It is through subjectivity that one experiences history and society, and it is subjectivity through which history and society speak. It is subjectivity through which the natural world also sometimes speaks, as Paul Wapner (2010, 209) points out:

> [O]ur thoughts, fantasies, and constructions are not self-originating but instead develop in relationship to the more-than-human world of which they participate. The nonhuman world works through us to the degree that we are the main agents of planetary change, but there is also something beyond us.

Installing the instrumentalization of teaching as preparation to standardized tests vitiates academic study by stripping it of both subjectivity and the world, leaving us with neither intellect nor soul.

IV Too Little Intellect in Matters of Soul

> We do not have too much intellect and too little soul, but too little intellect in matters of the soul.
> —Robert Musil (1990 [1922] 131)

Curriculum theory understands teacher education not as learning a new language for what teachers already do, although the language we employ to understand what we do structures, as well as represents, professional conduct. After Huebner (1999), we understand the limitations of the language of "learning," embedded as that term is in academic psychology, rather than in psychoanalysis (see Britzman 1998, 2009; Taubman in press). Canadian curriculum theorist Robin Barrow (1984, 97) is blunt: "[T]here is very little of importance for educators that can be gained from the study of such things as learning theory, child development and personality." After Huebner, we appreciate the significance of employing ethical, religious, and aesthetic languages to depict and structure our professional lives as educators.

Curriculum scholars are necessarily suspicious of rhetorical band-wagons such as "standards" and "accountability." Immediately we go to work to situate them historically, in terms of the discourse systems in which they operate, especially in politicians' obfuscating rhetorics. In studying curriculum theory, then, teachers are not being asked to "do" something "new" in the classroom, although their conduct there may well be altered, perhaps even transformed, as a consequence of study-ing curriculum theory. How it will be altered or transformed one can-not predict, however. We curriculum theorists do not regard our task as directing teachers to apply theory to practice, a form of professional subordination, in positions (as southern Baptists once described wives' relations to their husbands) of "gracious submission." Rather, curriculum theorists in the university regard our pedagogical work as the cultivation of independence of mind, self-reflexivity, and an interdisciplinary erudi-tion. We hope to persuade teachers to appreciate the complex and shifting relations between their own self-formation and the school subjects they teach, understood both as subject matter and as human subjects. It is this indirect expression of subjectivity attuned to the historical moment that enables one to answer the ongoing curricular question *what knowledge is of most worth?*

Curriculum theorists are skeptical of "business thinking," in which "curriculum producers offer something to curriculum consumers" (Aoki 2005 [1983], 113]). As well, curriculum theorists tend to be suspicious of military metaphors to depict what is at stake in education. Both business thinking and military metaphors continue to be invoked as correctives to the supposed lack of "rigor" in schools (which, as we will see in chapter 4, is also a gendered and racialized accusation). The profession of teach-ing requires us to understand and participate as colleagues in the school, including in the governance of the day-to-day life of the institution *and* in the administration of academic matters such as curriculum content, teaching styles, and the assessment of students' study. Participating in the governance of the school requires us to remain (or to become) self-aware of the multiple functions and potentials of the process of education and of the institutions that formalize them. This means becoming articulate about and exercising influence over curriculum content, including interdis-ciplinary configurations (such as women's and gender studies), theories of pedagogy, and various means of assessing student study. How all this gets worked out, including teachers' already overburdened schedules (too many students and too many classes continue to characterize teachers' under-paid and unprofessional lives in too many schools), is outside the purview of curriculum theory, but its scholarly understanding is not. Curriculum reconstruction, not its reorganization, typifies curriculum development.

Curriculum theory is, in effect, a form of autobiographically informed truth-telling that articulates the educational experience of teachers and students as lived. As such, curriculum theory speaks from concretely existing individuals' subjective experience of history and society, the inextricable interrelationships among which structure educational experience. The role of language—first articulated by Dwayne Huebner in the 1960s (his collected works are canonical: Huebner 1999)—in such "truth-telling" is key. As the legendary Canadian curriculum theorist Ted Aoki (2005 [1990], 369), has warned: "the danger ... is that we become the language we speak." If we employ, for instance, that bureaucratic language in which teaching becomes not an occasion for creativity and questioning and, above all, the cultivation of erudition and intellectual independence, but, rather, the "implementation" of others' "objectives," the process of education is mutilated. Whatever language we employ, we "become" the language. In "becoming" the language of "implementation," Aoki (2005 [1990], 369) notes, "we might become forgetful of how instrumental language disengages us from our bodies, making of us disembodied, dehumanized beings, indifferent to the nihilistic drying out of inspiritedness." "Instead of 'curriculum implementation'," Aoki asks, "how about 'curriculum improvisation'?" Such a shift in theoretical articulation, he notes, "provokes in us a vitalizing possibility that causes our whole body to beat a new and different rhythm."

Such a "new and different rhythm" is very much needed in U.S. teacher education, one that makes audible the generative roles of creativity and individuality in teaching and study. This requires shifting our attention from organizational issues (including "outcomes") to intellectual preoccupations, animated by ongoing academic study. Moreover, teacher education today threatens to become culture-in-the-unmaking as it is deprofessionalized by anti-intellectual interventions by government and by presumably professional organizations such as the National Council for Accreditation of Teacher Education (NCATE) (see Taubman 2009). In this "business-minded" and "technological" present, theory is not only severed from practice. It is banished from education schools. In Musil's analysis of European culture, quoted earlier, the problem of the age is crystallized in the severance of intellect from soul.

When Ted Aoki (2005 [1987], 357) recalled working as a public school teacher, his teaching seemed to reflect, rather than challenge, this cultural schism in which work is split off from play, mind from body, soul from intellect (where the soul is, presumably, merely a matter of "faith"). "What I was teaching," Aoki concludes, reflecting on his own practice as a public school teacher for nineteen years, "was a way of life that sees thinking as theorizing and doing as practicing." The title of the textbook he used to teach reading—We Think and Do— represents, he suggests, "a mundane version of what could be entitled We Theorize *and Practice*." "For educators," he notes, "it is a way of life that regards teacher preparation in education curriculum and instruction courses as theorizing and the practicing of theories as *practicum*" (2005 [1987], 358). "Must we be caught up totally in the linearized form of 'from theory into practice'?" Aoki (2005 [1987], 358) asks. Must we? The answer, in the United States at least, is "yes," as government and its enforcers—such as the NCATE—position teachers and those of us who teach teachers into positions of "gracious submission." This subjugation—rationalized by a rhetoric of "accountability" that even American business does not practice—is presumably in service of "learning."

Presumably. But, as Linda McNeil (2000, xiv) understands, "by increasing bureaucratic controls, these reforms inadvertently strengthened the very forces that are known to undermine teaching and learning, as teachers and students react against controls by limiting their own work." "Accountability" is not about "learning," but about controlling what we teach to our children. It is about controlling the curriculum. To achieve this control—which is, finally, control of the mind—the public schools are severed from both the social and the subjective. Teachers are reduced to technicians, "managing" student productivity. The school is no longer a school, but a business.

V The School as a Business

> No doubt there is a certain measure of inherent dissonance between business enterprise and intellectual enterprise.
> —Richard Hofstadter (1962, 233)

While the point of the American public schools has not changed much over the past one hundred years, the economy schools were designed to support has. The consensus is that the American economy is less and less industrial and more and more "service oriented," strongly "information based," increasingly organized around technological developments, including the Internet. It is said to be international or global in character. Rather than the assembly line of the early automobile factory, the major mode of economic production today is semiotic (i.e., production of signs, symbols, and other information), and it occurs not in factories but in committees and in front of computer screens in corporate offices.

During the first decades of the 20th century, many U.S. schools were modeled after the assembly-line factory, in which "raw material" (Bobbitt 1918, 77)—that is, children—were to be molded into saleable products (1918, 78). Such commodification of learning continued as, over the century, schools were remodeled after the contemporary corporation. That "profoundly undemocratic institution" (Lasch 1984, 51) represented, presumably, an improvement (Berliner and Biddle 1996, 295–297). So-called "smart schools" were touted as versions of the corporate model (Fiske 1991). Even the concept of "small schools" (Raywid and Schmerler 2003)—emphasizing "community" (Spring 2007, 135; Strike 2008, 247)—does not necessarily contest the economism of school deform. Still outcomes-based, the modes of cognition appropriate to even corporate schools are fewer and narrower than intelligence more broadly understood.

Because the organization and culture of the school are linked to the economy and structured by "business thinking," the school and U.S. curriculum studies have traveled different paths over the past thirty years. For the foreseeable future, most teachers will be trained as "social engineers," directed to "manage" learning that is modeled loosely after corporate work-stations, focused on test preparation. Certainly some segment of the U.S. curriculum field will devote itself to assist in the design and implementation of this corporate school curriculum. However, those of us who labored to reconceptualize the atheoretical, ahistorical field we found in 1970 have always seen a more complex calling for the field. The theoretical wing of the reconceived field aspires to ground itself not in the pressured everyday world of the corporate classroom but in worlds not present in the schools today, in ideas marginal to the maximization of profits, and in imaginative and lived experience that is not exclusively instrumental and calculative.

In its press for efficiency, outcomes, and standardization, the factory model reduced teachers to automata and administrators to managers (Shipps 2000, 83). In designing and teaching the curriculum in units that presumably "added up" to a logical even disciplinary "whole" (like products on an assembly line), the factory-model school achieved social control at the cost of intelligence, intelligence broadly understood as problem solving, critical thinking, and creativity as well as memorization and calculation. As Linda McNeil (2000, 3) has observed: "*Standardization reduces the quality and quantity of what is taught and learned in schools.*" Students who tolerate the routinized, repetitious nature of instruction that relies upon recitation and memorization sometimes are able to perform reasonably well on similar tasks, although the "transferability" of these task-specific skills has long been a problem for the factory model (Bobbitt 1918, 35; Bruner 1977 [1960], 5).

The corporate model emphasized "outcomes" as the goal of the school, despite the utter unpredictability of learning (Tyler 1949, 40). The contemporary reduction of learning to standardized test scores—themselves irrationally linked to upward social-economic mobility—relies on these unfounded assumptions of predictability, of "what works." Outcomes-based models permit a variety of instructional strategies to be employed in their attainment. Team teaching, small-group work, and other forms of so-called cooperative and collaborative learning (see Johnson and Johnson 2009) are encouraged so long as students do what is demanded of them. Moreover, the corporate model tends to acknowledge that intelligence is multiple in nature and function and includes aesthetic, intuitive, and sensory elements as well as linear, logical, narrowly cognitive ones (Gardner 1983). The social character of intelligence is also acknowledged as corporate classroom organization often permits the use of dyadic and small-group activities. The teacher in this scheme is a manager or, in Theodore Sizer's (1984) image, a "coach," a gendered metaphor Nancy Lesko (2000) associates with the remasculinization of the school. While masculinized, these images—*manager* and *coach*—are considerably less authoritarian than those associated with the teacher in the factory or—its contemporary incarnation—cram school.

Even in the presumably more flexible corporate model, the goal of instruction—the acquisition of that knowledge and the cultivation of those skills deemed necessary for productivity in a postindustrial economy—is not in question. Intelligence is viewed as a means to an end, the acquisition of cognitive skills, specialized knowledge, and social attitudes utilizable in the corporate sector. The maximization of profits remains the "bottom line" of the corporation as well as that of its earlier version, the factory. I am not suggesting that schools should have no relationship to the economy. Capitalism does require forms of knowledge and intelligence the corporate model of schooling is more likely than the factory model to produce. Nor could we have publicly supported schools in the United States that would *not* include economic considerations, at least for the imaginable future.

Curriculum theory reminds those of us committed to educating the public that for intelligence to be cultivated in fundamental and democratic ways, it must be set free of corporate goals. Such an idea hardly excludes instrumental reason, calculation, and problem solving as major modes of cognition. Intellectual freedom must allow, however, for meditative, contemplative modes of cognition, and for exploring subjects—especially those associated with the arts and the humanities—that may have no immediate practical pay-off and cannot be evaluated by standardized examinations (Fish 2008).

Intelligence is made narrow, and thus undermined, when it is reduced to answers to other people's questions, when it is only a means to achieve preordained goals. This instrumental and calculative concept of intelligence, while useful to the present form of economic organization—the corporation—is less helpful in investigations of more fundamental and enduring questions of human experience, experience that might not lead directly to economic development and increased productivity but might contribute to subjective well-being (Spring 2007). To study these questions is to "ride" intelligence to destinations perhaps not listed in the present economic and political agenda. Teachers cannot help students on such intellectual adventures when they themselves are conceived by others.

VI The Figure of the Schoolteacher

The figure of the schoolteacher may well be taken as a central symbol in any modern society.

—Richard Hofstadter (1962, 309)

Over the past one hundred years the American teacher's identity has been reconfigured from factory supervisor to corporate manager to cram school instructor. But if loyal to the cultivation of intelligence and the democratic project of education, teachers must become more than they have been conceived and conditioned to be. If we are submerged in identities conceived by others, the cultivation of intelligence is necessarily constrained. Of course, we teachers must meet contractual obligations regarding curriculum and instruction. However, we need not necessarily believe them or uncritically accept them. Curriculum theorists might assist teachers to avoid the disappearance of their ideals into the maelstrom of daily classroom demands. We might support teachers' identities apart from those constructed by corporatism by proclaiming the existence of other ways of conceiving education, noninstrumental ways of speaking and being with children.

We teachers are always, to some extent, conceived by others, by the expectations and fantasies of our students and by the demands of parents, administrators, policymakers, and politicians, to all of whom we are sometimes the "other." We are formed as well by their and our own internalized life histories. These various spheres or levels of self-constitution invite autobiographical investigation. Associating the process of knowing in the politics of identity suggests escaping the swirling waters created by the demands and pressures of others. The capacity to stand calmly in a maelstrom can come only with knowledge of other worlds, with living in other realities, not split off or dissociated from the everyday world of work. "Separate but connected" permits us to enter the work world larger, more complex, than the roles prescribed for us, making less likely that we will collapse upon the social surface, reduced to what others make of us.

We Americans might then model to our children how we can live in this society without succumbing to it, without giving up our dreams and aspirations for education. Teachers can become witnesses to the notion that intelligence and learning can lead to other worlds, not just the successful exploitation of this one. Theory is a "prayerful act" (see Macdonald 1995). But knowledge need not be regarded as a sacred text as in fundamentalist religions or an inviolate procedure as on the assembly line; nor is it only the more complex, sometimes even creative, means to an end that it is in the corporate model. Rather, knowledge and intelligence as free exploration become wings by which we take flight, visit other worlds, returning to this one to call others, especially our children, to futures more life-affirmative than the world we inhabit now. When we sink, submerged in those roles conceived by others, we become aborted possibilities, unable to realize in everyday life, in our relations with others, the politics of our individual and civic identities, the educational dynamics of creation and birth.

The pressure upon us is enormous. Through legislation, teachers are mandated to betray their professional calling to teach their subject as they deem appropriate, structuring the curriculum around their and their students' answers to the ongoing curricular question *what knowledge is of most worth?* Through the political complicity of pseudo-professional organizations such as the NCATE, the education professoriate is being pressured to comply with school deform (see Johnson, Johnson, Farenga, and Ness 2005; Pinar 2004, 210–222; Taubman 2009). Because school deformers reduce learning to test scores, they suspend key curriculum questions, such as: What does the school curriculum have to say to youth culture, specifically youth alienation and violence such as bullying? How can the school curriculum help us understand terrorism, the ecological crisis, globalization? In splitting curriculum from instruction, school deform turns teachers into technicians who have to pretend to know "what works." This anti-intellectual authoritarianism is disguised as "education science" (see Howe 2009; Slavin 2008). It is reflected in the organizational restructuring of a number of Colleges of Education wherein the historical designation "Department of Curriculum and Teaching" (first appearing at Teachers College, Columbia University in 1937) has been replaced with titles such as "Department of Teaching and Learning" or "Department of Instruction and Learning." Because teachers, and education professors, have little jurisdiction over the official school curriculum, it is no longer deemed by many to be a pressing professional concern. Like the public schools, schools of education are forced into positions of "gracious submission."

In colleges and universities many faculty—especially in the humanities and arts—remain clear that curriculum and teaching are profoundly linked, that the curriculum is the intellectual and organizational center of education. Most understand that the performance of their professional obligations as scholars and teachers requires us to retain the academic— that is, intellectual—freedom to choose those texts and topics we deem, in our professional judgment, most appropriate. Most of us appreciate that our professional labor requires that we decide how to examine our students, sometimes by research papers, other times by essay- or short-answer tests, and even, on occasion, by standardized examinations. The situation in higher education is, of course, hardly ideal: The general education curriculum in many public research universities is more a political than thoughtful and informed curricular arrangement—but my point is that the inseparable relation between curriculum and teaching remains intact, more or less, at many universities. Why it was never fully honored in elementary, middle, and secondary schools is a historical and specifically gendered and racialized issue, as I explain in chapter 4.

Because contemporary teacher education is about the "delivery" of instruction and focused on organizational accountability, many do not appreciate that the study of education is, first and foremost, a subjectively informed intellectual undertaking. The profession of teaching *is* academic. Too few appreciate the significance of studying the education field's intellectual history and cultivating its disciplinarity. In some schools of education, especially at prestigious private and public research universities, there has been a tendency to employ faculty with doctoral degrees in fields other than education, but who have claimed an interest in "education." In this scheme, "education" is a specialized interest, an "application" of a "true" academic field, such as psychology or sociology or history or physics (see Clifford and Guthrie 1988).

Aggressively self-promotional but having reached (for the moment) the physical size its enrollments and grant activities permit, academic psychology has long looked at the field of education as a potential colony. Rarely is academic psychology aware of the historical, political, gendered, and racial currents in which child and adolescent psychology appeared at the beginning of the 20th century (Baker 2001; Bederman 1995; Lesko 2000). Academic psychology focuses on "instruction" and "learning," evidently unaware of the central role of curriculum in the education of the American public. Ahistorical, imagining itself a "science," academic psychology "retreat[ed] from the challenge of Freud into the measurement of trivia," as Lasch (1978, xiv) appreciated. Harold Innis also knew how measurement narrowed the range of human experience that could be legitimately examined; he associated totalitarianism with quantitative social science (see Watson 2007, 475). Asserting an epistemological arrogance, academic psychology has often positioned itself the central discipline in the broad field of education, asserting it knows "what works" (Taubman 2009, 159). In its latest refashioning, as the so-called "learning sciences," psychology facilitates education's co-optation by business (Taubman 2009, 160).

Sometimes psychological research is stunningly simplistic. Consider the application of so-called social interdependence theory to education. Converting common sense into jargon—social interdependence theory discovers that we are affected by the actions of others (Johnson and Johnson 2009, 366)—Johnson and Johnson (2009, 367) report that research shows that working in groups (so-called collaborative learning) is insufficient in itself to "produce higher achievement and productivity." What is also necessary is vulnerability to peer pressure, which they recast as "positive interdependence" (2009, 367). Johnson and Johnson have also discovered that the greater the complexity of the task facing the group, the more slowly its work proceeds. They have discovered that unskilled members of a group can slow things down too. This is an example of "evidence-based" research reporting, presumably, "what works."

Curriculum theory rejects such reiterations of common sense and embraces the nuanced complexity of educational experience. To do so, it avoids the reductionistic protocols of quantitative social science as it explores hybrid interdisciplinary scholarship, utilizing philosophy, history, literary theory, the arts, and important interdisciplinary formations such as women's and gender studies, African American studies, queer theory, postcolonial theory. Employing research completed in other disciplines as well as our own, curriculum theorists construct textbooks that invite public school teachers to reoccupy a vacated "public" domain, not simply as "consumers" of knowledge, but as active participants in conversations they themselves will lead. In drawing—creatively but critically—from various academic disciplines and popular culture, curriculum theorists work to create conceptual collages for the public school teacher who understands that labor as aspiring to reconstruct that public space wherein students study academic knowledge to thread the subjective needle that stitches them to the world.

Given irresponsible, indeed libelous accusations made against public schools and colleges of education, many struggle just to show up. Not everyone succeeds. New teachers flee the profession at unprecedented rates (Dillon 2007). Despite the satisfaction of working with the young through ideas, we teachers must mobilize ourselves if we are to remain focused in the maelstrom of the present. Somehow, each evening we must replenish our reserves and hear anew the calling of our profession. Christopher Lasch's point about the political socialization of the young pertains, I think, to many educators as well:

> The socialization of the young reproduces the political domination at the level of personal experience. In our own time, this invasion of private life by the forces of organized domination has become so pervasive that personal life has almost ceased to exist.
>
> (Lasch 1978, 30)

Given this ongoing assault upon the profession, on our very personhood, teachers are forced to work from within.

Chapter 2

From Autobiography to Allegory

I To Run the Course: *Currere*

[I]gnorance seems to be mostly a matter of self-ignorance.
—Norman O. Brown (1959, 322)

Always academic, curriculum is also subjective and social. As a verb—*currere*—curriculum becomes a complicated, that is, multiply referenced, conversation in which interlocutors are speaking not only among themselves but to those not present, not only to historical figures and unnamed peoples and places they may be studying, but to politicians and parents alive and dead, not to mention to the selves they have been, are in the process of becoming, and someday may become. Education requires subjectivity in order for it to speak, for it to become concrete, to become actual. Without the agency of subjectivity education evaporates, replaced by the conformity compelled by scripted curricula and standardized tests.

Even in fields far from the humanities and social sciences, subjectivity is paramount (Shapin 2010). Understanding incorporates comprehension but expertise and the erudition upon which it depends require the cultivation of subjectively situated, historically attuned intellectual judgment. Such judgment is informed by academic knowledge and professional ethics, by technical know-how coupled with a passionate sense of public service, all threaded through the subjectivity of the socially engaged individual. Stripped of such a cosmopolitan cause, creativity is confined to careerism, and the individual—the lived and legal basis of human rights—can atrophy into an automaton, into what during World War II was called a "collaborator." Teaching by numbers (Taubman 2009) enacts the erasure of education as it ignores the intellectual judgment of the individual educator. The end of education foreshadows the defeat of democracy in America.

Focusing on teaching risks inflation of the concept. By subsuming "teaching" (or "instruction" or "pedagogy") into the concept of curriculum, the educator becomes a participant—albeit the key participant—in the complicated conversation that is the curriculum. Separating the teacher from curriculum reifies the role: too easily teaching becomes idealized. Idealized, the educator becomes a magician, mandated to a pull a rabbit out of a hat. Even conjoined—as in curriculum *and* pedagogy— teaching becomes a topic in itself, readily misconstrued as "technique," a bag of tricks to rescue a boring or irrelevant curriculum, or a sales pitch student-consumers demand before making a "purchase." Given the grade inflation that can only escalate thanks to politicians' demands for higher graduation rates, students' disinclination to study is likely reflected less in the grade received than in their evaluation of the faculty. While it is always pedagogically appropriate to attend to the experience of the student, the inflated emphasis upon evaluation during the last forty years has led to institutional neglect of the intellectual quality and character of the curriculum. The intellectual quality of the curriculum depends upon the erudition—only secondarily the savvy—of the teacher. Despite the profession's tragic assertion of the "priority of pedagogy over curriculum" (Green and Reid 2008, 23), what matters is what teachers know.

"Standards" and "accountability" signify the rhetorical means by which *study* has come to connote only test preparation, not self-cultivation or social democratization. Replacing the professional prerogative—indeed, the professional obligation—to communicate a situated, singular, and ongoing understanding of one's discipline addressed specifically to one's students, attuned to the historical moment, teachers are now scripted, delivering lessons not of their own making. Rather than students learning that academic study provides private passages to the public world wherein their own subjectivities come to form, too many students (knowing only the business model of schooling authoritarian politicians have espoused) have morphed into consumers of "educational services," not subjectively existing individuals struggling to understand themselves in the world through the curriculum they study.

To underscore a concept of education as self-formation through academic study, I devised the method of *currere*. The method of *currere*— the Latin infinitive form of curriculum meaning to run the course, or, in the gerund form, the running of the course—provides a strategy for students of curriculum to study the relations between academic knowledge and life history in the interests of self-understanding and social reconstruction. The two are reciprocally related, as David D. Roberts (1995, 52) makes clear:

> My being cannot be separated from the actual present world, which is the resultant of the totality of history so far and which, unstable and tension-ridden, is endlessly being remade through the responses of present individuals, including me.

"Response" means here not merely "reactive"; the term conveys the creativity, judgment, and knowledge a cosmopolitan education enables.

There are four steps or moments in the method of *currere*: the regressive, the progressive, the analytical, and the synthetical. To illustrate these I have used them to organize my answer to the question that is the title of this book. Enlarging the pool of memory, focusing on fantasies of the future, both understood in the contexts of history and present circumstances, mobilized for conduct not only in the classroom, these four concepts point to the temporal structure of the autobiographical—that is, self-situated—study of educational experience. Indeed, they characterize the temporal structure of educational experience. Through the subjective reconstruction of academic knowledge and lived experience—as each informs the other—we enable understanding of the public world as we discern our privately formulated way through it. In ways small and sometimes large, neither stays the same.

Put another way, the method of *currere* seeks to understand the contribution academic studies makes to one's understanding of one's life (and vice versa), and how both are imbricated in society, politics, and culture. Influenced by literary and feminist theory, *currere* is in this sense a form of cultural criticism. "Cultural criticism," Christopher Lasch (1978, 16) notes, "took on a personal and autobiographical character, which at its worst degenerated into self-display but at its best showed that the attempt to understand culture has to include the way it shapes the critic's own consciousness." Due to the dangers of exhibitionism and exposure (De Castell 1999), I decline to recommend the use of *currere* as an instructional device in the school curriculum, but as a sensibility it can become precious to educators committed to their—and their students'—ongoing self-formation through academic study.

The student of educational experience accepts that at any given moment she or he is located in history and culture, always in a singularly meaningful way, a situation to be expressed autobiographically (if indirectly) through the curriculum. "Biographic situation" suggests the self-restructuring of lived meaning that follows from past situations, meaning that contains, perhaps unarticulated, contradictions of that past and of the present as well as anticipation of possible futures. In the regressive step or moment I try to re-experience past "lived" or existential experience. "I think we are always burdened," Alan Block (2009, 67) acknowledges, "by the past that we don't remember." To stimulate memory one free associates, after the psychoanalytic technique, to re-enter the past, and to thereby enlarge—and transform—one's memory. In doing so, one regresses, that is, re-experiences, to the extent that is possible, the past. The emphasis here, however, is the past, not (yet) its reconstruction in the present. As the present ego is a distillation of all that has transpired, re-experiencing the past triggers reconsideration of present circumstances. As in psychoanalysis (Zaretsky 2004, 5), in the regressive phase free association enables recovery of repressed material that provides additional "information" for understanding the present I inhabit now.

In the second or progressive step one looks toward what is not yet the case, what is not yet present. Like the past, the future inhabits the present. Contemplatively, the student of *currere* imagines possible futures, including fears as well as fantasies of fulfillment. Each has significance for the self I have become now, the self I study through academic knowledge in the midst of my contemporaries, that is, colleagues and students. As is the past, the future is infiltrated with cultural content, but even aspirations for happiness are not only specific to the individual and his or her family history, but incorporate elements of national history and culture. After all, America's founding fathers associated the pursuit of happiness with liberty and life itself, not with home ownership and the avaricious accumulation of capital.

In the analytical stage the student examines both past and present. Etymologically, *ana* means "up, throughout"; *lysis* means "a loosening." The analysis of *currere* is akin to phenomenological bracketing; one's distantiation from the past and extrication from the future functions to create a subjective—third (Wang 2004)—space of freedom in the present. This occurs in the analytic moment, wherein we attempt to discern how the past inheres in the present and in our fantasies of the future. Here one works to understand how culture and history have become particularized in the specificity of the subjectivity within which I dwell and from which I work (Zaretsky 2004, 16).

The analytic phase is not self-scrutiny for the sake of public performance, a self-theatricalizing in which subjective life becomes a social spectacle. As Lasch (1978, 94) points out: "In our society, anxious self-scrutiny (not to be confused with critical self-examination) not only serves to regulate information signaled to others and to interpret signals received; it also establishes an ironic distance from the deadly routine of daily life." The point of *currere* is an intensified engagement with daily life, animated, paradoxically, by an ironic detachment from it. Such educational experience enables engagement with the world always, as Jackson Pollock described his painting, as working from within. So structured, the privacy of interiority becomes expressed through public service as one draws upon subjective resources to address the pressing issues of the day. This is worldliness, not virtuality.

The present becomes local and material, a situation, one populated with persons and with issues to be addressed. In the synthetical step— etymologically *syn* means "together"; *tithenai* means "to place"—one re-enters the lived present. Conscious of one's embodied otherness, one confronts one's own alterity in public. Listening carefully to one's own inner voice in the historical and natural world, one asks: "what is the meaning of the present?" This moment of synthesis—one of intensified interiority expressed to others—is expressed poetically by Mary Aswell Doll (2000, xii): "Curriculum is also ... a coursing, as in an electric current. The work of the curriculum theorist expresses this intense current within, that which courses through the inner person, that which electrifies or gives life to a person's energy source." This is the moment in which self-study becomes reconstructed as public service.

As Megan Boler (1999, 178) appreciates, "the Socratic admonition to 'know thyself' may not lead to self-transformation." By itself and especially as a narrowly psychological process, self-reflection "may result in no measurable change or good to others or oneself" (1999, 178). In contrast to psychologistic conceptions of self-knowledge, what Boler (1999, 178) terms "collective witnessing is always understood in relation to others, and in relation to personal and cultural histories and material conditions." As this volume makes explicit, self-knowledge and collective witnessing are complementary projects of subjective and social reconstruction. "Cultivating a sense of the wild within," for instance, "can enable us to care about and seek to nurture the wild without," as Wapner (2010, 163) appreciates.

The method of *currere* reconceptualizes curriculum from course objectives to complicated conversation. It is conversation with oneself (as a "private" person) and with others threaded through academic knowledge, an ongoing project of self-understanding in which one becomes mobilized for engagement in the world. Conceived as a complicated conversation, the curriculum is an ongoing effort at communication with others that portends the social reconstruction of the public sphere. Curriculum theory asks you, as a prospective or practicing teacher, to consider your positionality as engaged with yourself and your students and colleagues in the construction of a public sphere, a public sphere not yet born, a future that cannot be discerned in, or perhaps even thought from, the present. The present has been historically conceived, and so it is in the past we begin to seek the meaning of the present and our way to the future. It is the past that can dislodge us from submersion in the present, and its articulation can serve as an allegory-of-the-present. No longer a flat line between what is no more and can never be, the present becomes a palimpsest. In such a temporally structured, subjectively animated curriculum, the classroom becomes, simultaneously, a civic square and a room of one's own.

Undertaking the education of the public requires academic *and* self-knowledge, themselves reciprocally related. Our progressive predecessors imagined close associations among classroom protocol, personality, and democratic life, associations not even assumed by the authoritarian personality studies conducted at Berkeley in the 1950s (Adorno,

Frenkel-Brunswick, Levinson, and Sanford 1950). Despite the absence of any law-like association of personality with politics (although there *are* statistical correlations: see Hetherington and Weiler 2009), it matters very much who are you, how you are, with yourself *and* with others. Through the democratization of one's interiorized elements, none of which gets deported (projected, in psychoanalytic terms) onto the bodies of others who then themselves become *Other*, can the body politic be reconstructed as an organic community? Engagement with the world is not only self-mobilization but subjective reconstruction, however modest, occasional, and situation specific. As Christopher Lasch (1978, 206) appreciated: "Discussion of personal issues can no longer be dismissed as a form of 'bourgeois subjectivity'." Indeed, as an allegorical form, autobiography becomes pedagogical political practice for the 21st century.

Subjective engagement is not only anterior to classroom practice, it structures conversation in public, accords it life and meaning. Pasolini's conception of free indirect subjectivity denotes what Dominick LaCapra (2004, 3 n. 2), in another context, construes as the scholar's "strongly 'cathected' transferential relations with protagonists and problems." Focused on historians, LaCapra (2009, 213) wants:

> special constraints with respect to the use of a free indirect style ... the modern discursive analog of a middle voice. A free indirect style performatively intermingles the voice of the historian (or other inquirer) with his or her objects or subjects of analysis. When and how the use of such a free indirect style is legitimate should be questions for critical reflection and debate.

With LaCapra's caution in mind, I point out that Pasolini's free indirect subjectivity (see Greene 1990, 116) was no simple or naive self-expressivity, no unself-conscious projection of self onto the world. Indeed, it was always already complicated by contradictory currents that rewrote those transferential relations (into, for instance, what Pasolini sensed was a second screenplay), not triangulating them (in the ugly jargon of social science methodology), but ensuring boundaries between self and subject matter would not remain blurred but creatively redrawn as they were portrayed in public.

In U.S. school deform, wherein teachers are reduced to cram-school tutors, the call to free indirect subjectivity—expressing one's interiority through academic knowledge—becomes a form of political intransigence. Such teaching remains a performance, but one students can't copy, as it stipulates that study is always subjectively situated, socially engaged, and attuned historically. One must work from within. None of this adds up to "success," nor will it enable the nation to win some fantastically formed "race to the top." Subjectively engaged study is the prerequisite, hardly a guarantee, for erudition and understanding. Such understanding requires "dirt" research (Watson 2007, 120), Harold Innis' characterization of that academic labor prerequisite to understanding not only the history of political economy in Canada, but how, more germane to my present purpose, "to live inside of one's own times and learn to cope with them from within" (Watson 2007, 492 n. 3). School deform substitutes virtual reality—standardized tests divorced from the world—for the actual "dirt" (not only or simplistically "natural") world now walled off by technological insulation.

The degradation of the biosphere constitutes everyone's emergency, the impending catastrophe, the compelling "common democratic project" (Carlson 1998, 218). The intensifying ecological crisis requires us to cultivate what Spivak (2003, 71) terms "planetarity," in which, she suggests, we human beings constitute a "species of alterity" (2003, 72). As a species of alterity, we understand ourselves as the "they" who threaten Life itself. "If we imagine ourselves as planetary subjects rather than global agents, planetary creatures rather than global entities," Spivak explains (2003, 74), "alterity remains un-derived from us; it is not our dialectical negation, it contains us as much as it flings us away." We are the "other," not only to ourselves, but to Life itself. Rendered a "we" by a common enemy—ourselves—might we unite in a common curricular cause? "Internationalism," Spivak (2003, 92) asserts, "can, today, shelter planetarity," providing a "displaced site for the imagination of planetarity" (2003, 95). If we can imagine ourselves allegorically, as "we" and as "other," can we re-educate ourselves toward, and force our politicians to institutionalize, sustainability? Such "planetarity" requires, I suggest, subjective and social reconstruction through the ongoing education of the public. We find the future not in the present, however, but in the past.

II Allegories-of-the-Present

> The dead ... are never quite as dead as we think; they are part of us, not just genetically but psychologically.
>
> —Hilary Mantel (2009, 8)

To understand curriculum as complicated conversation, I invoke the concept of "allegory." It is, in my usage, interrelated with "reconstruction," as each reactivates the past in order to find the future. To *reconstruct* means to "establish or assemble again, to subject (an organ or part) to surgery to re-form its structure or correct a defect." Dewey underlined this last idea in his assertion that thinking—the means of reconstruction (1920, 134)—"takes its departure from specific conflicts in experience that occasion perplexity and trouble" (1920, 138). In my revision of Dewey, "reconstruction" becomes a form of "working through" in LaCapra's (2009, 25) sense, as "the attempt to connect the notion of working through the past to sociopolitical practice." It is important to note that my conception of "reconstruction" contrasts with its usages in historiography, that is, as aiming to reconstruct the past "as it was." In his discussion of Pasolini's *Il Vangelo,* Maurizio Viano addresses these distinctions. The film, he explains:

> eschews the idea of faithful historical reconstruction and opts for analogical rereading. Whereas reconstruction forgets the present and aims at an absolute past, analogy translates the past into the present and suggests a series of relations of resemblance and difference for the audience to recognize and to judge. If reconstruction ultimately abuses history, holding it up to the paranoid myth of discovering "what really happened," analogy uses personal and historical knowledge to gain insight for the present.
>
> (1993, 136–137)

In my view, allegory embraces both "resemblance" and "difference," the particularity of history *and* the past's significance for the present moment. Etymologically, "allegory" means to "speak publicly in an assembly." Its ancient Greek antecedents forefront its autobiographical, pedagogical, and communicative character. *A speech at once concrete and abstract, through allegory one narrates a specific story which hints at a more general significance.* Its characters are at once particular and symbolic, simultaneously historical and metahistorical, even mythological. Understanding curriculum allegorically self-consciously incorporates the past into the present, threaded through one's subjectivity. In speaking allegorically, we are not merely exchanging information. When we speak allegorically we do not do so for the sake of a future in which such information will, we imagine, become usable. Rather, we self-reflexively articulate what is at hand, reactivating the past so as to render the present, including ourselves, intelligible. As an ethical, political, always intellectual undertaking, the complicated conversation that is the curriculum enables *educational experience.*

Because each conversation is distinctive—that is, if it is enmeshed in the moment and expressive of the distinctiveness of those participating—it may not congeal into a conclusion. Nor does it necessarily mirror an anterior aim or objective. In the complicated conversation that is the curriculum, moments of synthesis may be deferred, and when invoked, they are contingently articulated, as "working through" what is the present requires the continual reactivation of the past, not the instrumental calculation of what will work in the future. For Pasolini such deferral recommended styles of "excess" and "contamination," in part to make vivid the palimpsest that is the present by emphasizing the present's noncoincidence with itself, by ensuring that the conversation does not devolve into a premature consensus or, at least, remain there (Rumble 1996, 13). Curriculum as *currere* emphasizes temporal distinctions, not for the sake of a simplistic proceduralism, but to enable the reconstruction of the present through the reactivation of the past, differentiating present-mindedness into the co-extensive simultaneity of temporal attunements, expressed individually in social context through the academic knowledge.

Allegory acknowledges academic knowledge as important *for its own sake*, even as it also encourages the articulations of its *educational* significance, the latter conveyed in the question: what might this knowledge signify for us as actually existing individuals at this time, in this place? In contrast to the information technologies (see chapter 5), allegory underscores that our individual lives are structured by ever *widening* circles of influence: from family through friends to strangers, each of whom personify culture, symbolize society, embody history. Allegory's movements are not only outward: they are also inward, as allegory provokes reflection on, say, the sciences not only as specific academic disciplines with distinctive intellectual histories and present circumstances, but also as social, as conducted in the public interest. Science is subjective, however subtextual and indirectly the subjectivity of science is expressed objectively.

Important in themselves, the academic disciplines as well as their interdisciplinary offspring are not only vocations (and/or paths to other vocations) for which the curriculum prepares. Questions of competence and skill are never severed from matters of meaning, fact, and significance; they are not only interwoven, they are mutually constitutive. The longer and more diligently we study a discipline the more we come to see its patterned detail and discern its porous boundaries, not only horizontally (with other contemporaneous disciplines) but vertically (both in terms of its own intellectual history and its emplacement in History). Allegory emphasizes the latter as it dwells not only on events (in the next chapter on Weimar Germany) but also questions of representation, as these follow from the curricular juxtaposition of past and present. "Allegory," Angelika Rauch (2000, 184) explains, "is an alternative way of reading that assembles fragmentary pieces in a collage that consists of various, if only once meaningful, representational elements." Discerning that meaning is the labor of academic study. And it is subjectivity through which I muster the prerequisite commitment as well as the cognitive and lived structures around which I reconstruct what others know and what I do not yet know but feel drawn, even compelled, to study.

"Subjectivity" is an abstract noun for the verb that means being alive and living to tell about it. However constructed, contingent, and even imaginary the "I" that speaks, it is "I" who is alive, for a little while longer at least. Being alive is no abstract or hypothetical phenomenon. Lived experience is not preconceptual but always already linked to our representations of it. While none of these (lived experience, representations, and their reciprocal relations) are necessarily simultaneous or transparent—in trauma, representation is belated because our experience of an event cannot coincide with it—it is "I" (in whatever reconstructed form) who must communicate the character and meaning of experience, including to myself. However finally elusive "I" am—not only to myself but often to others—it is "I"—however much the first person singular is a term of convenience—who exists, in whom history, culture, and society are personified in singular form. "I" am allegorical.

Study enables me to articulate the singularity of those forms, requiring me to discern their history and present associations. Study, then, becomes sensible not in an "environment," the long-time term of preference for a social and behavioral science that has too often stripped history and culture from its efforts to understand what it observes. Rather, study proceeds in a meaningful situation. As Madeleine Grumet (1978, 281) pointed out decades ago, the concept of "environment" conveys a blank slate, a space without people, a place without history and emptied of human intention. In contrast, "situation" specifies that what we face is already overdetermined by legacy, meaning, and intention. While no metaphysical bedrock, nevertheless it is "I" who testifies to the realities within and around us. "[N]either transcendent nor in process of self-realization," David D. Roberts (1995, 7) explains, each of us (as individuals, as collectivities):

> is rather bound up with some specific situation that is historical in a non-Hegelian sense. It would seem, then, that a post-Hegelian form of historical inquiry might replace subjectivity or consciousness as the key to self-understanding.

Allegory, then, follows autobiography. Allegory acknowledges both the specificity and distinctiveness of autobiography as well as the generalizing and common characteristics of History. And while it seems ill-advised to *replace* "subjectivity" or "consciousness" with History (to do so seems Hegelian), I endorse the concept of allegory because it forefronts both History and questions of its representation as central to understanding self and society through study.

So I offer to you this answer to the question "what is curriculum theory?" not on some blank slate implied by the term "environment" but in a situation with ever-widening circles of significance. I start in

U.S. school classrooms, wherein students are pressured to score higher on standardized tests that allegedly measure educational achievement. Never mind that test taking has never been—until now—conflated with educational achievement (always before it was only one indicator among others, and not necessarily the most significant one), and never mind that the "skills" these tests purport to measure are themselves abstractions severed from situations, reflecting the self-referential and enclosed world of standardization, academic versions of crossword puzzles. Driven by such self-enclosed rituals, educational institutions devolve into cram schools, no longer about the world but, instead, about themselves, about those tests, apparently technical but altogether ideological, as students learn to process information without raising questions about that information or the process. *What knowledge is of most worth?* is replaced with *"what's your test score?"* Such a shift in the curricular question ends critical thinking in the name of economic productivity. Obama's *Race to the Top* substitutes *nationalism* (which the *noblesse oblige* of "Teach for America" makes explicit) for the *social justice* implied in Bush's *No Child Left Behind*, as each administration forefronted the issue on which its adversaries deemed it most vulnerable.

No longer about the world, the education of the public in the United States is no longer the public medium of self-expression and site of social communication. Certainly it is no opportunity for social reconstruction. Reducing education to a means to others' political ends means muzzling those—schoolteachers and education professors—who might alert the public that testing condemns students to the inferior education it was presumably installed to correct. Teachers are now contracted to follow the scripts curricula provide and students are confined to study what test-makers have divined as "skills." Teacher education is to be aligned with these scripts. Once the sphere of open inquiry, "freedom schools" (see chapter 4, section IV) have been reorganized to serve as the sites of the "totalitarian temptation" (Peukert 1992, 241). That phrase references a historically specific configuration: Weimar Germany. Then and there, as the German historian Detlev J. K. Peukert (1992, 241) tells us, the totalitarian temptation was expressed:

> in a desire for highly personalized leadership; in the wish that middle class privileges should be restored; in the drive to dismantle the egalitarianism of the welfare state; and in a realization that the mass media could be used to shape public opinion and the public domain generally.

The secret site of totalitarianism in America today is hidden right out in the open. It is the school.

To help answer in late 2010 *What Is Curriculum Theory?* I replace the Bush-based allegory of the South (with its history of racial servitude, economic elitism, and anti-democratic authoritarianism: Pinar 2004, 93, 233) with Weimar Germany, accenting the Republic's intensifying political polarization, economic instability, and social prejudice. Historical facts are primary, but it is facts' capacity to invoke our imagination that marks them as allegorical. Their meaning is not confined to the past where they occurred; they spill into our experience of the present. That meaning is to be articulated, in solitude in study, with others in conversation, but these facts do not belong to us in the present. Bringing the past into the present while rigorously refusing to conflate the two incurs that "creative tensionality" (Aoki 2005 [1985/1991], 232) that structures an allegorical sensibility. Such a sensibility seems to me a curricular version of Du Bois' racialized "dual consciousness," enabling us to remain attuned to the specific in front of us while not losing sight of its antecedents and associations as we act on our not yet deadened desire for freedom through knowledge (Carby 1998, 17).

For Walter Benjamin, Rauch (2000, 186) reminds, allegory was a "model to represent the historical moment in terms of how a text affects us as readers even though we cannot determine its meaning." Allegory derived from Benjamin's conviction that the cultivation of a historical sensibility depended in part on the literariness of language and "its redemptive or memorial capacity in rhetorical structures" (2000, 186). Those structures are aesthetic, but what accords them immediacy and meaning is their saturation by the subjectivity of those who study them, in solitude and assembly. Through allegory we can build passages from the particularity of our situations to the alterity of others past. For Benjamin, Rauch (2000, 213) suggests, history becomes accessible through allegory.

It is this tensioned reciprocity between subjectivity and history that structures allegory. That is why school curriculum guidelines must never be more than guidelines, inviting reformulation according to the professional judgment of the individual educator. Subjectively situated, historically attuned teachers must be free to follow wherever their imaginations and instincts lead them, acutely aware that knowledge structures both instinct and imagination. Like speech, allegory is, then, not only self-referential; it extends beyond itself to comment on, connect to, what is past in the present, in those who are present among us. An allegory-of-the-present combines the uniqueness and authenticity that Walter Benjamin associated with the aura of an individually crafted work of art with the tradition such subjectively saturated art inevitably incorporates and reconstructs.

The teacher is in this sense an artist; complicated conversation is her or his medium. The curriculum becomes complicated through its "combinatory structure" (Rauch 2000, 188). When she reformulates allegory as "hieroglyphs," as "fragmentary remnants of historic cultural context which is lost," Rauch (2000, 231 n. 7) is acknowledging that such "combinatory structure" creates a "chaotic" image (i.e., Benjamin's "dialectical image") in tension with itself. Conversation is complicated as it unravels the present into its constitutive threads while acknowledging its unprecedented immediacy. This is simultaneously intellectual and psychological labor. Because intellectual labor is also an emotional undertaking, the individual teacher's judgment is necessary to rebalance and restructure these various elements each day, in each class. Standardization makes everyone stupid.

Allegory begins in the teacher's study, where it is transposed into curriculum design, or less formally, teaching (not necessarily "lesson") plans, as with what topic or exercise one chooses to start a given day's classroom dialogue. It might be helpful to reflect on one's intentions, but one's "objectives" are hardly primary or necessarily interesting. What matters is how complicated—simultaneously specific and general, literal and analogical—the conversation can be. Allegory "ends" in what students make of such conversation, a fate hardly removed from the province of the teacher but never definitively dependent on him or her. Even the most creative and provocative lesson can fall flat, as anyone who has ever taught knows. Attempting to force students' engagement (let alone "learning" more generally) becomes autocratic if not mediated by the subjective knowledge teachers have of the unique individuals in one's classroom. Moreover, what students make of their study may not be known for months or even years, and then only by the students themselves. Specific "core standards" such those promulgated by the Obama administration (Lewin 2010, July 21)—with the expectation that these will then be learned by students because teachers have taught them—amount to magical thinking.

Rather than making learning "accessible" (which often means watering down content so that students parrot it back), educators are engaged in an ongoing conversation. As in any conversation, one discerns misunderstanding, can supplement incomplete comprehension, and support questioning. There is both intimacy and formality in the classroom, familiarity and distancing. Can we know when those juxtaposed elements that comprise the curricular "hieroglyph" stretch credulity? There are logical relations between elements that cannot be violated at whim, but even apparently illogical relations can be grasped when contextualized in the moment, in an ongoing conversation. As Siegfried Kracauer (1995, 234) pointed out:

> The more reality opens itself up to man, the more foreign to him the average world with its distorted conceptual petrifactions becomes. He recognizes that a boundless plentitude of qualities inhabits each phenomenon, and that each is subject to widely differing laws. But

> the more he becomes aware of the many-sidedness of things, the more it becomes possible for him to relate them to each other.

Kracauer is acknowledging what has become in our era a commonplace: that reality is socially constructed. Of course, that hardly means that it is immaterial or arbitrary, but social constructionism does underscore that everyday life is not only what it seems, that ordinariness contains and expresses elements not on the surface, elements that, despite their apparent difference, could also be related to each other, although not necessarily due to contiguity. Difference becomes intelligible within relations of resemblances, as Kaja Silverman (2009, 74) teaches us through the concept of *analogy*, that which "links us to other beings." "But," she (2009, 74) continues, "analogy is also internal to our own being," as it is "what connects the person we were yesterday with the slightly different person we are today."

Sociality and subjectivity are, in this sense, analogous. As teachers, individuation denotes the developmental—and intellectual—specification of our individuality, informed as individuality inevitably is by society, history, culture. It is specifically formed through academic study and participation in the complicated conversation that is the curriculum. In so participating, Silverman (2009, 65) makes clear:

> we connect our lives to many others—to lives that are over, and to lives that have not yet begun, as well as to those proximate to us in time and space. Rather than a self-contained volume, authorized by us, our history is only one chapter in an enormous and ever-expanding book, whose overall meaning and shape we cannot even begin to grasp, let along determine. ... This volume is written from the inside, though the analogies we acknowledge and those we refuse.

Working from within, specifying the singularity of situations through threading the needle that is our individual subjective experience, we affirm resemblance through difference. Simultaneously abstract and concrete, such complicated conversation is allegorical.

III Allegory as Montage

> [T]he allegorical sensibility ... arises from a condition of radical designification, of an emptying out of (conventional) meaning.
> —Eric L. Santner (2006, 20)

"Allegory," Rauch (2000, 208) asserts, "becomes a new mode of signification that represents the past in a new, meaningful way as if to guide us in how we can sensibly live with this 'past in ruins'." While Rauch may overstate its "newness," she does point (if inadvertently) to the significance of allegory for curriculum theory. The central curriculum question—*what knowledge is of most worth?*—is no instrumental calculation of what skills students need to succeed in some imaginary workplace. Nor is it identification of the next step to take, as when so-called skills are to be mastered for the sake of learning more advanced "skills" later, as if the curriculum were a prolonged Ponzi scheme, later payouts dependent upon ever-increasing investments. Instrumental rationality itself has long been decried in curriculum studies as foreclosing educational experience, which is less a means to an end than an unforeseen and infinitely variegated consequence of study. Like art objects, outcomes of study cannot be known in advance, unless, of course, one's intention is to copy.

"Teaching to the test," Martha Nussbaum (2010, 134) knows, "[p]roduces an atmosphere of student passivity and teacher routinization. The creativity and individuality that mark the best humanistic teaching and learning has a hard time finding room to unfold." I'll say. In contrast to teaching to the test, asking *what knowledge is of most worth?* refocuses the question of curriculum on erudition and judgment threaded through subjectivity, attuned to (but not aligned with) history, culture, and politics. The existing individual is primary, and so the question is never answered once-and-for-all. The curricular question is a call to individuality, as it invites addressing the concrete other in one's midst. This is not the so-called "possessive individual" associated with capital accumulation, or the rationalistic self-interested hedonist associated with economics, but the actually existing, culturally variegated, historically sedimented, not always conscious human being for whom the question of academic knowledge is also a question of self-knowledge. These domains of lived experience—for cognition is no computerized processing of information but an embodied intellectual project structured by specificity of situation—reverberate reciprocally, requiring reconstruction, both subjective and social. Such reconstruction renders lived experience educational experience. Allegory demands both detachment and intimacy in its transfiguration of lived experience into educational experience. Allegory encourages educational experience by its representation of knowledge apparently unrelated to the present moment, knowledge the study of which counters the pull of the present. Depicting the Weimar Republic not only addresses but contradicts the present moment, relocating us in the past where we might find our way to the future (Rauch 2000, 132).

We cannot find the future if we are immersed in the present. In our era, present-mindedness ensures our submersion in the present, forever distracted by the steady stream of sensory experience stimulated by technological innovation. Gadgets can never substitute for the protracted labor of understanding and study. Such labor requires us to grasp the distinctiveness of situations—history *is* a series of particulars—but to appreciate as well how the present resembles the past, especially when we fail to discern its dangers. Presentism—the incapacity to discern the distinctiveness of the present, its historically sedimented and socially unstable nature, its foreshadowing of things to come—denotes an inability to *be* in the present. Only a historical sensibility enables us to "be here now." Present-mindedness is inevitably dissociation, especially from those unconscious elements inherited from the past that comprise the present. Understood as lived, history and memory are also unconscious history (Rauch 2000, 196), a history allegory resurfaces.

In this paradoxical sense, then, allegory underscores the distinctiveness of the present situation as it hints at its mythological implications. Like myth, allegories "present, in an encapsulated and powerful form, the essence of the circumstance of modern man" (Watson 2007, 301). Alexander John Watson is here discussing E. A. Havelock, who taught classics at the University of Toronto for seventeen years (1930–1947). He translated *Prometheus Bound*, emphasizing the tragedy of the play, in the specificity of which Havelock also discerned the tragedy of Western civilization, as:

> the very course of that civilization—technological advance—ends up undermining its basis. What could have led (and perhaps eventually will lead) to self-conscious freedom ends in the powerless enchainment of the intellect.
>
> (Watson 2007, 302)

When we imagine ourselves more "advanced" than those who preceded us—mistaking technological for moral and intellectual progress—we overlook what the past has to teach us. Our experience is not educational. Allegories are not only cautionary tales; they can precipitate shifts in subjectivity, as one "attempt[s] to develop an overall perspective that might counter somewhat the myopia of the modern mentality" (Watson 2007, 302).

Walter Benjamin's interest in allegory, Rauch (2000, 17) points out, had to do with "the psychological effect that it had, especially as a motive for developing our historical sensibility," our, in Peter Seixas's (2004, 8) term, "historical consciousness." Such a sensibility, Benjamin suggested, enables us to discern the "recursive" quality of eras of decline; these eras (in George Steiner's [1998, 24] paraphrase) "resemble each other not only in their vices but also in their strange climate of rhetorical and aesthetic vehemence." Thus, Steiner (1998, 24) continues, Benjamin's study of the baroque was "no mere antiquarian, archival hobby; it mirrors, it anticipates and helps grasp the dark present." Such allegory, like art, "might play a special role in a destitute time … enabling us literally to recover what we have forgotten or lost" (Roberts 1995, 127). Without the past, there is no present.

Subjectivity is indelibly historical, containing the traces of what is past and now forgotten as well as what remains uppermost in mind. But what remains uppermost for many of us in the press of the present is the next task that awaits us. Our emplacement in a present is structured by instrumental sequences of undertakings that only make sense within those sequences; such presentism precipitates stripping away the past, a fading of the future. The present comes to glare at us with "an empty stare" (1988, 116), Grumet's chilling visual image for a curriculum bleached of subjective intentionality, an environment of never-ending subjectively dissociated assignments.

Historicality is no preoccupation with what is past. By studying the past one hopes to work it through, however partial and halting and ongoing such intellectual–psychological labor must be. Trauma is inevitably displaced and deferred precisely because it cannot be worked through. More likely—although this is no simple binary—it is acted out, as in school deform. Trauma becomes the political unconscious of the present, belated, relocated sedimentation whose very illegibility blocks its working through. No narrowly therapeutic conception, such a concept of "working through," in LaCapra's (2009, 54) cumbersome but clarifying definition:

> is in general an articulatory practice with political dimensions: to the extent one works through trauma and its symptoms on both personal and sociocultural levels, one is able to distinguish between past and present and to recall in memory that something happened to one (or one's people) back then while realizing that one is living here and now with openings to the future.

It is such complicated conversation—acknowledging the trauma of historical experience while never ceasing to articulate its character and effects—that reactivates the past in the present. No esoteric activity, such engagement structures the labor of subjective and social reconstruction.

"To live in the present," Ross Posnock (1998, 91) observes, "demands a radical act of deracination." He thinks of Frantz Fanon as an "unprecedented" instance of such "willed exile and self-invention" (1998, 91). Born in Martinique, educated in France, the Algerian revolutionary and theoretician was simultaneously a Caribbean black man and a cosmopolitan citizen of the world, an "impure" ("contaminated" in Pasolini's term), "anti-organic, radically deracinated intellectual" like (Posnock [1998, 297

n. 3] offers) the U.S. feminist Margaret Fuller. That "strenuously intellectual woman" (see Kennedy 1995, 15) inspired Jane Addams (Knight 2005, 93) and Ralph Waldo Emerson (Townsend 1996, 16).

One of the greatest of New York's public intellectuals—Susan Sontag—also embraced the necessity of self-extrication through social analysis, evident in her "great themes of melancholic self-reflection, self-enervation, and intellectual exile" (Kennedy 1995, 10). Liam Kennedy (1995, 10) notes that the "mind as passion" and the "body in pain" are central themes in her writing. Sontag's passion and pain were physical and phenomenological, but they were also worldly, often political, as she enacted the tradition of the intellectual as *engagé*. No doubt it was intellectuals' commitment to "high culture"—and specifically as counterpoint to a degraded mass consumer culture—that triggered the reflex reaction of many Marxists. For self-proclaimed "materialists," any self-reflexive distantiation from the everyday—as in Maxine Greene's insightful conception of teacher as stranger (1973)—spells bourgeois quietism.

Even the work of Edward Said—whose conception of the activist intellectual as amateur I invoked in the First Edition (Pinar 2004, 181)—"emanates," according to Neil Lazarus (1999, 188), "a distinct whiff of modernist nostalgia—exilic, metropolitan, deracinated." Evidently unable to appreciate that these movements (exile and deracination) are prerequisite to political engagement, Lazarus (1999, 188) overlooks them in his reluctant affirmation of Said's intellectual achievements: "the opening up of horizons, the crystallizing of memories and experiences as legitimate aspects of a cultural heritage, the discursive contestation of dominating paradigms of knowledge, the production of counter-truths, etc." And while such movements are, Lazarus (1999, 188) emphasizes, "universalistic," that is, directed toward "internationalism," they are, I would add, also local, birthed in individual life history, present situation, and fantasies of the future. The profoundly fantastic character of intellectual practice—its transferential relation to its topic (as LaCapra notes), even when that topic is "material"—underscores that the public intellectual is also, must be (if s/he is no parrot), a private person.

Deracination provides the self-reflexive distance required to discern the past in the present, the concrete in the abstract, the local in the universal. The modernization of cities—for instance of Beijing for the 2008 Olympics—erases not only architectural history, but those cultural and subjective sites lived differently from the consumerist, secularized present. For Pasolini, it was Rome that provided the palimpsest only allegory could communicate, as the city's juxtaposition of ruins and everyday bustle only sharpened the disjuncture between now and then. But as Rome "became ever more derealized by the 'progress,' suggested by the Autostrada," John David Rhodes (2007, xiv) tells us, "Pasolini turned from documentarily specific representations located elsewhere, often in Africa." What he sought was deracination through relocation. This yearning for elsewhere becomes evident in several of his filmic characters, such as Emilia in *Teorema*, who becomes, Maurizio Viano (1993, 212) asserts, "an allegory of what exists outside the system." Such relocation (or exile) was not only personified in individuals but in communities as well. "What counted" for Pasolini, Patrick Rumble (1996, 139) explains, "was a politics of cinematic representation as an allegory of community, as a figuration of an impossible society." Structured as complicated conversation, synoptic texts—like the one you're reading now—aspire to act as allegories among the ruins of education, relocating ourselves from degradation of the present by reactivating the past.

Given the pervasiveness of calculation and instrumentality, it becomes imperative to acknowledge that "allegory" can complicate conversation. That is no outcome. In juxtaposing incommensurate fragments, allegory splits our attention while dissociating nothing, demanding that we discern what is distinctive in each fragment while at the same time appreciating the complexity of association that such a montage reveals. It requires (in Maxine Greene's terms, 2001, 122) the "release of imagination" in order to grapple with the tension of dissonance. But allegory makes no promises, as Avital Ronell (2003, 107) explains:

> Along with its capacity to mine and produce anxiety, however, allegory disturbs the very possibility of hermeneutic reflection. Disfiguring itself even as it unfolds, the allegorical attacks understanding as it profiles a power to defy comprehension. It defies the comprehension—indeed, the comprehensiveness—promised by the symbol, which offers an image of organic totality. By contrast, the allegorical desiccates the organic unity of the world potentiated by the symbol.

Allegory keeps open the question of the present, however conclusive the evidence, precisely because it declines to coincide with it.

The "allegorical script" (in Benjamin's terms: see Ronell 2003, 107) shifts our focus from what we see to what we can imagine, ignoring neither, emphasizing the disjuncture between the two. Such "dialectical images"—arranged "according to the cognitive principles of montage" (Buck-Morss 1993, 311)—do not fuse but remain destructured. Benjamin suggested: "Allegory established itself most permanently where transitoriness and eternity confronted each other most closely" (quoted in Santner 2006, 21).

Not to make a fetish of uncertainty—too often the case with postmodern theory (see Lather 2007, 70)—such "double consciousness" forecloses any singular (even "always" uncertain) perception or explanation. Nor would it accord any privilege to their multiplication, as if reality were a multiple-choice test. While signifying something else, allegorical fragments denote facticity, thereby resisting both historicism and presentism. Because these fragments—chapters 3 and 4 in the present volume—do not coincide with themselves, they resist their own transparency as well. Such "tension between metaphorical flight and documentary weight," Rhodes (2007, 137) points out, "is at the heart of Pasolini's practice." It is at the heart of any allegory-of-the-present, a complicated conversation between actuality and potentiality, specificity and generality, locality and universality. Such juxtaposition communicates the "structural contagion" (Rumble 1996, 69) that replicates rhetorically the structural presence of the past in the present.

IV Why Weimar?

> In certain epochs the image retains its power; the symbolic presentation becomes allegory.
>
> —Siegfried Kracauer (1995, 60)

Why did I choose Weimar as an allegory-of-the-present? Could that historical moment be any more different from ours? Germany had suffered defeat in World War I; the United States emerged victorious from the Cold War. It is true that we are now engaged in an unending "war on terror" that by definition precludes "victory," but the United States is widely acknowledged as the world's only superpower. The United States is a self-proclaimed (not without self-contradiction) and widely acknowledged (not without disputation) democratic republic without (relatively speaking) an authoritarian past. While George W. Bush personified an aggressive American Presidency, there is no public debate over restoring the monarchy or abandoning democracy, as there was in post-World War I Germany. Except for scattered gangs, there are no Nazis and no large Communist movement, as marked the far right and left during the Weimar Republic. There are no reparations to pay (although the national debt grows analogously enormous) and during 2010 it was deflation, not inflation, that threatened economic growth. Despite the disturbing degrees of national debt, the U.S. dollar's status as the world's reserve currency (the Japanese yen and European Union's Euro remain only back-ups) props up the currency's exchange value. The Weimar German Mark had no such international support.

The 2008 Recession *was* deep. Unemployment remains high by U.S. standards, especially for younger Americans. Generational differences in economic expectations and opportunities were also a factor during Weimar, undermining even university students' loyalty to a parliamentary system that seemed to spell primarily the freedom to be unemployed. Despite continued opposition, women and sexual minorities continue to make political gains, as they did during the Weimar Republic. The election of Barack Obama hardly signaled the end of racism in America; indeed, it seems to have provided an opportunity for its intensification through diffusion. While their historical experience was completely different from African Americans, Jews in the Weimar Republic also enjoyed greater integration into the public sphere while suffering an intensification of prejudice.

The two moments and places could not be more different, except for a few disturbing resemblances. What Peukert (1992, 251) termed the "totalitarian temptation" is simultaneously historically specific and timeless. When individual anxiety and social frustration build to some breaking point—itself always specific and under the influence of agency—there can be breakdown, and not only loss of control. There can be an intensification of control. In Weimar, as Peukert demonstrates, there were enemies of the Republic from the beginning, as well as those who were newly disaffected, those who became fatigued from the never-ending series of economic and political crises, whose desperation left them liable to believe the promises of the Nazis to set things right. While the contemporary United States also suffers the politics of *ressentiment*, without another Deep Recession or terrorist attacks (neither prospect is out of the question, of course) political extremism should be contained.

What has happened in the United States is the relocation of the "totalitarian temptation." Punitive action against the past and preemptive protection against the future have been acted out inside that institution wherein the past is reconstructed and the future is foretold. It was onto the American public school that Cold War anxieties were projected. The Kennedy administration's national school reform began as the response to the threat symbolized by Sputnik, whose launching provided evidence of the Soviet Union's technological superiority. As convoluted as the U.S. response was—why not a military response to a military threat?—it became even further convoluted as schools and universities became the sites of anti-Vietnam War protests, civil rights struggles, and the intellectual genesis of the counter-culture, that 1960s anti-capitalist, anti-bourgeois, multiracial and gendered refusal to follow in father's footsteps. In the presidential campaign of 1968, the splitting of the liberal left (among Hubert Humphrey, Eugene McCarthy, and Robert Kennedy) enabled the election of Richard Nixon and the onset of the Great Repression, first articulated as the restoration of "Law and Order" and its educational complement, "Back to the Basics." School reform has been, continues to be, a version of "reform school" for a delinquent generation, punishing them and their children and now grandchildren for taking too literally life, liberty, and the pursuit of happiness. This American expression of the totalitarian temptation is achieved not through Nazi-style burning of books but through standardized testing. Both accomplish the same. Testing controls what teachers teach and what students learn. In its political function, testing becomes "an allegory of the annihilation of differences in the name of one principle," as Viano (1993, 301) characterized Pasolini's portrait of fascism in *Salò*. Like the children kidnapped in that film, schoolchildren are subjected to constant surveillance and inspection, tests they can only fail.

While it had been the generals who led Germany to defeat in World War I, the German military managed to relocate responsibility for this fact, concocting a tale of accountability that excluded them and the soldiers they directed. In fact, the generals regained their reputations by persuading the public that Germany had been "stabbed in the back at home by Jews and Communists" (Gay 2001 [1968], 18), a ploy rightists have used in the United States, especially during the "Red Scares" of the early 1920s and the 1950s. To explain Sputnik, U.S. politicians deflected attention from themselves and the "military-industrial complex," not onto Jews and Communists, but onto teachers and the public schools. As political protests intensified during the 1960s, many fantasized the schools and the universities as havens for radicals and other treasonous subversives. As we see in chapter 4, textbooks—the formal school curriculum—became the battleground for ideological control.

Public school teachers became the traitors who "stabbed us in the back." They allowed Sputnik to happen, they complied with the 1954 Supreme Court decision to desegregate the public schools, they tolerated, even encouraged, un-American questions concerning race and gender. It was teachers who placed the nation at risk. It is teachers who must be controlled. "We" (legislators, coded male) will tie "their" (teachers, coded female) hands behind their backs and muffle their voices. Teachers will say what we tell them to say, as we will script their curriculum and align it with the tests on which students must excel. As in the military, children will be drilled on basic skills until they get them right. The visual images of "successful" classrooms—broadcast periodically on the nightly news—are now those of children chanting in unison, mesmerized by animated youth allegedly "teaching for America," students eager to please, determined to comply. No critical thinking necessary, no need to acknowledge uncertainty or ambiguity: in tests there are right answers. "As one reads through these tests," Peter Taubman (2009, 26) reports:

> a view of knowledge emerges that equates understanding or creativity or erudition with information retrieval, the ability to concentrate for long periods of time on a meaningless task, alacrity in making decisions, and compliance with directives that have no relevance to one's own interests, desires, abilities, knowledge, or understanding.

In such suspension of subjectivity and history for the sake of "excellence" one hears an echo of the German novelist, World War I veteran, and political theorist Ernst Jünger, who, Kaes, Jay, and Dimendberg (1995, 355) remind, "prophesied the overcoming of decadent bourgeois culture through violent struggle ... [and the] spiritualization of technology in the service of an authoritarian domination of nature." No longer confident we can dominate nature, what saves us from the apocalypse are the children and those teachers we have ordered to "reform" them. But the children, it seems, are rather busy, tweeting and bullying, as we will see in chapter 5.

School reform is a political reenactment of that repetition-compulsion characteristic of posttraumatic behavior. Trauma means "experience that is not fully assimilated as it occurs," Caruth (1996, 5) reminds. The anti-Vietnam War movement, the rise of the counter culture, school desegregation and the civil rights movement amounted to more "experience" than many European Americans could assimilate, as white reaction against it continues forty years later in the schools, where insistence on intellectual conformity compelled by standardized tests stifles dissent of any kind. Creativity, critical thinking, even the canon are all casualties of curriculum aligned with standardized examinations. "[T]he survival of trauma is not the fortunate passage beyond a violent event," Caruth (1996, 62–63) notes, "but rather the endless *inherent necessity* of repetition, which ultimately may lead to destruction." Test after test distracts teachers and students from facing the unresolved issues of the 1960s, prominent among them racialized, gendered, economic injustice. What gets destroyed is what school reform was installed to protect: democracy.

Surely that statement is hyperbole. No matter how test-after-test numbs minds, no matter how test-after-test installs submissiveness, no matter how skills render fact-less their memories, surely students will survive whatever we do to them. They will somehow, at some point, manage to self-reflexively realize what has been done to them. After all, many of the students who participated in the civil rights and anti-Vietnam War struggles of the 1960s had been educated in conservative classrooms. However conservative, they were not uniform, rendered standardized by tests. By stressing the ideals of democracy and the exceptionality of America, conservative classrooms inadvertently encouraged students to contest injustice. With academic knowledge replaced with "cognitive skills," on what can future generations draw?

Schools cannot ensure the future, but when controlled by ideologues they can efface the past. I am thinking here of the history of racial politics and violence in America, the history that makes contemporary economic inequality intelligible. Standardized testing reenacts racial subjugation as it commodifies black bodies as important only economically, ignoring black inquisitiveness and intellectual independence—the "freedom" in "freedom schools" (as we will see chapter 4)—as "skills" render the past irrelevant to a present where only the future matters. The focus on decontextualized "skills" quietly accomplishes that ideological suppression that before required raucous political debate (see chapter 4, section II). Rather than openly suppressing knowledge of slavery and lynching (for instance), skills-based curriculum and the apparent impersonality of standardized tests masks the historical amnesia, the racial violence, they reenact.

In the posttraumatic syndrome that is contemporary U.S. politics, accented by political polarization and the near collapse of the economic system in 2008, there is little patience or respect for academic knowledge, unless it leads to miracle cures or quick profits. Knowledge of the event is what gets suppressed in trauma, translated into belated "acting out" rather than "working through" (LaCapra 2004, 56). Skills are the solution, an empty promise that lends itself to the magical thinking that any problem is solvable with the right "skill set." In such a state of emergency, contemplation is simply too slow, and probably elitist anyway, requiring leisure: who has time for that? In the posttraumatic republic that was Weimar the very concept of classics was a casualty. Despite President Friedrich Ebert's invocation of both Goethe's *Faust* and the "spirit of Weimar" in his 1919 speech before the National Assembly, Matt Erlin (2009, 162) reminds, few believed that the concept of high culture could provide any rallying point for the new Germany. As many do now, many Germans questioned whether the liberal arts had any value in a politically tumultuous, economically imperiled present. In a 1929 discussion with Herbert Jhering, Erlin (2009, 162) reports, Bertolt Brecht traced the "death" of the classics in German cultural life to the trauma of World War I.

Replacing the literary classic in Weimar Germany was the detective novel (and its corollary, the crime film). Its portrayal of living in the aftermath of catastrophe by calculating its causes so that the crime becomes intelligible and justice can be rendered expressed the rudiments of emotional life in post-war Germany. Without those redemptive expectations strong religious faith enables, secular Germans converted the loss of the War into a structural and psychic "lack." In our time, images of "left behind" in the "race to the top" convey a similar sense of "loss" or "lack," a sense that America is falling behind, on the wrong path, increasingly at risk. In characterizing the detective novel as an allegory of "lack," Weimar critic Siegfried Kracauer was pointing to its representation of a world entirely dominated by a calculative rationality (Levin 1995, 14). There is no Truth and Reconciliation Commission in the United States to work through the nation's history of racial or economic violence. Instead, we have school reform. To deny the past and force the future, we teach to the test.

Part II

The Regressive Moment
The Past in the Present

Chapter 3

The Defeat of Democracy

I The Terrible Question

"How could it have happened?"

—Peter Gay (1978, 3)

"That terrible question," Peter Gay (1978, 3) affirms, "weighs" upon contemporary Germany. How could the Nazis have come to power; how could the Holocaust have happened? For German men born in the 1940s and 1950s, Kaja Silverman (2009, 207) notes, "the paternal legacy now meant defeat and guilt, not power and privilege, and ... the result was a widespread paternal disidentification." While the parallel is hardly exact, for U.S. schoolteachers the substitutions may be the similar. How could we have so fallen in the public's eye that we are no longer entitled to professional self-governance, the very prerequisite for professionalism? How—why?—did our "power and privilege" become stripped from us, no longer professionals but ventriloquists speaking others' lines, subjecting students to regimes of testing that ensure defeat and guilt (Taubman 2009, 144)? Like historians of Germany (as Gay describes), I, too, try to rewrite the tale whose "depressing end" (1978, 4) I fear I know already.

Grappling with the catastrophe of the Third Reich, German historians have looked everywhere for answers. Was the German family to blame (see Gay 1978, 4), with (according to one line of speculation) its authoritarian fathers? Did family structure, then, predispose citizens to submission to force? Were external events to blame? There was the calamitous defeat in War World I (lost, the generals lied, not on the front but at home: the infamous "stab in the back"). There were the putative terms of the Versailles Treaty. There was the fear (and manipulation of the fear) of the Bolshevik Revolution. From the outset there were enemies of the Republic, heartened by parliamentary gridlock, emboldened by runaway inflation, and finally provided their opportunity by the Great Depression.

Despite the range and variety of explanations, the "central ingredient," Gay (1978, 4) asserts, is that "hapless figure, the unpolitical

German" who preferred the realm of "culture" to "politics." In 1800 Friedrich Schlegel had written: "Do not waste faith and love on the political world, but offer up your innermost being to the divine world of scholarship and art, in the sacred fire of eternal *Bildung*" (quoted in Gay 1978, 4). The aim of German education had been the cultivation of the individual (to which politics was to be subordinated), as the advancement of culture required a hierarchy of claims, elite culture first among them; political and practical ones resided at the bottom (Gay 2001 [1968], 72). When, during World War I, the famous novelist and influential essayist Thomas Mann proclaimed he was no political man and proud of that fact, his preference for self-cultivation over public service was nothing new, as the predisposition was educationally, culturally, already well in place (see Gay 1978, 4). For many, this tension between culture and politics only intensified during Weimar. "There was a deep, widespread discontent with politics in the Republic," Gay (2001 [1968], 70) notes, quoting Hannah Arendt: "We young students did not read the newspapers in those years." When, a few years later Thomas Mann proclaimed allegiance to the Republic and to democracy (Gay 2001 [1968], 74), was he acknowledging that (as U.S. progressives appreciated) subjective and social reconstruction went hand in hand? Was it then—like now—too late?

The German cultural and political crisis during the 1920s was considered by some to be part of a broader crisis of European civilization. In his *Crisis of European Sciences*, Edmund Husserl had blamed a "misguided rationalism" (Rorty 1991, 11). For the Martinique-born, French-educated, Algerian revolutionary Frantz Fanon, Gordon (1995, 8) points out, it was racist, not disintegrated, reason that structured the sickness of Europe. For Gordon, there was an indelible relation between the two (see 1995, 8–9), as European culture had split off the "barbaric" from itself, projecting it onto Africans and other colonized peoples. Many have suggested that the two 20th century European wars represented colonialism come home, but others have argued that colonial savagery was already culturally inscribed within European civilization. Whatever its sources, the German right exploited racism in its rhetoric of "respectability" and "revenge" (Mosse 1985, 132). While France had before World War I played "the leading role" in European racism, during the Weimar Republic racism became "part of the mass politics practiced by 'respectable' nationalist political parties as well as by the extreme political right" (1985, 132). German Jews found themselves caught between full emancipation and intensifying discrimination (Peukert 1992, 150).

For Robert Musil—an Austrian who considered himself a German writer (see Luft 2003, 97)—the decisive feature of Weimar culture was the antirationalism of the German distinction between spirit and intellect; he associated this dissociation with "despair, conservatism, and a yearning for great ideological superstructures" (Luft 2003, 124). Here Musil took issue with Hegel, Marx, Spengler, and their journalistic heirs in the Weimar Republic. Musil's point was that history has no *sense*, but this he regarded as an *optimistic* view, as it implied that human beings are free to invent their own history. What worries Ulrich—a character in Musil's masterwork *The Man Without Qualities* (referenced earlier)—is that human beings seem to take history seriously only in times of crisis. Most people think of history as a distant, even muffled, sound made by an orchestra over which they have no control, not as embedded in the psychology of their own daily lives, as determining the very continuance of their physical lives. What allegory emphasizes is that not only does the present resound in the inner languages of emotion and fantasy; its progenitor, the past—splintered into millions of indecipherable fragments—is the sourcebook for the future.

In an allegory-of-the-present one reassembles loose pieces, not according to a grid the present implies, but in fact "to disrupt the smooth surface of present circumstances," as Martin Jay (2005, 338) describes Walter Benjamin's depiction of the old photograph. "By preserving a moment of the past in this manner," Jay (2005, 338) suggests, the possibility of a different future is also protected. Referencing the same Rauch study I invoked in chapter 2, Jay (2005, 338 n. 96) appreciates that her distinction between nostalgia and melancholy turns on this issue of the past's promise for the future. No regression to an imaginary past, melancholy is not only incomplete mourning, but, rather, an ongoing acknowledgment of the past and its irrevocable loss, exhumed for the very sake of finding the future that the present forecloses (Jay 2005, 338 n. 96; Rauch 2000, 210). Such subjective and social reconstruction is no instrumental foraging through ruins for something we might use to exploit the present. As in the regressive phase of the method of *currere*, such mourning permits the past to reconfigure the present, as more of it seeps in, through memory, through academic knowledge, thereby reconstructing the subjectivity that embodies its traces. In Santner's terms, historical investigation is "not so much of discovering in the past resources for working through crises in the present as discovering in the present a new legibility of the past that in some sense redeems it" (Santner 2006, 130). For LaCapra (2009, 40 n. 8), that *is* "working through."

To enact such historical consciousness in the service of answering the question "what is curriculum theory?" I will thematize my depiction of Weimar, juxtaposing synopses of non-equivalent categories: art, the economy, education, politics. In making such a curricular montage, I am not hijacking history for my pedagogical purposes, but, rather, attuning myself to the period in order to relocate myself in the present. "If a master narrative of Weimar history with collapse and horror as its telos is no longer viable," Kaes, Jay, and Dimendberg (1995, xvii) assert:

the principle of montage suggests itself as a more appropriate strategy for comprehending the fragments of an untotalizable whole. Indeed, the multiperspectivism of montage was often praised during the period itself as the technique that challenges synthesis and closure.

Our calling as teachers is to challenge synthesis and closure, and not only about Weimar, but in the sphere where they least belong but are now legislated: the school. We are teaching in a state of emergency.

II States of Emergency

> [T]he perception of a state of emergency ... distinguished Weimar culture.
> —Patrizia C. McBride (2006, 21)

Early in 1918, General Paul von Hindenburg promised the Kaiser that the Germans would capture Paris by April 1. Confronted with more than two million recently arrived American troops, however, he was forced to face the opposite prospect: surrender seemed inevitable. On the afternoon of September 28, General Erich Ludendorff raged around his office, cursing the Kaiser (Friedrich 1995 [1972], 16–17). The next day, the two commanders—Ludendorff and Hindenburg—summoned the Kaiser and his chief ministers to military headquarters and informed them that the war had been lost. An armistice must be signed immediately. The Kaiser was shocked, but the generals insisted he initiate contacts with the American government to bring the war to an end (Weitz 2007, 14). They hoped the Americans would offer more generous terms than the British and French.

Those generals who were responsible for the defeat declined, however, to accept responsibility, instead blaming their loss on sabotage at home, the infamous "stab in the back" committed by, in Hitler's phrase, "the November criminals" (Friedrich 1995 [1972], 17). To many Germans, Friedrich explains, "any accusation seemed plausible," as "the defeat itself was so shattering, so sudden, and so inexplicable" (1995 [1972], 17). The generals would not endure the ignominy of defeat for long. In regaining their prestige and power, they undermined the Republic by their obsessive allegiance to fantasies of what might have been (Gay 2001 [1968], 18), not unlike the Confederates in the United States (Pinar 2004, 242). Their political rehabilitation was institutionalized by those Weimar leaders who positioned the defeated army as indispensable to the preservation of public order in the Republic (Gay 2001 [1968], 19).

On November 9, 1918, with tens of thousands assembling in the public squares in Berlin and thousands more marching on the city, the liberal Prince Max von Baden (who on October 3 had been summoned by the Kaiser to form a new government) handed over the Reich chancellorship to Friedrich Ebert, the head of the Social Democratic Party (SPD). Perhaps Ebert could preserve public order. Just blocks away, from the balcony of the royal palace, the radical socialist and antiwar activist Karl Liebknecht proclaimed a socialist republic. This schism—from time to time it seemed a civil war—between the liberal center and the left would disable the formation of any united democratic front, thereby allowing the right (itself divided until Hitler's appointment as Chancellor on January 30, 1933) to challenge the very legitimacy of parliamentary government in Germany (Gay 2001 [1968], 19).

On November 10, the day after the proclamation of the Republic, the new President, Friedrich Ebert, concluded a far-reaching agreement with General Groener, accepting the aid of the army in keeping order. (Kurt von Hammerstein and Kurt von Schleicher—the latter of whom would later serve as the last Chancellor of the Republic before Hitler—were also key [Kirsch 2010, 52]. We will return to von Hammerstein at the book's end.) Regular troops, supplemented by a hastily formed *Freikorps*, murdered militant leftists—the Spartacists—having been authorized to do so for the sake of social order. On November 11, representatives of the new government traveled to France and signed the armistice that ended the war. The formal peace treaty—Versailles—would be signed later (Weitz 2007, 20). More than thirteen million men, 19.7 percent of Germany's 1914 male population, had served in the army during World War I; nearly eight million of them remained in arms on November 11, 1918, when the armistice was signed (Weitz 2007, 8).

Almost two million—Friedrich (1995 [1972], 15) specifies 1,773,000—German men died during the War. That number constitutes, Friedrich (1995 [1972], 15) points out, the "greatest loss" by any one nation in a war that claimed at least 8.5 million lives overall. Approximately four million—Eric Weitz (2007, 8) sets the figure at 4.2 million—German men were wounded, including some twelve thousand Jews. For the first time Jewish officers had been permitted to serve in a German war effort, a fact defaced later by allegations of Jewish war-profiteering and shirking of military duty, part of the "stab-in-the-back" fantasy aggressively advanced by defeated generals like Hindenburg (Kaes et al. 1995, 248). The generals may have been defeated on the battlefield, but they were determined not to lose on the domestic political front; they relocated the responsibility for Germany's military defeat from where it obviously belonged—themselves—onto scapegoats, primarily Jews. While the persons and circumstances are completely different, the scapegoating process—and the motives of those who deploy it—seem sickeningly similar in U.S. school deform.

Appalling reminders of the military defeat were visible every day in Weimar Germany, as survivors struggled with wounds physical and psychological. Traumatized, many suffered from "shell shock" (Weitz 2007, 9); they became "Germany's lost generation" (Weitz 2007, 23). The great social theorist Max Weber's wife Marianne was among those who tried to imagine veterans' suffering:

> How the years of living rootlessly, homelessly in foxholes and trenches, in the wet and filth, *in ghastly spiritual uniformity*, how the experience and commission of unspeakable things have stamped the souls of our male compatriots, is difficult to measure. We can only hope that their inner natures were protected by some kind of immunity to poisonous influences.
>
> (Weber [1919], in Kaes et al. 1995, 197, emphasis added)

It became clear that this hope of immunity was unfounded. Many of those who had served—and still could—were unable to leave behind the state of emergency that was the war. Afterward, many become involved in a "wide array of right-wing paramilitary formations that so marred the political landscape of Weimar Germany" (Weitz 2007, 115). Their officers, from the top down, fantasized themselves as the "true bearers of the German spirit and the German state, and were only biding their time until something different, whatever that might exactly be, replaced the republic" (Weitz 2007, 116). Many hoped for an "authoritarian alternative" (Weitz 2007, 121). They would get it.

Between 1919 and 1923 political assassinations became "commonplace," Weitz (2007, 82) reminds, "conducted by shadowy yet well-connected right-wing groups." When apprehended by the authorities, they were treated leniently by the courts, which were "notorious bastions of conservatism," that aggressively sentenced those on the left (2007, 82). Between 1918 and 1922, Gay (2001 [1968], 20) points out, assassinations attributable to left-wing persons numbered twenty-two; of these, seventeen were rigorously punished, ten with the death penalty. In contrast, right-wing extremists found the courts sympathetic: of the 354 murders attributable to them, only one was punished, and he not by the death penalty. The average prison sentences mandated by the courts reflected the same ideological bias: fifteen years for those on the left, four months for those on the right (Gay 2001 [1968], 20). Socialist and Communist newspapers and politicians brought these inequities to the attention of the public, but to no avail (Gay 2001 [1968], 21).

There were periodic states of emergency during the Weimar Republic, always political, often economic, but also cultural—including gendered—as well. The so-called "new woman," the heightened visibility of lesbians and gay men, especially in Berlin, the importation of jazz and all things American: these developments scandalized conservative Germans. Because the Republic had begun in revolution it was always compensating, seeking order and stability. Not only the right threatened: Gay (2001 [1968], 17) notes that the "confusion, irresponsibility, bloodthirsty language, and dictatorial pretension of the Spartacist left—forestalled decision and action in area after area." The political culture of Weimar was an ongoing state of emergency.

Giorgio Agamben (2005, 2) characterizes the Third Reich as "a state of exception that lasted twelve years." A concept derived from the work of Carl Schmitt, the most widely read and respected political scientist of his day (Herf 1984, 44), "states of emergency" are said to occur during crises that obviate normative law, thereby requiring political authority to act. "In this sense," Agamben (2005, 2) explains:

> modern totalitarianism can be defined as the establishment, by means of the state of exception, of a legal civil war that allows for the physical elimination not only of political adversaries but of entire categories of citizens who for some reason cannot be integrated into the political system. Since, then, the voluntary creation of a permanent state of emergency (though perhaps not declared in the technical sense) has become one of the essential practices of contemporary states, including so-called democratic ones.

As a contemporary example Agamben (2005, 3) cites the so-called Patriot Act enacted under U.S. President George W. Bush, which, in effect, "radically erases any legal status of the individual, thus producing a legally unnamable and unclassifiable being." He points out that the Taliban captured in Afghanistan do not enjoy the status of Prisoners of War as defined by the Geneva Convention. Agamben rejects (see 2005, 17) the assumption animating such suspension of normative law, namely that during crisis "necessity is the primary source of law."

The infamous Article 48 of the Weimar Constitution allowed the German Chancellor to govern by decree during a state of emergency. In 1930 President Hindenburg invoked Article 48, and for the next three years, until he appointed Hitler Chancellor on January 30, 1933, Germany was governed by a presidential dictatorship. Originally conceived as a "stopgap measure" to establish order during a state of emergency, in 1930 the article allowed the enemies of the Weimar Republic to set about dismantling it (Weitz 2007, 122). Article 48 did contain, Peukert (1992, 214) points out, a "safety device in the form of Parliament's right to override presidential emergency decrees at any time by means of a majority vote." In the midst of a crumbling economy and political infrastructure, that device was insufficient.

III The "Highly Fissured" Republic

—Noah Isenberg (2009, 10)

[I]t is a travesty to see Weimar only as a prelude to the Third Reich.
—Eric Weitz (2007, 5)

Still, there were those who seemed to know what was coming. In his lecture at the University of Munich, "Politics as a Vocation," delivered only a short time before his death in 1920, Max Weber expressed his concern that Germans faced a "polar night of icy darkness and severity," a time requiring heroism and patience, passion and judgment (quoted in Kaes et al. 1995, 86). Of course he—no one—could know the calamity to come. What Weber did know was that the Weimar Republic was born out of national defeat and amidst social chaos. These events precipitated a series of political aftershocks that were deepened by a set of international economic crises. Peukert (1992, 249) insists that no one factor caused the Republic's demise. Economic and political events were not always even primary in the ongoing crisis that was Weimar: education, the arts, technology, and culture itself seemed askew as well. The novelist Hans Ostwald recalled:

> It was a time of intense revaluation—in the economy and culture, in material as well as psychological things. ... *The family, too, seemed to be in rapid decline.* An ecstasy of eroticism cast the world into chaos. ... Nudism was no longer confined to specific circles and to theatrical revues and cabarets.
>
> ([1931], quoted in Kaes et al. 1995, 77, emphasis added)

For many Germans, George Mosse (1985, 131) suggests, the Weimar Republic *meant* decadence.

Certainly cosmopolitanism characterized the Weimar Republic, especially in Berlin. Cosmopolitanism—recoded by conservatives to denote decadence—had not appeared suddenly, Gay (2001 [1968], 8) points out; it had been "commonplace" during the Kaiser's time. In that respect the "Weimar spirit" was born before the Weimar Republic (as, Gay adds, was its nemesis). Peukert (1992, 5), too, acknowledges the complexity of historical "periodization." The Protestant theologian Ernst Troeltsch insisted that the Weimar Republic:

> was no break with the German spirit and its history. We want to ground ourselves anew in this history and draw from it its great treasures in order to stamp it with a new vitality and unity. In this respect we want to establish the idea of a conservative democracy, since novelty will be sufficiently looked after on its own.
>
> ([1918], in Kaes et al. 1995, 91)

Others, as Weber's 1920 sense of foreboding makes clear, were not so sanguine. "These middle-class citizens of Germany are antidemocratic through and through," the journalist Kurt Tucholsky complained; "they know no middle ground between patriarchal domination and the banditry of a degenerate bolshevism, for they are unfree. They accept everything so long as they are allowed to continue earning money" ([1919], in Kaes et al. 1995, 96–97). Some say the same of Americans.

No doubt contradictory currents and powerful impulses were at work during Weimar, intensified by profound cultural change, social disorder, political crisis, and economic upheaval. Despite this turbulence, Weitz (2007, 2) reminds, Germans enacted a "highly liberal political order with very substantial social welfare programs." The working day was reduced to eight hours, unemployment insurance promised workers some protection from the business cycle, women won the right to vote, and the press was free to report the news as it saw fit (2007, 2).

These reforms had been enacted in the constitution, proclaimed in the city of Weimar, on August 11, 1919. Berlin was bypassed as the site of this historic event because the situation in the capital remained "dangerous," Weitz (2007, 32) explains, and the new government hoped that the "spirit of Weimar"—as a symbol of classical German culture—would enlist the loyalty of conservative Germans as well as the Allies. The new constitution had been drafted by Hugo Preuss, a professor of law at the University of Berlin, a liberal and a Jew (Friedrich 1995 [1972], 48). Whatever the weaknesses of the constitution (including the infamous Article 48), the crisis of Weimar did not follow from it, Friedrich (1995 [1972], 49) asserts:

> but from the society that the Constitution was supposed to represent. It was a society fiercely divided against itself, divided not only between extremes of radical and conservative ideology but between classes, regions, and religions. It was a society shattered by both the psychological and economic consequences of military defeat, and still facing the crises of reparations, inflation, foreign invasions, and intellectual demoralization.

In addition to these fissures, it was, Peukert (1992, 254) suggests, the "failure of the welfare state" to honor its promises that played a major role "robbing the Republic of its legitimacy."

This failure followed the onset of the Great Depression, as declining revenues disabled the federal government from providing even basic services. But its political genesis occurred at the Republic's founding. Apart from a few theorists such as Rosa Luxemburg, Peukert (1992, 30) reports, even German socialists envisaged socialism not as a revolutionary process of "spontaneous self-organization by the masses," but, instead, as an "expansion of public administration designed to promote the general welfare." In the election of the National Assembly, held on January 19, 1919, the workers' parties failed to secure a majority of votes, results, Peukert (1992, 33) observes, that "display a considerable degree of electoral continuity between the monarchy and the Republic." While the constitutionalist movement had "carried the day," he continues, "it had bought its victory at the cost of a heavy reliance on the old elites in the military and the bureaucracy" (1992, 34). The thwarting of hopes for a mass movement (which had never been likely) led to an ongoing and fractious conflict between the majority Social Democrats and the more radical sections of the working class—the latter some 10 percent of the electorate (1992, 72)—that Peukert (1992, 35) describes as "tantamount to civil war." By the summer of 1920, he (1992, 35) suggests, "the pattern that was to typify the remaining years of the Weimar Republic was fixed: the forces of democratization were split, and their capacity to act effectively was checked."

Add to these divisions within the left and between the left and the center, a continuing German nationalism, still powerful even after the discrediting of the Supreme Command in the defeat of 1918. German nationalism represented a tendency toward totalitarianism (Peukert 1992, 49). As the "truly significant alternative" to the republican constitutionalism of 1918, this same nationalistic tendency toward totalitarianism "reasserted itself, in radicalized form," when the Nazis took power in 1933 (Peukert 1992, 49). It is in the context of these "fissures," Peukert (1992, 50) argues, that the "achievements of Weimar constitutionalism, then, need to be judged." Further fracturing German political culture were events that undermined the stability and credibility of the Republic, including the financial and psychological burdens of the Versailles Peace Treaty and (not unrelatedly) the ongoing indignation of the elites, with their often stridently anti-republican attitudes. Moreover, the elites were positioned in the higher echelons of state where their influence would prove decisive. Not only the elites undermined the Republic: even the middle class, whose net worth would be erased by a decade of inflation, aggravated by the inability of government to come through on its promises (as it was strapped by the stagnation of the post-war economy), finally lost faith in the Republic (Peukert 1992, 50). These fissures and events, Peukert (1992, 51) acknowledges, "made the future of the democratic experiment highly uncertain."

While the Great Depression intensified the crisis and emboldened the Republic's enemies, the economic crisis struck Germany more harshly than it did even the United States. As one indicator of social distress, note that in 1932 there were 133 suicides per million inhabitants in the United States, compared with 85 in Great Britain and 155 in France. There were 260 in Germany (1992, 280). Note as well that this was the *second* economic collapse—we will review the calamitous 1923 inflation momentarily—Germans would undergo in less than a decade. "But the real scale of the economic crisis," Peukert (1992, 257, emphasis added) suggests, "was perhaps less important than the *symbolic meaning* of the crisis as Germans perceived it. ... The answer seemed obvious: to join the headlong rush to abandon the Weimar 'system' altogether." The Weimar "system" was not only political; it comprised the entire public sphere.

IV The Regimented Mass

Mass structures had become a species of ornamentation.
—Detlev J. K. Peukert (1992, 163)

As was the case in the United States, the 1920s saw "fundamental changes" in the character of the public sphere in Germany, changes, Peukert (1992, 161) points out, that were political, socio-cultural, and technological in character. "The dominant common image symbolizing these changes," he (1992, 161) continues, "was that of the regimented mass." He cites several examples—huge rallies with mass marches, huge sporting events and mass spectacles in the theater, mass production in industry, and mass construction in the anti-traditional styles of the new architecture—that emphasized the ocularcentrism of the era, but "underlying this generally more regimented public sphere was the *standardization of the individual unit*" (1992, 161, emphasis added). During the 1920s, then, more uniform behavior was demanded of individuals—the assembly line with its coordinated movements of workers is the image familiar to many Americans—that, in Peukert's (1992, 161) terms, "replicated basic units and served to produce new massive geometrical structures." These orchestrated bodies of workers formed, Kaes (2009, 176) reminds, what Siegfried Kracauer called a "mass ornament," in which the individual is "radically submerged" in "highly structured formations." While the purpose of such assemblages might have been functional in the service of social efficiency, nonetheless they constructed "a species of overwhelming, unprecedented monumental mass ornamentation ... a huge, choreographed totalitarian spectacle" (Peukert 1992, 161). Note that regimentation is associated with organization and supervision through observation. Visuality—the emphasis upon vision as the arbiter of reality—restructures a public sphere toward totalitarianism in the name of productivity. Mosse (1985, 134) puts the matter succinctly: "Stereotyping through looks was basic to racism, a visually centered ideology." We will return to this point in the final chapter.

Among those Weimar intellectuals who discerned this new reality was Siegfried Kracauer. Thomas Y. Levin introduces an important collection of Kracauer's cultural criticism by recalling the moment Kracauer fled France in August 1940, two months after Paris had fallen and the Vichy government had installed Nazi authority. There were, Levin (1995, 1) tells us, many refugees gathered in Marseilles hoping to escape, among them Kracauer and his "long-time" friend Walter Benjamin who would be detained a month later trying to cross into Spain. Benjamin committed suicide. Kracauer and his wife Lili, however, succeeded in escaping to New York where he was able to make a living as a writer, publishing articles in a wide range of journals (including the *Nation*, *Commentary*, the *New Republic*, *Harper's Magazine*, *Public Opinion Quarterly*, and *The New York Times Book Review*).

During the Weimar Republic, Kracauer had written for the renowned newspaper the *Frankfurter Zeitung*. Founded in 1856 as a trade and finance newspaper by the Jewish banker and politician Leopold Sonnemann, the *Frankfurter Zeitung* had become, Levin (1995, 4) reports, "one of the leading and internationally acclaimed organs of the liberal bourgeois press, highly regarded in economics and business circles." The newspaper was also a strong supporter of Weimar constitutional democracy, even advocating nationalization of major branches of the economy. Kracauer's Weimar prose, Levin (1995, 4) concludes, is nothing less than "astonishing," and notable not only for its "freshness" and "relevance" but for its "decidedly philosophical character" as well.

Somewhat equivalent to arts and culture sections in today's newspapers, Kracauer wrote in the tradition of the *feuilleton*, a genre that had existed, Levin (1995, 5) explains, since the 19th century. To the legendary Karl Krauss—Franz Kafka, Wilhelm Reich, Gershom Scholem, Theodor Adorno, Franz Werfel, and Arthur Schnitzler all testified to Krauss' profound influence—this "elegant, impressionistic personal essay," so "popular" in the culture sections of Vienna's newspapers, was a marker of "intellectual disintegration," as it emphasized "superficial phrase-making at the expense of objective reporting and analysis" (Kirsch 2008, 65). In Kracauer's hand, however, the genre had become serious cultural criticism. Comprising book reviews, conference reports, and various assessments of the state of intellectual and cultural life in the Republic, Levin (1995, 5–6) continues, the feuilleton was derived from the quotidian, referencing the scenes of daily life: unemployment offices and arcades, bestsellers and boredom, mass sports events, dance clubs, and even hotel lobbies. All of these and more became the focus of Kracauer's perceptive analyses, very much in the tradition, Levin notes, of Kracauer's teacher, the social theorist Georg Simmel.

Philosophical reflection gave way to polemical intervention, Levin (1995, 6) reports, as political developments during the late 1920s escalated. But these interventions conflicted with the shifting (and finally forced) political allegiances of the *Frankfurter Zeitung*. Kracauer had become "highly respected," Levin (1995, 8) observes; he could have supported himself as a freelance writer. Despite deteriorating political circumstances at the newspaper, Kracauer resolved to stay, in part to contest the growing threat from the right, and from the Nazis in particular. "The responsible intellectual in the late Weimar Republic," Kracauer observed, "did not feel called upon to serve the interests of the 'absolute,' but rather felt duty-bound to articulate for himself (and for a wider audience) a sense of the current situation" (quoted in Levin 1995, 10). Such intellectual independence became intolerable by the Republic's end, and Kracauer was dismissed from the *Frankfurter Zeitung*.

In contrast to Kracauer's embattled interventions during the late 1920s and early 1930s, Levin (1995, 13) points out, his early 1920s work exhibits a "resigned" and "even lapsarian metaphysical tone." Levin (1995, 13) attributes this melancholia to Kracauer's reading of the historical moment, one characterized by "an evacuation of meaning, a bifurcation of being and truth ... a modernity bereft of unity and substance." That is unsurprising, as for many—including Franz Rosenzweig—"modernity is but the total secularization of Christianity" (Mosès 2009 [1992], 33). Unlike many of his more hopeful intellectual contemporaries, Kracauer worried that the Weimar Republic was no new democratic beginning for Germany but, rather, the "final stage" in a process of "decay" (quoted in Levin 1995, 13). Among the fissures of Weimar culture was the divide between organic community (*Gemeinschaft*) and technological–functional society (*Gesellschaft*), terms that now conveyed, in Levin's (1995, 13) fine phrasing, the "presence" and "absence" of "meaning (*Sinn*)." Today, there are those who imagine the former is contributing to the formation of the latter (see Ling 2008, 185). We examine that claim in chapter 5.

During the 1922–1925 period, Levin (1995, 14) reports, Kracauer focused on the detective novel as as an allegory of "lack." For Kracauer, Levin (see 1995, 15) explains, the allegorical significance of the detective novel had to do with its presentation of a rationally decipherable meaningless world. Kracauer (1995, 175) claimed: "The composition of the detective novel transforms an ungraspable life into a translatable analogue of actual reality." In this structural homology between the detective novel and contemporary society, the quotidian—also a key concept in curriculum studies in Brazil—the apparently unintelligible public sphere provides "clues" for the social detective to decipher. For Kracauer, especially "low culture" provided clues for contemporary critics, as it reflected (in Kracauer's terms) "the face of de-realized society more purely than any other means by which one can catch a glimpse of it" (quoted in Levin 1995, 15). For Kracauer, Levin (1995, 15) explains, it was the very insignificance of quotidian artifacts that converted them into markers of historical crimes in the making.

The mass ornament, Kracauer argued, was a "new type of collectivity," one organized not according to the bonds of community but, in Levin's (1995, 18) fine gloss, as a "social mass" of "functionally linked individuals." Rather than emotion or sexual attraction or sport, wherein subjectivity in its embodied singularity remains the focus of attention, the mass ornament glitters as condensation of instrumental rationality, an "abstract unity" of "reified elements" (Levin 1995, 18). Discerning the devolution of reason into compulsive calculation earned Kracauer the respect of other public intellectuals, prominently among them Theodor Adorno, who claimed in 1933 that Kracauer "was the first of any of us to seriously tackle once again the problems of the enlightenment" (quoted in Levin 1995, 19).

In Kracauer's early work the social surface was the locus of loss, Levin (1995, 19) explains, displaying a world emptied of meaning, flattened by a distracting superficiality. What was at first characterized as a *cul-de-sac* becomes, in Kracauer's later work, passages to realities freed from functionality and instrumentality. The phenomenology of the surface in Kracauer's writings after the mid-1920s, Levin (1995, 20) continues, portrays varieties of the social surface—Levin lists hotel lobbies, dancing, arcades, bestsellers—in order to move to some other side, not metaphysical, but a material and political otherwise. By focusing on scorned quotidian locations, artifacts, and practices—"material expressions of a particular historical condition" in Levin's precise phrasing (1995, 20)—Kracauer was insisting on the possibility of a messianic moment, what he called the "revolution of the negative." Examining, like a detective at the scene of a crime, the "relationless jumble that is the signature of modernity" (Levin 1995, 22), Kracauer was confident that the truth of things could become discernible. Like progressive cinema—on which he also focused—the cultural critic was "to look the dire situation straight in the eye" (quoted in Levin 1995, 23).

As a film critic, Kracauer was clear that very few late 1920s German commercial movies looked reality straight in the eye. (Momentarily we will glimpse one movie that did.) Most films disguised reality by substituting (compensatory) daydreams and (forbidden) wishes, often presented in an "alienated form" that simultaneously expressed "denial" (Levin 1995, 24). Another such "alienated form," for Kracauer, was photography, which he judged as a "depersonalized technology" (1995, 53). "For fashion," Kracauer wrote, naming another such depersonalizing technology, "effaces the intrinsic value of the things that come under its dominion by subjecting the appearance of these phenomena to periodic changes that are not based on any relation to the things themselves" (1995, 67). Kracauer cataloged the culture industry's recasting of "political and social exploitation" into entertaining distractions like "adventure, romance, and triumph" (Levin 1995, 24). Such recasting also occurred through cinematic representation itself, which converted concerns over economic insecurity and political violence into "consumption" and "compensatory leisure" (1995, 25). One memorable site of "conversion" was the cabaret, made vivid for American movie audiences in the 1972 production of *Cabaret*, starring Liza Minnelli and Michael York.

All was not inevitably ideological obfuscation, however. Kracauer argues for an "emancipatory potential" in distraction, as it restructures perception (here Levin sounds like Marshall McLuhan) for the new "sensorial economy," the most striking features of which are its "speed" and "abrupt transitions" (Levin 1995, 26). In what Walter Benjamin would also embrace as potentially progressive, Kracauer identified "shock" as "one of the medium's most progressive features" (Levin 1995, 26). (Surely shock's potential has now been thoroughly exhausted due to its overuse. How much violence can Hollywood peddle?) For Kracauer, Levin suggests, it was less the phenomenology of the shock for the individual that was potentially politically progressive than it was its effect on the collectivity that is the movie audience. Cinema, he thought, could stimulate a structural reconfiguration of the public sphere so that it might actually become a site of enlightenment, an emancipatory expression of a mass-cultural aesthetic politics (see Levin 1995, 26–27). Here Kracauer—as decades later would Pier Paolo Pasolini—demonstrates his faith that the visualistic banality of the social surface is not the final stage in social devolution, but, rather, that it can provide, if the film is structured appropriately, a passage to insight and action. It is a faith I so want to share.

V Art as Allegory

> With film there arises a new region of consciousness.
> —Walter Benjamin ([1927], in Kaes et al. 1995, 626)

It may not be possible to know why, at a particular time and place, aesthetic and intellectual culture flourishes, and artists, writers, and philosophers achieve breakthrough after breakthrough, but, Weitz (2007, 293) asserts, "there can be no question that Weimar Germany was just such a place and time." The very founding of the Republic, he (2007, 39) suggests, "unleashed one of the greatest periods of artistic and intellectual creativity in the twentieth century." Especially, "young artists," Gay (2001 [1968], 4) tells us, "broke away from the pomposity of academic art and sought to rise above the bombast of their surroundings to cultivate their inner life, articulate their religious yearning, and satisfy their dim longing for human and cultural renewal." In architecture, dance, literature, music, opera, photography, painting, theater, and marked by the movements known as Surrealism, Cubism, Dada, Expressionism, and the New Objectivity (*Neue Sachlichkeit*, or matter-of-factness), Weimar art was characterized, Kaes et al. (1995, 474) suggest, by its "syncretism, a propensity for blurring styles and genres which was as ubiquitous as the hyperbole of its manifestos. No less notable was the internationalism of its aesthetic horizons." "Weimar art," Weitz (2007, 170) concludes, "was about the totality of being and was infused with powerful, utopian visions of transforming society—and humanity—once and for all."

No institution represents the aesthetic innovation of the Weimar Republic like its signature art school: the Bauhaus founded in 1919 by Walter Gropius. The term, Martin Filler (2010, 27) explains, conjoined the monosyllabic root of the German verb *bauen* ("to build") with the noun *Haus*, homophone of cognates in both English and Dutch, according the neologism a "snappy assonance as well as intimations of universality." Fourteen years later, Filler (2010, 27) notes, the very word "Bauhaus" would become a "red flag" to the Nazis; within months of their ascendancy in 1933 the school was closed. Several of those who taught at the Bauhaus—among them Paul Klee, Wassily Kandinsky, Joseph Albers, and Laszlo Moholy-Nagy—escaped to the United States where they became influential architects, designers, and teachers (Kaes et al. 1995, 421).

The "hallmark innovation" of the Bauhaus, Filler (2010, 26) tells us, was the *Vorkurs* (preliminary course). This was a required introductory class that provided an intensive experience of immersion in color theory and composition, emphasizing the "arrangement of tonalities to achieve specific optical effects, and on recombinations of pure geometric form as the elemental building blocks of design" (2010, 26). The *Vorkurs* was conceived and taught by Johannes Itten, the "extravagantly eccentric" and "mystically inclined" (Filler 2010, 26) Swiss expressionist painter hired by Walter Gropius as "form master" for the school's metalwork, sculpture, wall-painting, weaving, and wood-working workshops. Itten left the Bauhaus in 1923 in protest over Gropius' shift in curricular emphasis to commercial rather than purely theoretical design (Filler 2010, 26).

These two dispositions—theoretical and commercial—converged in Weimar cinema, which, Kaes et al. (1995, 618) report, "epitomized modernity: speed, motion, simultaneity, and the predominance of the visual. A product of both science and the imagination, film was the site of an uneasy symbiosis between technology and magic." Art, science, money: add to these cinema's social functions, the emphasis (as noted) of Siegfried Kracauer, the influential critic of the *Frankfurter Zeitung* from 1925 to 1933. Film's social functions were said to be various: through shock (Kracauer's interest) it could edify, distract, even propagandize. That last function fell infamously to Leni Riefenstahl, whose *Triumph of the Will* (1935) obscures not only her directorial debut with the "mountain film" *The Blue Light* (1932), but another film also made by a woman, and one that was not only a national but an international success, one with very different, indeed "anti-authoritarian" politics (McCormick 2009, 271).

Given the frequency and intensity of the demonization of new models of gender and sexual behavior that emerged during Weimar, it is noteworthy, Richard McCormick (2009, 271) argues, that the 1931 film *Girls in Uniform* (*Mädchen in Uniform*) was directed by a woman, Leontine Sagan; the movie "celebrated" a sexuality that "threatened the status quo." Indeed, *Girls in Uniform*, McCormick (2009, 271–272) emphasizes, endorsed Weimar's most "democratic" and "emancipatory tendencies" as it opposed those "authoritarian" forces determined to destroy the Republic. While his initial reaction to the movie had been "more positive" (McCormick 2009, 287 n. 1), writing in 1947, McCormick (2009, 272) informs us, Kracauer judged the film insufficiently anti-fascist.

Acted by an all-female cast, the film is embedded in several progressive discourses circulating during the late Weimar Republic, among them, McCormick (2009, 272) notes, demands for homosexual rights, the proliferation of urban, queer subcultures suggestive of Surrealism, the "New Objectivity" and other avant-garde movements in the arts; indeed, the film positioned itself at the "intersection" of "modernity" and "democratic egalitarianism." And at that intersection was a "fairly overt homoeroticism" (McCormick 2009, 272). McCormick (2009, 272–273) cites B. Ruby Rich's 1984 insistence that the film's sexual politics and its anti-fascist politics are inseparable. For himself (see McCormick (2009, 273) the film is best contextualized in the "New Objectivity" of the middle and later years of the Weimar Republic.

"New Objectivity," Kaes et al. (1995, 568) explain, was the term accorded to the "comprehensive realignment of all arts in relation to society." And, they point out, it was a society "increasingly dominated by industrial production and its operating principles of rationality, practicability, and functionality" (1995, 568). Rejecting its antecedent movement—Expressionism—the New Objectivity (*Neue Sachlichkeit*) was "austere" (1995, 455), a "cool and critical view of social reality" (Hall 2009, 139). For some it was associated with "Americanization"—the mirror of Weimar Germany (Peukert 1992, 178)—and for others with World War I. For still others it was both an evocation of the assertive "new woman," and the reactionary response to "her" (McCarthy 2009, 220). For Franz Kafka's friend and editor Max Brod ([1929], in Kaes et al. 1995, 206), it was all of these:

> But if objectivity means Americanization, a refusal of the heart, of problems, of love, then it is not a protest against war but rather against its result, its continuation and, finally ... its approbation. It will be the task of the woman of tomorrow, full of instinct and cleverness, to distinguish the good components of the New Objectivity from the bad. In this task I see her significance, not simply for man and the masculine spirit ... but for the development of a genuine society, one no longer based on exploitation, but rather a true community of nations.

This admixture of themes achieves visibility in *Girls in Uniform*.

The film tells the story of 14-year-old Manuela, who is brought by her aunt (the girl's mother is deceased) to a boarding school (not unlike the one where Torless is sent: see Musil 1955 [1905]) structured by the "rigid, authoritarian discipline" enforced by its headmistress, who is determined to raise obedient "mothers of soldiers," a gendered fate taught long before Weimar was born but resurrected after its demise. The one "sympathetic" teacher—Fraulein von Bernburg—shows kindness and affection, including kissing each of her girls' foreheads when saying goodnight (McCormick 2009, 275). After learning that Manuela lost her mother, Bernburg shows her special attention, to which Manuela responds by throwing her arms around Bernburg. Moved, Bernburg kisses the girl on the lips, one of the "most famous close-ups" in the movie (2009, 275). Now infatuated, Manuela cannot concentrate while in class. Upon learning that Manuela's underclothes are old and inadequate, Bernburg presents her pupil with a chemise from her own underwear drawer (2009, 275).

Thrilled, Manuela excels in the school play, acting the role of a man in Schiller's *Don Carlos*. Celebrating afterward, she confesses to her classmates her love for the teacher, to which the headmistress (who has overheard) responds by isolating her from everyone and forbidding Bernburg to see her again. Bernburg is defiant, threatening to resign rather than comply with a system emptied of human affection. Manuela attempts suicide, but is spared by the intervention of her classmates. Bernburg confronts the headmistress who is "stunned and for the first time silent," and, "seemingly defeated," she walks away as military bugles sound in the distance (McCormick 2009, 275).

One is reminded of Miss Sill and Jane Addams at Rockford Seminary, but this situation is rather different. True, in both instances there is a clash among generations, gender, and politics. McCormick (2009, 276) regards *Girls in Uniform* as attuned to its historical setting, asserting: "The political warning in the film about the situation in Germany is actually fairly explicit." During the Weimar Republic Addams is living out her final decade, embroiled in controversy the right wing in the

United States had manufactured in response to her refusal to endorse America's entrance into World War I. Like the fictitious Bernburg, Addams broke from her headmistress's conservatism, embodying an "emerging modern, democratic, egalitarian order" (McCormick 2009, 278). This tension between the authoritarian values of the school—now disguised by rhetoric promising to "leave no child" behind in the "race to the top"—and the more democratic demands of the students and the servants reinscribes, McCormick (2009, 281) points out, the "deep political polarization" that had fissured the Weimar Republic from the start.

There were more than a dozen memorable films produced during Weimar. While Fritz Lang's *M* (1931) is the "most critically acclaimed" (Herzog 2009, 291), for Anglo-American viewers the visual impression of Weimar is linked less to the great films of the period—among them *Dr. Caligari* (1920), *The Indian Tomb* (1921), *Dr. Mabuse, the Gambler* (1922), *The Last Laugh* (1924), *Metropolis* (1927), *Pandora's Box* (1929), or *The Blue Angel* (1930) (despite Marlene Dietrich's memorable performance)—than it is to Bob Fosse's *Cabaret* (1972). Not a Weimar film at all, the "divine decadence" acclaimed by American showgirl Sally Bowles (Liza Minnelli) and the androgynous worldliness of the host (Joel Grey) communicate the coming calamity that would end the Weimar Republic (see Isenberg 2009, 3).

VI Economic Crisis

[A]ny verdict on the Weimar Republic must take account of the fundamental social and economic fact of stagnation and crisis.
—Detlev J. K. Peukert (1992, 12)

"The constant factor throughout the decade 1914–24," Peukert (1992, 61) emphasizes, "was inflation." When it ended (in the complete collapse of the German currency in 1924), the economy stabilized, in part due to the revision of the reparations schedule (mandated by the Versailles Treaty) orchestrated by the American finance specialist Charles Dawes. Published in April 1924 and accepted by the Reichstag in August that year, the Dawes Plan, Peukert (1992, 60–61) points out, ended inflation and inaugurated economic growth. But, he (1992, 109) also points out, the economic foundation of the Weimar welfare state had been inflation, enabling employers to pass on higher costs as higher prices and the state to finance its social policies. Stabilization removed the leverage that inflation had created, and with it the economic basis for the welfare state.

Inflation had begun during World War I. The "incredible fact," Friedrich (1995 [1972], 60) observes, "is that Imperial Germany's conservative finance officials never levied a single Mark in extra taxes to pay the gigantic costs of World War I." The total cost had been approximately 164 billion Marks (the Mark was then worth 4.20 to the dollar), he points out, and of that amount some 93 billion Marks had been raised by war loans, some 29 billion by Treasury bills. The rest was produced by the government, which simply printed the money on its printing presses (1995 [1972], 60). Sound familiar?

Following the 1918 defeat, there started a second round of inflation, this time due to the Republic's need to finance demobilization. After all, "millions of soldiers had to be brought back home and found work; millions of war victims had to be cared for" (Peukert 1992, 47). Peukert (1992, 48) points out that the government's open-handed "inflationary financial measures" were effective in the short term, consolidating the peacetime economy by keeping unemployment figures relatively low and protecting Germany from the effects of the world economic crisis of 1920–1921.

Still, purchasing power eroded. The wholesale price index had risen from 1 in 1913 to 2.17 by war's end in 1918; in just five years the mark had lost half of its pre-war value! Not only did everyday expenses double, but those who had savings saw a substantial reduction in the value of those savings. Those living on fixed incomes suffered the most. But things were about to get worse, much worse. In 1919, the first year of peace time, the wholesale price index (taking 1913 as 1) rose to 4.15, doubling prices once again. In 1920, it more than tripled from that level, rising to 14.86. That means that an item that cost one Mark (or, let's say, one dollar, to use the more familiar unit) in 1913, now cost almost $15! In 1921 the German currency stabilized somewhat, as the wholesale price index rose "only" to 19.11, but in 1922 inflation accelerated dramatically, and the index reached 341.82. During 1923 the German currency gradually lost its function as a medium of payment, and many, including businesses and government authorities, resorted to substitute forms of currency. In January 1923 the whole price index was already 2,783 times higher than its 1913 level; by December 1923 it was 1,261 thousand million times higher (Peukert 1992, 62–64).

Not only pensioners and others on fixed incomes were impoverished by the inflation, working and middle-class people (including academicians and intellectuals) were devastated as well. Among many a "profiteering ethic" replaced restraint, and Germany underwent "an inversion of values" (Peukert 1992, 66). Recorded adult crime had risen from 1919 to 1921, but not significantly. During the inflation of 1922–1923, however, crime "exploded," occurring on a scale never seen in Germany since statistics had been kept (Peukert 1992, 149). Filmmakers were among those who represented the reality around them. In G. W. Pabst's *The Joyless Street* (1925), Sara F. Hall (2009, 145) observes, "the economic reality no longer accommodates emotional response based on old-fashioned values and assumptions." This experience of hyperinflation, Peukert (1992, 64) points out, "left a profound imprint on the German psyche." Hyperinflation left a profound and, if recent events are considered, continuing imprint. Following the 2008 economic crisis, fiscally conservative Germany—Europe's most powerful economy—threatened to trigger a deflationary spiral throughout Europe as it refused to countenance any policies that could possibly trigger inflation (Soros 2010, 29).

Germans took the 1920s economic crises personally, feeling that their country had not only been humiliated by the terms of the Versailles Treaty—the so-called war-guilt clause blamed the war entirely on Germany—but that reparations mandated by the Treaty had made them victims of "economic enslavement" (Peukert 1992, 122). By the terms of the Treaty, Germany was made to pay compensation not only for the war damages that the German Army itself had caused, but for all costs of the war as a whole. The total reparation, then, was "so colossal as virtually to defy imagination" (1992, 53) but in fact, Peukert (1992, 54) points out, the actual payments were "perfectly manageable." The 1924 Dawes Plan (see above) had made payments even more reasonable, but the Young Plan of 1929 made them more so. Given the collapse of the economy in the Great Depression, payments were allowed to be suspended for one year; in 1932 reparations were suspended altogether (Peukert 1992, 196–197). Peukert (1992, 197) concludes: "Reparations did not, in fact, bleed the German economy." While that may have been the case, reparations made it easy for Germans to blame their economic ills on "foreigners" (1992, 122). Germans were embittered by the "dictate from Versailles" (quoted in Weitz 2007, 38). Reparations, Weitz (2007, 144) suggests, was an "issue handed on a silver platter to all the forces opposed to Weimar democracy."

Following the collapse of the German currency in 1923–1924 due to hyperinflation, stabilization was successful, and the economy rallied. From 1924 to 1929 the economy improved, not only statistically but in terms of lifestyles: Germans, Weitz (2007, 146) reports, "went on a consumption binge, and they did it with modern flair." If conspicuous consumption signaled the "golden years" of the Weimar Republic, he (2007, 149) continues, "rationalization" marked the baser side of economic life. Imported from the United States, "rationalization" meant the application of scientific methods to production in order to increase output while reducing labor costs. "Technological and managerial improvements were all the rage," Weitz (2007, 149) tells us, as "businesses combined, mechanized many processes, and shed workers." Sound familiar?

While rationalization enriched business owners and investors, it only made life more difficult for ordinary German workers. While wages rose between 1924 and 1929, so did rates of unemployment, and many found the "intensified pace of work nerve-rattling and destructive of their health" (Weitz 2007, 152). Working women suffered most of all, Weitz (2007, 153) notes, as household labor had to be completed after a long day at the factory: "sleep-deprived: never enough rest, always waking groggy, usually at 5:30AM or even earlier, and not getting to bed until 11:00PM or even later." He (2007, 155) admits the Communist Party was not inaccurate when it condemned German rationalization as "American factory and exploitation methods, American profits, but no American wages, only German hunger wages."

Things were no better in white-collar jobs or on farms. The office was, Weitz (2007, 157) tells us, "extremely hierarchical." Advancement was reserved for the elites, linked by family, education, status, and class. "While they lingered in their positions until comfortable old age," he (2007, 157) reports, "many employees found themselves unemployed at forty, victims, like their blue-collar colleagues, of their inability to keep up with the faster pace of work." Nor did the "golden years" apply to Weimar's farmers. They had been accused of hoarding commodities during the inflation; afterward they saw prices for their commodities collapse, even before the U.S. stock market crashed in 1929. Like many white-collar workers, farmers blamed economic misfortune on socialists and Jews (Weitz 2007, 159–160), two groups closely associated with the Republic. "All talk," Peukert (1992, 140) reports, was of the "crisis of the welfare state and the need to curb its 'excesses'." As in the United States, such rhetoric recoded racial resentment.

By the beginning of 1932, six million Germans were officially unemployed, almost one-third of the labor force. But, Weitz (2007, 161) notes, another two million were "unofficially" unemployed: altogether some 40 percent of the workforce had no income. German unemployment rates were thus higher than even those in the United States. As unemployment increased, political polarization intensified. Like farmers and many small shopkeepers (especially outside Berlin), the lower middle class became attracted to the Nazis as the Communists continued to concentrate not on the threat from the right but on the less left-wing Social Democrats who were, they alleged, "social fascists" (Herf 1984, 20). While the Depression provided the conditions for its collapse, the right had opposed the Republic from the outset, working quietly (and not so quietly) for over a decade to destroy its legitimation. Known collectively as the "conservative revolution," opponents of the Republic associated democracy with the lost war, with Versailles, the inflation of 1923, Jews, cosmopolitan mass culture, and liberalism (Herf 1984, 21). To many Germans living through year after year of crisis, the earlier era of monarchical rule began to look like the "good old days" (Peukert 1992, 13).

VII The Great Age of Educational Reform

[T]he Weimar era is rightly seen as a "great age" of educational reform.
—Detlev J. K. Peukert (1992, 142)

The great cultural figures of Weimar, Eric Weitz (2007, 293) reminds, were the "beneficiaries of Germany's phenomenal educational system." Even those like Thomas Mann who only completed *Gymnasium* (high school), Weitz (2007, 293) continues, had a received a "superb grounding" in literature, philosophy, history, and classical and modern languages. Perhaps due to the intellectual sophistication of this curriculum, the founders of Weimar knew that the future of the new republic rested on its becoming a *Kulturstaat*: a "culture state" or "civilized society" (Peukert 1992, 141). What was at stake in the education of the public, they knew, was not preparation for the workplace, but the intellectual cultivation of the human spirit. Upon *that*—more intellect in the matters of soul, in Musil's terms—democracy depended.

Not that economic considerations were absent from the public sphere; it was that they were not assumed. In fact, the very idea of construing education economistically was hotly debated, especially as such a view was associated with America and its "rationalization" of the workplace (as noted in the previous section). In his discussion of F. W. Murnau's film *Faust* (1926), Matt Erlin (2009, 162) underscores Faust's relevance to debates concerning the cultural–educational mission of Weimar classicism, noting that commentators, from *Reichspresident* Friedrich Ebert to Oswald Spengler to Bertolt Brecht, all spoke to the national significance of Faust. Despite Ebert's invocation of both Goethe's *Faust* and the "spirit of Weimar" in his 1919 speech before the National Assembly, many Germans doubted that what was arguably an elitist, late-18th-century concept of culture could in fact provide a "rallying point for the new Germany" (Erlin 2009, 162). Critics on the left, Erlin (2009, 162) notes, questioned if classical literary texts were significant for contemporary readers. He (2009, 162) cites Brecht's 1929 exchange with Herbert Jhering, in which Brecht associates the "death" of the classics with to the "trauma of the war experience."

Throughout the 19th century, Dennis Shirley (1992, 20) points out, many educators judged Germany to have the "finest public school system of any country in the world." Germany had been among the first in the West to make education compulsory. Moreover, Shirley continues, those secondary school and university reforms undertaken by Wilhelm von Humboldt during his tenure as Minister of Education in Prussia had resulted in a rigorous academic curriculum emphasizing ancient languages and history. Shirley (1992, 20) reminds that 19th-century German schools were destinations of pilgrimages undertaken by foreign (including U.S.) school reformers:

> who marveled at classes with clear and sequential instruction, professionally trained teachers with thorough competence in their subject areas, and diligent, obedient students. The high standards set by the school, and the state's willingness to invest in superlative teacher education programs, were credited by many with creating the scientific and technical expertise that fueled Germany's economic takeoff in the last quarter of the century.

Theoretically structuring German schools was not economism—reducing all intellectual activity to those modes of instrumental calculation key to profit-making—but the notion of *Bildung*, or self-cultivation through study.

An authentic German life was to be sought spiritually, Daniel Tröhler (2003, 759) explains. Originally a religious idea that became secular, *Bildung* was associated with German art, and specifically German music. The person was no isolated individual, but, rather, characterized by that inwardness and spirituality resulting from self-effort and self-cultivation, or *Bildung* (2003, 759). Accompanying this "inward personhood" was the complementary conception of nationhood. The national spiritual life was *Volksstaat*, a notion of nation as "ethnocultural," and "detached" from politics (2003, 759). In fact, a German could cultivate him- or herself as a person only if s/he also cultivated him- or herself as a German, that is, in terms of his or her people: the German *Volk*. In contrast to English concepts of democracy that depicted the nation as an "aggregate of individuals," in Germany—conceived then as an ethnocultural Nation (today, however, almost 20 percent of the German population are immigrants)—the *Volk* constituted an organic unity that incorporated the individual. *Bildung*, in Tröhler's (2003, 759) formulation, depicts the "spiritual formation" of "integrated, cultivated personalities" oriented to the *Volk*. "To be free," Tröhler (2003, 760) states succinctly, "meant the embedding of the individual into the harmonious beauty of the whole."

Twentieth-century German educational discourse—the so-called *Geisteswissenschaftliche Padagogik*, education as one of the humanities or arts rather than as a science—triumphed around 1925, Tröhler (2003, 760) continues. Philosophy, not social science, was the key influence, evident in a conception of life (*Leben*) that was not empirical (as in the United States), but, instead, expressed the notion of the "mystic-holistic experience of life" (Tröhler 2003, 762). With the individual person conflated with the ethnocultural nation on the one side, and embroiled in politics and economics on the other, a dualism emerged, Tröhler (2003, 763) argues, and not only in educational thought. To illustrate its pervasiveness, he (2003, 763) references (as I have earlier in this chapter) Thomas Mann, who criticized American democracy and capitalism as "unGerman." Mann associated democracy with materialism and capitalism; he attacked all three, not only as anti-German but as anti-Christian as well (2003, 764). During Weimar, however, Mann underwent a change of heart, arguing that only through democracy could Germans achieve *Bildung* (Weitz 2007, 255).

Mann was not the only famous figure to articulate what was at stake for the nation in public education. Albert Einstein did as well, if in negative terms. Einstein, Friedrich (1995 [1972], 221) informs us, loathed the German process of education. "To me," Einstein reflected later, "the worst thing seems to be for a school principally to work with methods of fear, force, and artificial authority. Such treatment produces ... the submissive subject. It is no wonder that such schools are the rule in Germany and Russia" (quoted in Friedrich 1995 [1972], 221). Conservatives dismissed Einstein as "a Jew, a liberal, an internationalist, a pacifist, a skeptic, an innovator, and a scientist whose work baffled the average intelligence" (Friedrich 1995 [1972], 225). Groups of conservatives would wait for Einstein outside his apartment on the *Haberlandstrasse*, or outside his office in the Prussian Academy of Science. They would shout at him whenever he appeared. Others stuffed his mailbox with obscene and threatening letters. On one occasion, a gang of right-wing students disrupted Einstein's lecture at Berlin University, shouting "I'm going to cut the throat of that dirty Jew" (quoted in Friedrich 1995 [1972], 215).

Not all Germans shared these sentiments, of course. Sometimes influenced by U.S.-style progressivism and John Dewey in particular (despite German criticism of Dewey: Tröhler 2003, 766), many Germans undertook, in Shirley's (1992, 51) phrase, "a dizzying array of initiatives." Eager to pioneer new theories of curriculum, he (1992, 51) reports, Weimar educators undertook ambitious art education projects as well as experiments in industrial and vocational training, creating, for instance, "folk colleges" where working-class adults were able to continue their education on evenings and weekends, reminiscent of the courses offered at Hull House in Chicago by Jane Addams and Ellen Gates Starr. "By the time of the Weimar Republic," Shirley (1992, 51) concludes, "a broadly based movement of 'new education' or 'reform pedagogy,' which sought to transform schools root and branch, had gained a firm foothold in German society." Like much else in the Weimar Republic, progressive educational experiments too had started earlier.

In 1910, Paul and Edith Geheeb decided to open a new school they called the *Odenwaldschule*, after the nearby Odenwald forest. Unlike institutions of "correctional" education—which I describe in the next section—this school was strongly progressive. Students were placed in pedagogical "families": Geheeb discarded the concepts of "students" and "teachers," replacing them with "comrades" and "co-workers" respectively (Shirley 1992, 40). Each morning the school day began with "air baths," exercises taken outside in the nude. At *Odenwaldschule*, Shirley tells us, such practices reflected the German youth movement and back-to-nature "life reform" (*Lebensreform*) movement, the latter of which had begun around 1900 in an appropriation of Eastern (and specifically Indian) thought (Rogowski 2009, 64). Students did these exercises in the woods behind the school (Shirley 1992, 41). There were also hikes in the countryside, some of which lasted as long as a week or ten days. Paul Geheeb hoped the hikes enabled students to appreciate nature, to experience their own physical strengths and psychological resources, as well as providing opportunities to assist each other in various ways, teaching them the importance of social responsibility (Shirley 1992, 42).

Another pedagogical practice Geheeb promoted was the reading of quotations once a day before mealtime. While typically taken from classical works, such as those by Goethe or Fichte, these sometimes came from the writings of late-19th-century cultural critics such as Friedrich Nietzsche or Paul de Lagarde, who had criticized German schools for destroying the individual's creativity for the sake of a spiritually impoverished utilitarianism (Shirley 1992, 21). On occasion, Shirley (1992, 42) reports, Geheeb read aloud from newspaper articles, including those espousing feminist causes. "Whatever the source," Shirley (1992, 42) reflects, "the purpose of the reading was to stimulate the students to reflect for a moment about the deeper issues and purposes of life before settling in to their meals." Such practices also helped attune students and faculty to the moment and place where their academic study proceeded.

There was no standardized curriculum. Instead of grade levels, the *Odenwaldschule* organized "course communities" in which students met for two hours each day to study specific subjects. While these "communities" usually comprised students of similar ages, Shirley reports, on occasion there were communities of mixed ages that continued working together for several years. Students selected their areas of study; in cooperation with their instructors, students themselves were responsible for evaluating their work (Shirley 1992, 43). Indeed, Geheeb—often quoting the Greek poet Pindar's injunction to "become who thou art!"—encouraged students to resist coercion and to actualize their inner strengths (Shirley 1992, 46). "Become an individual," Geheeb enjoined his students, "become that individual who in the entire world only you, irreplaceably and uniquely you, can become through the development of your latent and fundamental personality" (quoted in Shirley 1992, 46). As Shirley (1992, 47) records, Geheeb regarded individuality as the most significant feature of human existence. Realization of this fact provided a corrective to the devolution of *Bildung* into cultural capital or political passivity. Geheeb wrote:

> If we really follow the imperative to 'Become who thou art!' then self-cultivation (*Bildung*) is neither a collection of cultural goods nor an object which we can own, but a being and a becoming. This formation of individual, which develops according to its own inner laws, stands in continual interaction with nature and the cultural products of the individual's environment, which it sometimes accepts and sometimes transforms, but which never reaches a conclusion. Whereas the dominant school system is most concerned with the quantitative learning of children and understands learning almost exclusively in intellectual terms, the organization of a true educational workshop for children must consider their individual differentiation.
>
> (quoted in Shirley 1992, 46–47)

The democratic significance of these pedagogical views were appreciated by many during Weimar; it was during the Republic that the *Odenwaldschule* entered the period of its greatest prosperity and fame (Shirley 1992, 50). As Weimar crumbled, Geheeb and his colleagues were stalwart in their opposition to the conservative restoration, especially to its most radical form, the Nazis. Not so for German teachers generally: by May 1933, only months after Hitler's ascendancy, almost a quarter of all teachers belonged to Nazi paramilitary groups (Shirley 1992, 218).

VIII Correctional Education

> The final myth Europe still possesses is—the Jew.
> —Efraim Frisch ([1921–1922], in Kaes et al. 1995, 253)

The first Jewish settlement on the Rhine was established in the second century C.E., Friedrich (1995 [1972], 108) notes, meaning that "the tormented relationship between Germany's Jews and gentiles has endured for nearly two millennia." And even though a Prussian royal edict of 1812 conferred full citizenship, Friedrich (1995 [1972], 109) adds, Jews were not accorded full civil rights until Bismarck (whom W. E. B. Du Bois had once admired [Townsend 1996, 251]) promulgated the Constitution of a united Germany in 1871. Even then the rights of Jews were disputed by many.

During World War I, over 100,000 (one out of six) Jews expressed their patriotism by joining the German army. Of these, 80,000 served in front-line trenches, and 35,000 were decorated for bravery (Friedrich 1995 [1972], 110). On November 7, 2010, German soldiers filed silently through a leaf-covered cemetery in Frankfurt to lay wreaths at a memorial for these Jewish soldiers. The memorial, a semicircular stone marker erected in 1925, honors 467 of the 12,000 Jewish soldiers who died fighting for Germany during the war (Ewing 2010, A8).

There were relatively few Jews in Germany, never more than 1 percent of the population. Most lived in Berlin. Even so, Berlin's Jews never numbered more than 5 percent of the city's population. Despite this low number, Friedrich (1995 [1972], 110) registers that "the spectacular culture of Berlin in the 1920s, the culture dominated by men like Max Reinhardt and Bruno Walter and Albert Einstein, was a Jewish culture." One-quarter of all the Nobel Prizes won by Germans in the first third of the 20th century were won by German Jews (Friedrich 1995 [1972], 111).

The establishment of the Weimar Republic, Peukert (1992, 158) judges, "completed the process of Jewish emancipation in Germany." Remaining barriers to full participation in German public life were finally removed. Not only in Berlin, but in the Republic generally, Peukert (1992, 159) emphasizes, "Jews now assumed an important part in post-war public life." Serving as leaders in the liberal parties and in the parties on the left, in universities and in the mass media, and in certain branches of business (especially commerce), Jews were, simply, central to the Weimar Republic. Certainly Jews were central to art, and many embraced the various avant-garde movements (noted earlier). For the first time, in Peukert's (1992, 159) words, there were glimpses of "the possible emergence of a new international, secularized culture which would sweep aside the traditional and nationalistic barriers on which anti-Jewish discrimination had rested." Anti-Semites would associate such cosmopolitanism with Jews; both Hitler and Stalin denounced Jews as "rootless cosmopolitans" (Appiah 2006, xvi).

Accompanying Jewish emancipation was an "alarming rise" (Peukert 1992, 159) in anti-Semitism. Despite their sacrifice during the War, Jews were denied membership in veterans' organizations, forcing them to form their own group (Mosse 1985, 131). Despite the long history of anti-Semitism in France and England, Jewish veterans were not excluded from veterans groups there. In post-War Germany, however, stung by the military defeat and the sudden appearance of democracy, the right relied on racism to deflect its responsibility for the defeat, in part by demanding revenge. In Weimar, Mosse (1985, 132) notes, "racism forged ahead … as part of the mass politics practiced by 'respectable' nationalist political parties as well as by the extreme political right." For no faction within the right was anti-Semitism as obsessive a concern as it was for the National Socialist German Workers' Party (NSDAP), founded in 1920 (Kaes et al. 1995, 119).

The threat to Jews was not only external, as many feared for the survival of Jewish identity given the steady decline in the population, due to low birth rate, loss of faith, and mixed marriages. From their different points of view, both Orthodox Judaism and the Zionist movement acted to counter this loss of Jewish identity (Peukert 1992, 159). For liberal and secular Jews, the family became the locus of safety and rejuvenation, "as a haven in an anti-Semitic world" (Gillerman 2009, 46–47). Policymakers turned to population policy as a means to encourage both the quantity *and* the quality of Jewish peoples (2009, 53). Sharon Gillerman (2009, 55) characterizes this policy as "biopolitics." She reminds that our attention (from the present) tends to be focused on Weimar's end, meaning that we invariably frame the Jews only as a potential group of victims. Such analyses thus fail to consider German Jews as a community that consciously and thoughtfully attempted to create an ethnically inflected program of biopolitics aimed at cultivating the Jewish population both as a valuable human resource and as the realization of an age-old religious tradition. Paralleling broader German concerns, then, Jews associated demographics with national—and specifically Jewish—survival (Gillerman 2009, 57). As with other Weimar developments, this Jewish preoccupation with survival also had its origin during the Wilhelmine period.

Not only the numbers of Jews was of concern, so was physical, mental, and moral deterioration. Such concern had intensified with the 1911 publication of *The Decline of the German Jews* by Felix Theilhaber. Sometimes compared to Spengler's *The Decline of the West*, Gillerman (2009, 60) explains, the culturally pessimistic Theilhaber argued that Jews' very success—becoming modern, adjusting to dominant German culture and the German economy—had "prepared the way for the degeneration and even eventual disappearance of German Jewry." Theilhaber associated Jewish moral and physical decline with urbanization, excessive individualism, the spread of chronic diseases (in our time "pandemics"), and a reduction in the size of Jewish families (especially the declining number of births among the healthy, productive strata of the population). While much criticized, by the time of the second edition (1921), Gillerman (2009, 61) points out, the book had become a "standard point of reference" in Jewish public debate. "The salient feature," Gillerman (2009, 61) emphasizes, "of all reproductive discourse, whether left or right, Orthodox or Liberal, was the conflation of private reproductive behaviors with social and national well-being." Complying with the biblical commandment to "be fruitful and multiply"—what Theilhaber deemed Judaism's "categorical imperative"—was not only the key to the survival of Judaism and Jewry, Gillerman (2009, 68) notes, it was as well "a measure of the subordination of individual desire to the general good."

Questions of the "general good" were at stake in efforts to accom-
modate new immigrants, especially the *Ostjuden*, or Jews from Eastern
Europe. By 1925, Jews from Eastern Europe made up 19.1 percent of
Germany's Jewish population (Gillerman 2009, 24). These immigrants
differed from German Jews socially and culturally, including in their
forms of worship. This provoked tension, even conflict, within Jewish
communities. There were commentators, Kaes et al. (1995, 248) note,
including the novelist Joseph Roth, who portrayed the new arrivals with
"considerable sympathy." Others, like Arnold Zweig, felt inspired by the
communal solidarity and vibrant religious feeling they discerned among
the *Ostjuden*, whom they had first encountered on the eastern front
during the War (1995, 248). Easily identified, however, the *Ostjuden*
quickly became a target for anti-Semitic prejudice (Peukert 1992, 159).

During the fourteen years of the Weimar Republic, German Jews created a wide array of welfare programs and social institutions addressed
to the needs of not only the *Ostjuden*, but of nearly all Jews and at every
stage of life. This pervasive "engagement in improving, normalizing,
and regulating the social sphere," Gillerman (2009, 6) argues, "not only
helped to bring a unity of purpose to the community but also constituted
a new kind of holy work for Weimar Jews." Similar to Tröhler's (2006)
characterization of U.S. pragmatism as a secularized Protestantism, this
relocated religiosity did not, however, efface its spiritual antecedents,
but incorporated them in a spiritual–social vision of Jewish and German
rejuvenation (Gillerman 2009, 7).

Just as U.S. school deform cannot be understood apart from U.S.
gender and racial politics, Weimar social welfare initiatives cannot be
grasped without understanding gender and racialization in early 20th-
century Germany. Suffice to say here that, as the "primary agents" of
social work, women—in Gillerman's (2009, 7–8) phrase—became the
"key practitioners" in these efforts at social and educational reform,
"bringing their 'motherly' qualities to bear on the problems of other
families within the Jewish community and the nation as a whole." This
gendered influence followed modernization generally—as traditional
patterns of patriarchal authority eroded—and not only due to women's
increasing participation in the workforce. Just as the absence of fathers
was racialized and gendered during U.S. Cold War politics, absent
fathers played a powerful role in the social crises of Weimar Germany
as well. Just as World War II would play a pivotal role in the American
family in the 1950s, war also reshaped Weimar families, as World War I
had resulted, in the phrase of Viennese psychoanalyst Paul Federn, in a
"fatherless society" (quoted in Gillerman 2009, 27).

Conservatives concluded that it was the combination of absent fathers
and working mothers that was to blame for a rise in male and female
juvenile delinquency during and immediately after the war. By the early

1930s, Gillerman (2009, 27) reports, over 60 percent of those teenagers deemed "endangered youth" by the courts and placed in correctional education facilities came from families split by divorce, separation, or the death of at least one of the parents. Because youth were regarded as both the greatest threat to society and the greatest hope for the future, educating "endangered" adolescents—in our time "at risk" kids from poor neighborhoods and often associated with ethnic minorities—figured as the most important specialty within Weimar youth welfare (Gillerman 2009, 108).

In the state of emergency following the war—leaders judged the German nation as in "a state of collapse" and foresaw only a "dark future with little hope"—legislators passed the Reich Youth Welfare Law (RJWG). Citing the Weimar constitution's proclamation of every child's "right to education," the RJWG gave the state the coercive power to remove children from homes that failed to protect that right (Gillerman 2009, 110). Correctional education was then "designed specifically" to correct socializing failures of the family, parents, school, and other social institutions in German society (Gillerman 2009, 113). In theory and in law, Gillerman (2009, 114) explains, the state served as "substitute parent," and as such, "superseded parental authority and operated independently of the wishes of the responsible adults or the minor himself." In entrusting the responsibility for child rearing to state representatives, she (2009, 114) notes, correctional education represented a "radical and decisive educational measure." No child would be left behind.

According to the Youth Welfare Law, the point of correctional education was countering the *Verwahrlosung*—neglect leading to "social unusefulness" (Gillerman 2009, 116)—of children. Gillerman (2009, 114) points out that *Verwahrlosung* was the "key concept" for summarizing a child's inappropriate care as it legitimated state intervention. By definition, she continues, *Verwahrlosung* could not be corrected by the individual efforts alone; it "required" social intervention (2009, 114). Moreover, the term conveyed strong class concerns: since its use in the 1880s *Verwahrlosung* had been associated with the threat to social order that the middle-class public projected onto working-class youth. In the late 19th century, with industrialization fully under way, masses of young men—as young as 14 years of age—entered factories, no longer in school but not yet old enough to be drafted into the German army. Some number of these young men spent their wages in leisure activities deemed unsuitable, even alarming, by more conservative middle-class Germans (Gillerman 2009, 115). So even the socially useful could be judged to be in a state of *Verwahrlosung* if, after working all day, they engaged in socially disruptive activities.

Unsurprisingly, students eligible for correctional education came disproportionately from the urban–industrial working classes (Gillerman

2009, 118). Also unsurprising, given that they were disproportionately middle class, Jews were under-represented in correctional education facilities, accounting for only 0.05 percent of the national correctional education population, while their percentage of the general population in 1933 was 0.077 (Gillerman 2009, 200 n. 29). (Catholics were over-represented [2009, 201 n. 46].) But composing almost 50 percent of Jewish youth in correctional education were young east European Jews (Gillerman 2009, 108). The arrival of east European Jews in Germany had increased the size of both the Jewish working and the lower middle classes (Gillerman 2009, 118).

Gender also played a prominent role in determining those who were "endangered" (Gillerman 2009, 121). In the boys' cases, Gillerman notes, the most common concern was their failure to work. After this work-related concern, the next most common concern among boys was crime, specifically theft (Gillerman 2009, 123). But, Gillerman (2009, 124) notes, symptoms of *Verwahrlosung* could also be rather vague, among them "general incorrigibility, 'running around,' and 'lying'." Some 20 percent of at-risk boys were charged with one of these. In contrast, fewer than one-third of the girls, compared with over one-half of the boys, were judged as irresponsible in their working lives. The most common sign of *Verwahrlosung* in girls was said to be sexual: some 80 percent of the girls sent into correctional education were judged guilty of sexual misconduct. The tell-tale sign of sexual misconduct was having had an abortion or a sexually transmitted disease, but the charges were also often vague, even without evidence. Many girls, Gillerman (2009, 125) reports, were charged with conducting an "immoral lifestyle, having a bad reputation, or keeping bad company." In the cases of both boys and girls, it was 19th-century notions of self-restraint and social responsibility that informed the interests of many correctional educators. The effects of *Verwahrlosung* could be reversed, it was thought, only by developing youth's rational capacity, teaching them to resist succumbing to their passions and "baser instincts" (Gillerman 2009, 128).

Not only the moral and psychological well-being of German youth was at stake; presumably also was the economy. Educators believed that youth's capacity to learn self-discipline was the prerequisite for the acquisition of marketable job skills. (Sound familiar?) And the rationale worked the other way: schools that emphasized job training were said to be producing "responsible citizen-workers" (Gillerman 2009, 129). For both girls and boys, correctional education emphasized learning a trade, requiring self-discipline and submission to authority. But with the Weimar economy so "volatile" (2009, 129), it was not always obvious what training would be demanded by the market. Neither is it obvious today.

As a symbol for the Republic, correctional education became the subject of increasing controversy throughout the 1920s. Those on the left criticized it as "repressive" and anti-working class (2009, 132). Public pressure to abandon the authoritarianism associated with correctional education persuaded many Jewish educators to reform their practices; in 1929, leading Jewish educational and social reformers issued a statement calling for the fundamental reform of correctional education (2009, 133). The directors of the Commission on Endangered Youth hired Dr. Hans Lubinski to direct the new Jewish correctional education facility at Wolzig, on the outskirts of Berlin. Gillerman (2009, 133) reports that Lubinski eliminated punishment and granted boys greater freedom of movement. He acknowledged the influences of the German youth movement, among them education of youth by youth, education for responsibility and autonomy, and the creation of "youth community." Rather than *Verwahrlosung* being constitutionally produced (i.e. genetically), it was, Lubinski argued, a consequence of childhood experiences, which could be corrected (2009, 134).

Yet if the Jewish educational experiment at Wolzig came to embody the ideal of the "new education"—extending to "at-risk" youth the progressive education more privileged students had enjoyed at *Odenwaldschule*—it did so at a moment when this trend was in retreat in much of the rest of Germany. Gillerman (2009, 134) points out that the economic crisis forced the federal government to retreat from its commitment to support those in need, rendering progressive education's support for subjective and social reconstruction irrelevant. After Hitler's ascendancy to power in 1933, the boys' home at Wolzig was closed and many of the students sent to *Sachsenhausen* on fabricated political charges. Once the pride of the Jewish community, Wolzig became the property of the Hitler Youth (Gillerman 2009, 169).

Recall that non-Jewish German youth had been radicalized during the various crises they associated with Weimar. By 1927, when the Prussian Student Organization took a poll of its members on the question of whether Jews should be allowed to join, fully 77 percent of the young intelligentsia voted NO. Far more than their parents, Friedrich (1995 [1972], 222) informs us, German youth were not only anti-Semitic but pro-Nazi—60 percent by actual count—and "ready for violence." Despite the broad support for progressive educational ideas within the teachers' associations, when Hitler took power, many educators were quite willing to work with the Nazis (Peukert 1992, 143–144). Thirty years later, on the other side of the Atlantic, a different state of emergency was invoked to persuade U.S. schoolteachers to comply with federal directives.

Chapter 4

Mortal Educational Combat

I Gracious Submission

> [T]he post-Sputnik educational atmosphere has quickened the activities of those who demand more educational rigor, who can now argue that we are engaged in mortal educational combat with the Soviet Union.
>
> —Richard Hofstadter (1962, 358)

The "combat" to which Hofstadter refers turned out to be a civil, rather than foreign, war, one in which public school teachers and professors of education were soundly defeated by a coalition of liberal and conservative politicians dedicated to business models of education. "[S]ince the 1960s," Richard Elmore (1993, 39) summarizes, "reformers usually agree that educators are not to be trusted, any more than another parochial special interest group, with major decisions about the direction or content of public education." Today, multiple "stakeholders" (not the least among them politicians, textbook publishers, and commercial firms promising higher test scores) have replaced public schools with cram schools. These are increasingly privatized, meaning that public budgets are now plundered by commercial firms (Molnar 2002; Taubman 2009). How did this happen?

The story starts in the 1950s. One of the early and most vocal academic critics of public school education was Arthur Bestor, a graduate of Teachers College's experimental Lincoln School at Columbia University, a historian at Teachers College and the University of Illinois, and leader of the Council for Basic Education (Clifford and Guthrie 1988; see Hofstadter 1962, 358). Anticipating Richard Hofstadter's even more influential attack a decade later, Bestor (1953, 14) charged that public education suffered from anti-intellectualism:

> The nation depends on its schools and colleges to furnish this intellectual training to its citizenry as a whole. Society has no other

institutions upon which it can rely in this matter. If schools and colleges do not emphasize rigorous intellectual training, there will be none.

While polemical, indeed overdetermined, this charge of anti-intellectualism was not without substance.

Bestor had also been critical of colleges and schools of education, complaining about what critics came to call "the ed. school monopoly." Bestor complained about the "interlocking directorate" of influential figures in schools of education, state departments of education, public school administration, and the United States Office of Education, who together (presumably) decided the quality and character of schooling. To break the stranglehold of "educationists" on schooling meant to intervene in the training, licensing, and employment of teachers (Clifford and Guthrie 1988). Soon after the 1957 Sputnik satellite launching—which qualifies, in LaCapra's (2009, 203) terms, as "the founding trauma ... a shattering, often divisive, event that splits self and/or society," in our case, schooling from education—Bestor would be joined by military critics, among them Vice-Admiral Hyman Rickover (1959, 1963).

In *Education and Freedom*, Rickover (1959) accused the American public of indifference to intellectual achievement and excellence. He insisted that Americans valued athletic over academic accomplishment, a point with which few curriculum theorists would take issue, but which would be aggressively ignored by the soon-to-be-elected Kennedy administration, as we see later in this chapter. Like Bestor, Rickover was sure that a *curricular* reconfiguration was the answer to the *military* crisis: "Our schools must return to the traditional task of formal education in Western civilization—transmission of cultural heritage, and preparation for life through rigorous intellectual training of young minds to think clearly, logically, and independently" (Rickover 1959, 18). While complaining about the American preference for muscles over mind, Rickover's call conflates the two, echoing those 19th-century classicists who believed that the mind was a muscle.

Christopher Lasch divides these critics of public education into two groups. Bestor, he suggests, belongs to those who attacked public education as "anti-intellectual and undemocratic" (1978, 139). But Rickover, James B. Conant, and Vannevar Bush were critical because schools failed to produce enough scientists and high-level technicians, the reason, they insisted, why the United States lagged behind the Soviet Union in the arms race. This "analysis" deflected responsibility from those most obviously responsible for this state of affairs, that is, military leaders and scientists. Rickover, Conant, and Bush, Lasch (1978, 139) emphasizes, "did not question the school's function as an instrument of military and industrial recruitment, they merely sought to make the selection process more efficient."

Lasch (1995, 76) singles out Conant for redefining the Jeffersonian notion of democracy. From a notion (which, Lasch suggests, Abraham Lincoln shared [see 1995, 69]) in which education was to be encouraged among all citizens for the sake of *intelligent and engaged civic life*, in Conant's criticism education merely replaced European aristocracies of wealth with an American aristocracy of talent. The principle of aristocracy remained intact. Lasch (1995, 76) comments: "In the name of the 'Jeffersonian tradition,' which envisioned a community of intelligent, resourceful, responsible, and self-governing citizens, Conant proposed merely to ensure the circulation of elites."

The specific event that led to the intensification of criticism of public education—and its association with national survival—was the launching of the Soviet satellite Sputnik in 1957. This was a traumatizing event because it was interpreted by many as declaring that the United States no longer enjoyed military superiority over the Soviet Union. Given the terrible tensions of the Cold War—millions of public school students practiced air raid drills weekly—the Sputnik satellite launching set off a national reaction that 1960 presidential candidate John F. Kennedy exploited in his campaign promise to "Get America Moving" again. Significantly, the Kennedy campaign exploited American anxieties not only over military competition and space exploration, but its tacticians sensed that education—hitherto a local matter—could be exploited as a national campaign issue.

Contra evidence and common sense, then, politicians, arts-and-sciences academicians, and military men all argued that the Soviets' satellite success cast doubt on the quality not of the American military or of American science, but of the American *educational* system. Had U.S. schools been academically strong, would the Soviets have defeated us in the space race, calling into question America's military superiority? Hofstadter (1962, 5–6) observed:

> The Sputnik [launching] was more than a shock to American national vanity: it brought an immense amount of attention to bear on the consequences of anti-intellectualism in the school system. ... Cries of protest against the slackness of American education, hitherto raised only by a small number of educational critics, were now taken up by television, mass magazines, businessmen, scientists, politicians, admirals, and university presidents, and soon swelled into a national chorus of self-reproach.

The alleged consequences of this ill-defined "slackness in the school system" would change from military to economic setbacks over the next forty years, but the political exploitation of public education would continue and intensify. The era of professional autonomy—negatively characterized by Bestor as a "monopoly"—had ended. An era of scapegoating public schools and university-based colleges of education was under way.

In the preface to the re-issued *The Process of Education* (summarizing the proceedings of the 1959 Woods Hole Conference at which was set the academic agenda for 1960s national curriculum reform), Jerome Bruner reflects on how his book functioned in three nations. In the Soviet Union, he tells us, the book was seized as "a weapon" in the struggle against ideological dogmatism in the school, and the academic-discipline-based curriculum the book demanded was viewed as supporting "more independence of mind" (Bruner 1977 [1960], x). In Japan, the book functioned to challenge the emphasis upon rote memorization in Japanese education. In Italy, Marxists attacked the book as a form of epistemological (i.e., bourgeois) idealism while classicists condemned it as an assault on scholasticism and humanism. "In all of these confrontations," Bruner (1977 [1960], xi) observes, "it was quite plain that debate about education was not just about education but about political ideals and ideology." What Bruner fails to note is that the same was true in the United States.

In the United States, Bruner's book—and the curriculum reform movement it rationalized—functioned in favor of academic vocationalism, against progressivism, as a means to "strengthen" and make more academically "rigorous" (or intellectually "muscled") young Americans' educational experience. These objectives were to be achieved through an intellectually challenging "teacher-proof" academic curriculum that forefronted scientific knowledge. Avowedly "liberal" during the Kennedy–Johnson years, such academic vocationalism would become explicitly "conservative" then "reactionary" after the election of Richard Nixon in 1968, as political and cultural conservatives began appropriating school "reform" to their own ideological ends. School deform begins, then, in a displacement of military and scientific failure onto public education. Uncritically participating in the displacement Bruner (1977 [1960], 74–75) declared,

> Today many Americans have become conscious, not just of the practical virtues of education, but of its content and quality. ... Unquestionably, there has also been a surge of awareness born of our sense of imperiled national security. The Soviet Union's conquests in space, its capability of producing not only powerful weapons but also an effective industrial society, have shaken American complacency.

Twenty years later economic, not military, matters prompted politicians and their collaborators to displace their failure onto the schools. During the early years of the Reagan administration the presumably "lax" condition of American schools was alleged to have placed the nation "at risk." After Reagan's election in 1980, Republican tax cuts created federal budget deficits that imperiled the stability of the American dollar (as federal deficits do today), then (as now) vis-à-vis the German (now the Euro) and Japanese currencies. But the crisis manufactured by the Reagan administration in the early 1980s was not only economic. Aggravated by its aggressive foreign policy, there was, as Lasch (1984, 73) observes, a "deterioration of Soviet–American relations," an "escalation of the arms race," and a "revival of the Cold War." But it was not fiscal irresponsibility (aggravated by tax cuts and military aggressivity) that was to blame for the state of the nation: somehow schools were (National Commission on Excellence in Education 1983).

During subsequent presidential administrations the declining economic competitiveness of the nation presumably imperiled America's ability to compete in the "global marketplace" in the "new millennium." Although few educators would dispute the significance of public education for the fate of the nation, politicians' exploitation of public education as a national political issue—onto which myriad other issues, especially military and economic ones, were grafted—has been disingenuous at best, diverting public scrutiny from the politicians themselves onto a largely politically passive professional sector unlikely to aggressively mount a counter-campaign. America's public school teachers have been and remain, politically speaking, "sitting ducks."

The consequences of this politicization of public education have been numerous, catastrophic, and continuing. The first has been to focus curriculum funding on science, mathematics, and technology, marginalizing (even more) programs in music and in the visual and other arts. The current and unrelenting hype about the computer occurs within this national fantasy—fabricated and reiterated by politicians—that education is too important to be left to the teachers (and education professors). There is a gendered dynamic at work here. Legislators (who are overwhelmingly male) feel entitled—compelled—to intervene in teachers' (coded female in the American popular imagination) domain of professional activity, as if "mother" cannot be trusted to raise "father's sons" properly. There is a long history of male suspicion of women's primacy in childcare, a suspicion that women's dominance in young men's lives may imperil their very manhood (see Kimmel 1994, 1996; Tyack and Hansot 1990; see also Cannella 1998). In section V we glimpse this dynamic at work in the Kennedy administration's obsession with physical education, especially the education of the adolescent male body.

The gendered character of teaching, fueled as it is by popular (male) imagination, is grounded in fact. Geraldine Clifford and James

Guthrie (1988, 328) characterize public school teaching as "a feminized occupation," noting that, at the time of their writing, women formed two-thirds of the nation's teachers. This "feminization of teaching" (Grumet 1988) has been the case for a century. By 1870, Richard Hofstadter reports, women represented approximately 60 percent of the teaching force, a percentage that increased in the decades following. By 1900, more than 70 percent of teachers were women, and in another quarter of a century the percentage peaked at more than 83 percent (see Hofstadter 1962, 317). Jane Addams (2002 [1902], 87) appreciated this gendering of the profession: "'Teacher' in the vocabulary of many children is a synonym for women-folk gentry, and the name is indiscriminately applied to women of certain dress and manner."

"In 1953," Hofstadter (1962, 320) writes, "this country stood almost alone among the nations of the world in the feminization of its teaching: women constituted ninety-three percent of its primary teachers and sixty percent of its secondary teachers." The gender politics of Hofstadter's critique of public education becomes even clearer when he imagines the problem male public school teachers face from other (presumably more masculine) men:

> But in America, where teaching has been identified as a feminine profession, it does not offer men the stature of a fully legitimate male role. ... The boys grow up thinking of men teachers as somewhat effeminate and treat them with a curious mixture of genteel deference (of the sort due to women) and hearty male condescension.
>
> (Hofstadter 1962, 320)

What was fifty years ago a "hearty condescension" is now contempt. Since *No Child Left Behind*, education schools have been directed to find "what works," an expensive and quixotic search derived from an early 20th-century gendered (see Seigfried 1996, 194) faith that "the scientific study of the nature of human learning will lead to principles for effective teaching" (Egan 2002, 74). We have known for a long time (see, for instance, Bauman 1978) that as long as human beings are capable of creativity, human conduct (except in trivial matters) cannot be predicted. As Egan (2002, 135) points out, authoritarianism works (at least for a while, sometimes a long while, as the Soviet example suggests):

> Unless the school has enormous power and authority over children, which in a democracy we are unwilling to allow, the dominant values and behavioral norms will be those the children bring to the school and against which any competing values and norms of the teachers' will be largely helpless.

This is the political point of accountability: to force teachers to force children to accept "new" norms: docility, dependence, and an unquestioning trust of authorities. Complementary to the obsession with "what works" is the fantasy that new teachers from elite institutions can pull rabbits out of hats, a pedagogical version of *noblesse oblige*.

While gender politics in education have a long history (Tyack and Hansot 1990), their present versions became imprinted during the post-Sputnik era, and especially in the administration of President John F. Kennedy. During that time men's long-standing suspicions of women's influence on children, specifically on boys, were stimulated as the nation—in many men's minds gendered masculine—was imperiled. Never mind that it was men in the Eisenhower administration and in the military establishment who were responsible for this heightened sense of peril, having lost to the Soviets the race to launch the first satellite in space. Other men—in this case, the Kennedys—sensed the political dividends to be paid should they convince an uneasy American public that women—public education, gendered female—were to blame.

The origin of the convoluted present is not only gendered; it is racialized. The racialization of public education, begun in the South one hundred years earlier (Trelease 1971, 293; Williamson 1984, 51), intensified during the Cold War era as the Supreme Court mandated desegregation and white flight (in the North to the suburbs, leaving urban cores painted black) followed. The civil rights movement—animated by student-led organizations such as the Student Nonviolent Coordinating Committee (SNCC)—intensified the racialization of education in the (white) public mind, where desegregation was fought both in school buildings and in school textbooks (Carson 1981; Zimmerman 2002).

The educational architect of the 1960s national curriculum reform movement, Jerome Bruner, came close to realizing that the national concern over curriculum was not strictly "educational" in nature. In the preface to the 1977 edition of *The Process of Education* (first published in 1960), Bruner (1977, xi) suggests that curriculum reform as a "means of cultivating intellect" was "swamped" by "deep social forces," among them, the civil rights and the anti-Vietnam War movements. I would supplement Bruner's verb choice—*swamped*—with another, *expressed*. Although I do not doubt the sincerity of those who participated in the 1960s national curriculum reform movement, I do think that movement was not only *swamped* by deep social forces, it *expressed* them, including the (white and, especially, male) public's resistance to these social movements. It did not *only* do that, but curriculum reform did—and school reform would thereafter—express deep social forces, among them gendered and racialized forces and, especially, white and masculinist reaction to these. Politically exploiting these forces, politicians allege that lazy or incompetent teachers—gendered female and racialized black—are to blame when children do not succeed in school. The phrase "No Child Left Behind" was no doubt intended to exploit black and poor parents' concerns for their children's futures by demanding that schools be held accountable for student learning as measured on standardized examinations. That schools alone—rather than government or the corporate sector or "faith-based" communities—are accountable for the future goes unchallenged. Despite indisputable evidence that the ongoing school "crisis" is "manufactured" (see, for example, Berliner and Biddle 1996), *school deform* continues to garner bipartisan support, politicians who refuse to acknowledge the absurd assumptions that underpin it, namely that the school is *the* lever for social and economic improvement and that teachers are responsible for student learning.

II The Racial Politics of Curriculum Reform

[T]he Cold War would spark the most furious textbook controversies that America had ever seen.
—Jonathan Zimmerman (2002, 80)

As early as 1913, the historian William Dodd complained that "two distinct histories are taught in the schools" (quoted in Zimmerman 2002, 34). One was taught above the Mason–Dixon Line, the other below it. While the racialization of the public school curriculum—in the public mind—would intensify after the Supreme Court's 1954 decision, in *Brown v. Board of Education*, to desegregate the public schools, the racialization of the curriculum had begun at least one hundred years earlier. But in the years surrounding the 1957 Sputnik incident, this racialization intensified and took the form of curricular control, which is to say a systematic effort at ideological control.

Pressured by public intellectuals and activists such as W. E. B. Du Bois and Carter Woodson, the National Association for the Advancement of Colored People (NAACP) convened in 1932 a textbook committee to coordinate the efforts of local branches to examine history, literature, and civics schoolbooks, and to protest those that misrepresented the facts. It reissued this recommendation in 1938 and again in 1939, publishing a pamphlet entitled *Anti-Negro Propaganda in School Textbooks* as a guide for community activists. NAACP officials visited publishers to demand revision of their textbooks, while calling on the students themselves to join the fight (Zimmerman 2002).

As the school curriculum expressed the white racism of the nation at large, many hoped that correcting the curriculum might influence the larger society. To illustrate this hope, Zimmerman (2002, 49) quotes a black Kansas City newspaperman: "I do not say that a change in our anti-Negro text-books will kill prejudice, but I am convinced it is a major step in that direction." Zimmerman points out that as Du Bois came to reject the NAACP's commitment to racial integration, he also came to doubt whether "integrated" textbooks could temper white racism. Carter Woodson remained committed to mixed-raced schools *and* to specialized black history courses in African American schools (Zimmerman 2002).

The Cold War attack on textbooks was animated at first, and foremost (at least initially) by the paranoid anti-Communism of the right wing. From elitists like William F. Buckley Jr. to low-brow anti-Semites like Allen A. Zoll, thousands of Americans converged on local school boards and classrooms to protest textbooks' allegedly "communistic" preference for public housing, progressive taxation, and other markers of presumed left-wing subversion (Zimmerman 2002). During 2009 debates over the "public option" in health care reform, the same tactic was invoked, this time by the specter of "socialism."

Zimmerman points out that the three themes of right-wing assaults on textbooks in the 1950s—Communism, internationalism (especially the United Nations), and sexual depravity—came to include, by mid-decade, a fourth one: race. Across the country, conservative critics pressed publishers and school boards to omit any mention of the Ku Klux Klan, lynching, or segregation. Teaching the truth about the racial violence in the United States amounted to complicity with Communism, as such information would presumably foment what was then commonly called "racial agitation." In Georgia, Zimmerman points out, the mere mention of black poverty in Magruder's *American Government* textbook provoked threats of white retribution. Magruder "should be shot as a traitor to our Country," one citizen proclaimed in 1950. "This type of stuff might be expected in the Harlem district of New York, but that it should be taught in the Public Schools of Georgia is unthinkable" (quoted passages in Zimmerman 2002, 88).

When in 1952 Alabamans discovered that one of their textbooks included a chapter on the Fair Employment Practices Committee and other efforts to fight racial injustice, they demanded that the publisher delete the entire chapter. To "protect" Alabama schoolchildren against further "subversion," the state legislature passed a law requiring all subsequent textbooks to carry a statement confirming that neither the author nor the people quoted had been members of a Communist or "Communist-front" organization. This very broad and ambiguous designation was used whenever it suited right-wing fanatics. In this instance, Zimmerman tells us, the law was directed at the NAACP, considered by many white southerners to be a "Red" organization. Given the NAACP's bitter and expensive fight with the Communist Party USA over the legal defense of the "Scottsboro Nine"—young black men falsely convicted of raping white women in 1930s Alabama—one wonders how any southerner could entertain such nonsense (Carter 1979 [1969]).

While nationwide, right-wing assaults on school textbooks were most intense south of the Mason–Dixon Line. The regional difference became apparent, Zimmerman suggests, in the controversy surrounding the 1958 publication of *Brainwashing in the High Schools* by E. Merrill Root, a former English professor and right-wing zealot. Root alleged that studying subversive textbooks in high school had led to American prisoners' vulnerability to Communist indoctrination during the Korean War. The allegation was greeted with widespread ridicule in the North, where critics pointed out that eighteen of the twenty-one "traitors" had not even completed high school, making their study of the textbooks in question unlikely (Zimmerman 2002).

In the South, however, Root's fantasy was treated as fact. Southern lawmakers hired Root to analyze supposedly subversive texts in their high schools. No segregationist, Root was of little help. Despite his acknowledgment, in a report to Mississippi legislators, of his own support for voluntary racial integration, Root's rabid anti-Communism proved useful to southerners in their segregationist cause. Zimmerman points out that Root's list of "Reds" who were cited—or worse, celebrated—in "collectivist" schoolbooks included William O. Douglas, Eleanor Roosevelt, and other advocates for racial justice. After Root (1958) condemned twelve Mississippi textbooks for the "pink political fog," lawmakers immediately demanded that schools remove them (see Zimmerman 2002, 104). The color of his visual image is not incidental; right-wing fanatics often linked political betrayal with gender betrayal. In the decade to follow, "Pinko-Commie-Fag" was hurled at more than one long-haired Vietnam War protester.

Perhaps compensating for the treason of their Confederate ancestors, many white southerners embraced the anti-intellectual attacks on school textbooks by presumably "patriotic" societies. Apparently inspired by Root's *Brainwashing in the High Schools*, Zimmerman tells us, the Daughters of the American Revolution issued a list of 170 objectionable texts in 1959. Unlike Root, whose diatribes were limited to history textbooks, the DAR went after literature, biology, music, and even arithmetic textbooks. Like Root's book, Zimmerman reports, the DAR list was taken seriously only south of the Mason–Dixon Line.

In Mississippi, segregationist governor Ross Barnett criticized southerners for failing to take seriously enough the Communist threat in school textbooks. Taking control of the state's text-selection system, Barnett promised all textbooks adopted by Mississippi would defend "the Southern and true American way of life" (quoted in Zimmerman 2002, 106). Originating in the North as a campaign to defend America's "free enterprise system" from "creeping collectivism," Zimmerman points out, the assault on textbooks became a southern assault on the prospect of racial integration.

Civil rights movement activists were not silent in the face of this nonsense. In 1961 a NAACP resolution demanded that school textbooks "properly present the contribution of the Negro to American culture"; in 1963 Urban League officials called for a "nationwide struggle" against "all-white" textbooks; and in 1965 the Congress for Racial Equality condemned "stereotypes and distortions of the roles of Negroes" in school textbooks (quoted passages in Zimmerman 2002, 112). That same year, Zimmerman (2002, 112) tells us, the Urban League convened a "tense" meeting between black leaders and representatives of the publishing industry. While proclaiming allegiance to responsible racial representation, most of the publishers present cautioned against "moving too fast," fearing that white school boards would refuse to adopt "integrated" textbooks. Publishers should produce "what people ought to know, not just what will sell," Urban League Whitney Young pointed out. "Don't approach integration like castor oil," Young told the publishers. "For once, look at something not as a problem but as an opportunity. ... Your job as human beings is do what is right. Take a position" (quoted passages in Zimmerman 2002, 112).

Civil rights activists knew they could not rely on publishers to place ethics over profits. Like other civil rights struggles in the sphere of public education, the textbook battle would be won or lost "on the local level," district by district, school by school. In addition to identifying racist schoolbooks, then, the NAACP also asked local affiliates to organize against them. Across the country, thousands of African Americans responded, demanding racial justice in the school curriculum. Activists used two basic arguments, both connected to the era's civil rights movement. First, activists pointed out that accurate history textbooks might help persuade stubborn (especially southern) whites to revise their racist views. Second, activists pointed out that if the school curriculum texts continued to misrepresent African Americans and their experience in America, black children would suffer "feelings of separateness and inferiority," as several Philadelphia activists wrote in 1965 (quoted in Zimmerman 2002, 114). On this point they were in agreement with the theories of Kenneth B. Clark and other "damage" theorists, whose ideas were influential in *Brown v. Board of Education*. If physical segregation was harmful to African Americans, "segregated" textbooks were damaging as well (Zimmerman 2002). Martin Luther King Jr. employed both arguments; he pointed out that biased school curricula supported both "white supremacy" and "the Negroes' sense of worthlessness" (quoted in Zimmerman 2002, 114).

White liberals brought federal power to bear on the matter. On occasion, they used the "bully pulpit," as when Vice President Hubert

Humphrey condemned the "Negro history gap" in American schools (quoted in Zimmerman 2002, 115). On other occasion, liberals used legislation. Under the Elementary and Secondary Education Act of 1965, $400 million was allocated to schools and libraries for the purchase of "multi-racial" and "multi-ethnic" books (quoted in Zimmerman 2002, 115). Such actions on behalf of an "integrated" school curriculum were—like actions on behalf of integrated school buildings—bitterly contested, especially by southern whites (Zimmerman 2002).

While white resistance and recrimination were hardly limited to the South, it was especially widespread and intense there. Southern whites insisted that racial integration was unacceptable, whether in classrooms or in textbook illustrations. As late as 1969, in Birmingham, Alabama, whites blocked the adoption of a textbook that alluded to the church bombing that had killed four black girls in the city in May 1963. In truth, Zimmerman (2002, 116) points out, the authors of the textbook "bent over backward to appease local sensibilities," attributing the crime to lower-class "white extremists," thereby absolving Birmingham's political and economic elites. Even through the early 1970s, Zimmerman (2002, 116) notes, "*any* reference to racial violence, hostility, or prejudice often spelled the removal of a textbook."

Even the most modest mention of distinguished African Americans in the textbooks of time was met by white protest. In Florida a teacher who used a text showing black Union soldiers during the Civil War found the tires of her car slashed and warnings scrawled across the windows. Other critics objected to even the mention of Frederick Douglass simply because such acknowledgment implied criticism of racist whites. "For God's sake," demanded one white Virginian in 1970, "give us some history to be proud of" (quoted in Zimmerman 2002, 116). By resisting the inclusion of important African Americans in school textbooks, these same southerners were insuring that America would have no future of which to be proud. Today such key figures disappear as the curriculum contracts to so-called cognitive "skills" to be assessed by standardized exams.

Racists in the North and West tended to be less direct than those in the South. There they made their objections to integrated textbooks in class rather than in explicitly racial terms. Rarely, Zimmerman (2002) points out, did northern white resistance to integrated textbooks—or, for that matter, to integrated classrooms—employ long-discredited arguments concerning inherent differences between blacks and whites. Rather, racists in the North complained that liberal elites were smearing hardworking, patriotic Americans (Zimmerman 2002). "Of course, we do have much of which we are not proud," acknowledged one Californian, "but why play up our mistakes, downgrade our heroes, and please our enemies?" (quoted in Zimmerman 2002, 117–118).

Such an "argument" would be trotted out again during the 1995 history curriculum controversy, when, led by Lynne Cheney, former head of the National Endowment for the Humanities and wife of future Vice President Richard Cheney, conservatives maligned the National History Standards that she had funded (along with the Department of Education) for giving insufficient attention to Confederate General Robert E. Lee and far too much to presumably obscure figures (such as Harriet Tubman) or patriotically embarrassing episodes (such as the Ku Klux Klan and McCarthyism). Such straightforward ideological indoctrination is also evident in recent efforts of the Texas school board to require the school curriculum to portray "conservatives" in a "positive light," to "emphasize the role of Christianity in American history, and include Republican political philosophies in textbooks" (McKinley 2010, March 10, 1). It's back to the future.

III Students and the Civil Rights Movement

[F]or a while all of us seemed to go crazy with hope for another kind of America.

—Audre Lorde (1982, 172)

While the physical integration of public schools and the intellectual integration of the curriculum racialized public education in the white mind, there were other events that associated African Americans with schooling. Recall that the struggle for civil rights generally was, in no small measure, conducted by students. True, these were college and university students, but for many whites such distinctions blurred into one conflated impression. To further appreciate this phenomenon of racialization inflecting 1960s curriculum reform, let us review, briefly, moments in the history of one of the major civil rights organizations in the 1960s, the Student Nonviolent Coordinating Committee (SNCC).

I choose the SNCC because it was the most student-affiliated wing of the civil rights movement. Born during a period of extensive student protest activity, the SNCC was widely regarded as the "shock troops" of the civil rights movement. SNCC activists established projects in areas such as rural Mississippi considered too dangerous by other organizations. Over time, the SNCC's activities shifted from racial desegregation to political rights for African Americans, and its philosophical commitment to nonviolent direct action gave way to a secular, humanistic radicalism influenced by Marx, Camus, Malcolm X, and, concretely, by the SNCC organizers' own horrifying experiences in southern black communities (Carson 1981).

The SNCC's founding conference was held April 16–18, 1960, in Raleigh, North Carolina, called by the Executive Director of the

Southern Christian Leadership Conference, Ella Baker. The initiating role of the Southern Christian Leadership Conference (SCLC) had established the leadership over the southern black struggle by Martin Luther King, Jr., and those ministers associated with him. But Baker understood the psychological significance of independence for student activists, and she resisted efforts to undermine their autonomy. Students at the conference affirmed their commitment to the nonviolent doctrines advocated by King, yet they appeared to be drawn to these ideas due less to their association with King than because they provided an appropriate rationale for student protest. The founding of the SNCC was, as Clayborne Carson (1981, 19) points out, "an important step in the transformation of a limited student movement to desegregate lunch counters into a broad and sustained movement to achieve major social reforms." Not only the public school was at stake, it seemed to many (especially southern) whites, it was the public sphere itself.

At first, the SNCC appeared to outsiders and even to many black student leaders as merely a clearing house for the exchange of information about localized protest movements. To SNCC leaders, it was potentially an organization for expanding the struggle beyond its campus base to include all classes of blacks. At a fall conference in Atlanta on October 14–16, 1960, the SNCC attempted to consolidate the student protest movement through the establishment of an organizational structure and by clarifying its goals and principles. In brief, the movement's goals were "individual freedom and personhood" (quoted in Carson 1981, 27).

At the end of 1960 the SNCC was still a loosely organized committee of part-time student activists who were uncertain of their roles in the southern struggle. Their political orientations could be said to be more or less conventional. Yet within months, the SNCC would became a cadre of full-time organizers and protesters. Its militant identity was forged during the "freedom rides," a series of challenges to southern segregation that for the first time brought student protesters into conflict not only with white southern legal officials, but with the Kennedy administration itself. The SNCC's militancy was further deepened by the experiences of student activists in Mississippi jails during the summer of 1961. It had been after attending a Congress of Racial Equality (CORE) workshop in December that a few students decided to remain in jail after being arrested rather than posting bond. Imprisonment, many decided, constituted a crucial learning experience (Carson 1981).

The freedom rides not only contributed to the desegregation of southern transportation facilities, they accelerated the formation of a self-consciously radical black student movement which would soon direct its militancy toward other, even more controversial issues, including questioning the good faith of the federal government. Increasingly, the

SNCC charged the federal government with hypocrisy, as it failed to act forcefully to achieve domestic civil rights for African Americans while self-righteously proclaiming democratic values abroad (Carson 1981). This understanding would provide the foundation for a coalition with mostly white student groups opposing the war in Vietnam.

The SNCC sent representatives—as did other civil rights organizations—to a meeting with Attorney General Robert Kennedy on June 16, 1961. (In light of his volatile relationship with black activist groups, Kennedy's concern with the state of American manhood was not only gendered but also racialized.) At that 1961 meeting Kennedy suggested that the freedom ride campaign be refocused toward the goal of registering southern blacks who had been disenfranchised through violence, intimidation, and more subtle techniques such as literacy tests and poll taxes. Students affiliated with the SNCC were divided over whether to become involved in voter registration work. While they understood that this was an important activity, many were reluctant to abandon the direct action tactics that had placed them at the forefront of the civil rights struggle (Carson 1981).

The black-dominated southern civil rights movement would have a profound effect on the white student left. Without the knowledge of the nonviolent tactics and organizing techniques developed by the SNCC in the South, white student activism would probably not have expanded as quickly or as successfully as it did. Tom Hayden and other leaders of the student-led anti-Vietnam War movement learned much from their experiences in the South. Students for a Democratic Society, the northern radical student movement, as well as other predominantly white student organizations, attracted students whose induction into political activism had occurred during their engagement in the struggle for civil rights in the South (Carson 1981).

The pace and scope of protest in the years following accelerated and expanded, respectively, intensifying white southerners' sense of emergency. During 1963, Southern Regional Council researchers estimated that 930 public protest demonstrations took place in at least 115 cities in eleven southern states. More than 20,000 persons were arrested during these protests, in contrast to approximately 3,600 arrests in the period of nonviolent protests prior to the fall of 1961. In 1963, ten persons died in circumstances directly related to racial protests; at least thirty-five bombings occurred. Those SNCC activists who were engaged in mass protests became aware of a militancy, especially among urban African Americans, that surpassed their own. This militancy among the people compelled them to reassess their own convictions regarding nonviolent protest (Carson 1981).

As the 1960s progressed and anti-Vietnam War and civil rights movements gained momentum, black and white women working within male-dominated protests groups—among them the Students for a Democratic Society (SDS) and the SNCC—began to express their frustration with their own situation of powerlessness. In some fundamental way the struggle for civil rights, for black power and culture, was also a "matter of manhood." Certainly many experienced it as such. Michelle Wallace (1978/1979) reports that many African American women felt they were being shut out of what seemed increasingly to be a men's affair. Wallace quotes Cynthia Washington, director of a freedom project in Mississippi in 1964:

> We did the same work as men—organizing voter registration and community issues in rural area—usually with men. But when we finally got back to some town where we could relax and go out, the men went out with other [white] women. Our skills and abilities were recognized and respected, but that seemed to place us in some category other than female. Some years later, I was told by a male SNCC worker that some of the project women had made him feel superfluous. I wish he had told me that at the time because the differences in the way women were treated certainly did add to the tension between black and white women.
>
> (quoted in Wallace 1978/1979, 6)

At an SNCC meeting held at Waveland, Mississippi in November 1964, the mostly male staff members were confronted by black women on these issues. Just as the origins of the 19th-century women's rights movement can be traced to the involvement of women in the abolitionist struggle (Ware 1992), so the contemporary women's movement underwent incubation in the SNCC and the civil rights struggle of the 1960s (Carson 1981).

At Waveland a workshop on the role of women was held, and from this workshop came the demand that SNCC men confront the issue of sexual discrimination within the organization. A paper was written by a group of female staff members, including some of the most influential white members, charging, among other things, that women were routinely asked to perform mundane office chores while rarely being asked to chair meetings or take important roles in policymaking. The paper likened the status of women to that of blacks. Further, the SNCC should "force the rest of the movement to stop the discrimination and start the slow process of changing values and ideas so that all of us gradually come to understand that this is no more a man's world than it is a white world" (quoted in Carson 1981, 148). Male SNCC workers at Waveland dismissed these complaints, arguing that sexual discrimination was a minor matter compared with other issues, namely racial ones. The feminist paper had little impact on most of the male SNCC staff (Carson 1981).

Stokely Carmichael was one of those at Waveland who regarded these charges of sexual discrimination as a bothersome diversion from the SNCC's important work. To a question regarding the proper position of women in the SNCC, Carmichael jokingly responded, "prone." The comment was widely circulated in feminist circles and became a source of embarrassment for Carmichael. It reflects the lack of serious attention given to women's concerns by many men at the time. Additionally, the fact that the principal supporters of the paper were white led many black staff members to discount its significance. The paper produced no noticeable changes in the SNCC's policies, although it did raise the issue and anticipated the feminist movement to follow (Carson, 1981). Reflecting a decade later on gender relations in the civil rights movement, Michele Wallace would write:

> Now that freedom, equality, rights, wealth, power were assumed to be on their way, she had to understand that manhood was essential to revolution—unquestioned, unchallenged, unfettered manhood. Could you imagine Ché Guevara with breasts? Mao with a vagina? She was just going to have get out of the way. She had had her day. Womanhood was not essential to revolution. Or so everyone thought by the end of the 1960s.
>
> (Wallace 1978/1979, 13)

African American women are haunted, Wallace argued, by the mythology that surrounds African American men. This mythology is drawn from the actual historical persecution:

> castrated black men hanging by their necks from trees; the carcasses of black men floating face down in the Mississippi; black men with their bleeding genitals jammed between their teeth; black men shining shoes; black men being turned down for jobs time and time again; black men watching helplessly as their women go to work to support the family; black men behind bars, persecuted by prison guards and police; jobless black men on street corners, with needles in their arms, with wine bottles in their hip pockets; black men being pushed out in front to catch the enemy's bullets in every American war since the Revolution of 1776—these ghosts, rendered all the more gruesome by their increasing absence of detail, are crouched in the black woman's brain.
>
> (Wallace 1978/1979, 15–16)

Barbara Christian (1985, 91) testified to the "unwillingness of many black women to acknowledge or address the problems of sexism that affect them because they feel they must protect black men." But by protecting their men, Michelle Wallace worried, African American women were not always taken seriously.

In the fall of 1964, the SNCC accepted the invitation of Harry Belafonte to send a delegation to Africa. A loyal SNCC supporter, Belafonte arranged for the trip through his contacts with the government of Guinea. On many occasions SNCC activists had rhetorically linked their struggle with the African nationalist movements in which Frantz Fanon had been so completely engaged (Sekyi-Otu 1996). SNCC activists had appealed to Africans for support of American civil rights efforts. In December 1963—two years after Fanon's death to the month—a group of staff members met with Oginga Odinga, the Kenyan leader, during his brief visit to Atlanta. The SNCC's African tour began on September 11, 1964. The experience had a profound impact on the SNCC delegation, composed, in part, of James Forman, John Lewis, Julian Bond, and Fannie Lou Hamer (Carson 1981).

Learning how the American struggle was perceived by Africans, SNCC members discovered that the United States government had far more control than they over the image of the American civil rights movement abroad. The son of the famous educator Horace Mann Bond and soon to be nominated for Vice President of the United States, Julian Bond expressed shock at the blatant misinformation disseminated by American information offices in Africa: "There were all these pictures of Negroes doing things, Negro judges, Negro policemen, and if you didn't know anything about America, like Africans would not, you would think these were really commonplace things. That's the worst kind of deceit" (quoted in Carson, 1981, 135).

Perhaps the most memorable episode of the SNCC trip to Africa was an unexpected encounter in Nairobi with Malcolm X, who told SNCC activists he was determined to support the radical elements in the civil rights movement. Malcolm X was eager to meet with representatives of the SNCC which, he said, was his favorite civil rights organization. Although he worried that Africans would not endorse specific American groups or factions, Malcolm X hoped that his recently formed Organization of Afro-American Unity (OAU) would bring together African Americans who were interested in closer ties with Africa (Carson, 1981). One form those closer ties would take would be "Afrocentricity" (Asante 1987, 1992; Young-Bruehl 1996, 492) itself gendered, associated with "feminist epistemology" (Awkward 1995, 52; Braxton 1989, 59; Higginbotham 1996, 23) and with "black masculinism and black nationalism" (Harper 1996, 69). That Africa was the mother of ancient Greek—and subsequent Western—civilization was not news; in the second volume of the *Journal of Negro History*, for example, Carter Woodson had published an article by George Wells Parker asserting the "African Origin of Grecian Civilization." African studies should constitute the core of every Negro history course and textbook, Woodson had argued; he devoted the first five chapters of his most popular text to black Americans' African origins (Zimmerman 2002, 51). In the 1960s, the civil rights struggle would also take educational forms.

IV Freedom Schools

> Love is the central motif of nonviolence. Love is the force by which God binds man to Himself and man to man.
> —SNCC Statement of Purpose (quoted in Carson 1981, 24)

During this period of increased student militancy, plans were developed for a "freedom school" program. The idea for the school program had been conceived by SNCC worker Charles Cobb in the fall of 1963. Cobb had recognized the inadequacy of public education in Mississippi, due, in part, to its "complete absence of academic freedom" and its repression of "intellectual curiosity and different thinking." (Sound familiar?) He proposed that schools be established to "fill an intellectual and creative vacuum" in the lives of young black Mississippians. He was especially interested that teachers "get them to articulate their own desires, demands and questions." Cobb proposed that teachers be employed from the hundreds of northern college students who would be arriving in Mississippi during the summer: "These are some of the best young minds in the country, and their academic value ought to be recognized, and taken advantage of" (quoted passages in Carson 1981, 109).

The curriculum for the freedom schools was developed in March 1964 at a meeting of educators, clergymen, and SNCC workers in New York. The curriculum would include the usual school subjects, plus courses on contemporary issues, cultural expression, and leadership development. This last course would teach the history of the civil rights struggle (characterized in those heady days as the black liberation movement), including the study of political strategies. Staughton Lynd, a white radical intellectual teaching at the time at Spelman College in Atlanta, became director of the freedom school program (Carson 1981).

Mississippi children and parents responded favorably to the freedom schools. While encouraging to many students, the innovative educational program only partially removed the barriers of distrust and fear that separated white teachers from black residents. The SNCC had conducted educational programs before, preparing black residents for Mississippi's voter registration test. In 1963 SNCC's Maria Varela had established an adult literacy project in Alabama. Despite these precedents, the freedom schools were the SNCC's first comprehensive educational program designed for a large number of black youngsters. A statewide enrollment of about one thousand students had been expected for the freedom schools, but more than twice that number attended classes in forty-one schools. Participation was greatest in those areas where there had already been civil rights activities. In Hattiesburg, Mississippi, for example, more than 600 students enrolled (Carson 1981).

In plantation areas participation was much lower. The reasons were not only ideological. A teacher in Shaw explained that black youngsters in that plantation community attended public schools during the summer so as to be available to pick cotton in the fall (Carson 1981). After leaving public school in the afternoon, many youngsters preferred to sleep rather than going to the freedom school to study "in the blazing heat of the Mississippi sun and dust" (quoted in Carson 1981, 120).

Freedom school teachers tended to ignore traditional classroom routines, employing innovative teaching methods in an effort to encourage the free expression of ideas. A curriculum guide developed for boycotting students in Boston was adapted for use in the Mississippi freedom schools. As part of the leadership training, students discussed the role of freedom schools and, specifically, the educational importance and political necessity of preserving and advancing African American culture. Uncritical assimilation to white culture must cease (Carson 1981).

Students were offered courses in creative writing, drama, art, journalism, and foreign languages. There were evening classes in literacy, health, and typing. Many students attended performances of the Free Southern Theater, a touring company organized as part of the freedom schools by John O'Neal at Tougaloo College. The Theater performed *In White America*, a play written by (white) historian and, later, queer theorist Martin Duberman, depicting the history of American race relations from slavery to the murder of the three civil rights workers at the beginning of the summer (Carson 1981).

Freedom school teachers were both encouraged and frustrated by their experiences during the summer. The students "hardly trust whites," a volunteer in Indianola wrote, "and there is a lot of 'Yes Ma'am' and constant agreement with what you say." Overcoming the students' reticence was, Carson reports, the schools' major accomplishment. Another teacher described her delight when students discovered they could "translate ideas into concrete written words. After two weeks a child finally looks me in the eye, unafraid, acknowledging a bond of trust which 300 years of Mississippians said should never, could never, exist" (quoted passages in Carson 1981, 120).

The schools represented one of the first attempts by the SNCC to replace existing institutions with alternative ones. As Howard Zinn (1965, 10) noted, these schools represented a challenge to American education, embodying "the provocative suggestion that an entire school system can be created in any community outside the official order, and critical of its suppositions." For Zinn, the freedom schools raised questions regarding the future of American education. Could teachers and students work together *"not through the artificial sieve of certification and examination* but on the basis of their common attraction to an exciting social goal?" Could teachers teach values "while avoiding a blanket imposition of the teacher's ideas?" Would it be possible for teachers "to declare boldly that the aim of the schools is to find solutions for poverty, for injustice, for race and national hatred, and to turn all educational efforts into a national striving for those solutions?" (Zinn 1965, 10, emphasis added). Instead, America's "national striving" has shriveled into (rather than expanded and complicated the curriculum of) the schools, no longer "freedom" but cram schools, where education is no academically informed articulation of a "common attraction to an exciting social goal" but, simply, sadly, student submission to socially evacuated "cognitive skills" employable in the corporate state.

Few SNCC workers were involved directly in the operations of the freedom schools after the Summer Project of 1965. However, the schools continued to be characterized by the SNCC's anti-authoritarianism. They constituted important if unacknowledged models and testing grounds for later alternative schools and tutorial projects throughout the nation (Carson 1981; Lomotey and Rivers 1998). While I do not share Zinn's faith that schools can "find solutions" to injustice, they can be indispensable in educating the public to understand its history and analyze its present circumstances. The academic curriculum can be attuned to society and its history without reducing it to a means to predetermined ends, even laudable ones. For the sake of understanding and erudition "objectives" of any kind must be discarded, as the instrumentalism they institutionalize destroys the academic freedom prerequisite to intellectual life. Freedom, as SNCC teachers knew, is not something to be requested but taken (see Chun 2006, 293).

By 1965, the SNCC had become, in the eyes of supporters as well as critics, not simply another civil rights organization. The SNCC was very much a part of the New Left, that amorphous body of young student activists seeking ideological alternatives to conventional liberalism (and certainly to conservatism, which had become more radicalized due to the Goldwater presidential campaign of 1964 and its recasting of the Republican Party as primarily right-wing: see Black and Black 1992, 126–131). Some observers have attributed the SNCC's ideological radicalism to the presence of white leftists in the southern struggle. The truth is, Carson (1981) concludes, that the SNCC is more accurately understood not as derivative from white student radicalism, but, rather, as a *source* of insights and inspiration for the New Left. Just as its unique and often spontaneous style of unstructured, rebellious activism broke through decades of southern black accommodation, the SNCC helped transform those pervasive patterns of political and cultural conformity exhibited by white college students in Cold War America.

While FBI Director J. Edgar Hoover did not include the SNCC in the FBI's Counterintelligence Program (COINTELPRO) until 1967, concerted FBI surveillance of the SNCC's activities had begun years earlier. As early as October 1960, the FBI was receiving reports on SNCC activities. In 1965, Hoover received permission of Attorney General Nicholas Katzenbach to institute wiretaps on the SNCC's phones. None of the FBI reports during the period from 1964 to 1967 presented evidence that any member of the SNCC's staff was or had been a member of the Communist Party (Carson 1981). Despite the facts, Hoover persisted, defaming not only the SNCC but the Black Panthers, Martin Luther King, Jr., and, later, the American Indian Movement (see Churchill and Wall 1988).

On August 25, 1967, Hoover ordered FBI field officers to begin a new effort "to expose, disrupt, misdirect, discredit, or otherwise neutralize the activities of black nationalist, hate-type organizations and groupings, their leadership, spokesmen, membership and supporters, and to counter their propensity for violence and civil disorder." Among the groups identified for "intensified attention" in this extension of COIN-TELPRO were the Deacons for Defense and Justice, Nation of Islam, the Congress of Racial Equality (CORE), the Southern Christian Leadership Conference (SCLC), and the SNCC. FBI offices were instructed to "establish" the "unsavory backgrounds" of "key agitators" to discredit them. FBI agents were reminded that these projects were to be kept secret. No actions were to be taken without prior Bureau authorization (quoted passages in Carson 1981, 262).

In a COINTELPRO proposal submitted on July 10, 1968 to Hoover, it was recommended that:

[c]onsideration be given to convey the impression that [SNCC leader Stokely] Carmichael is a CIA informer. One method of accomplishing [this] would be to have a carbon copy of informant report reportedly written by Carmichael to the CIA carefully deposited in the automobile of a close Black Nationalist friend. ... It is hoped that when the informant report is read it will help promote distrust between Carmichael and the Black Community. ... It is also suggested that we inform a certain percentage of reliable criminal and racial informants that "we have heard from reliable sources that Carmichael is a CIA agent." It is hoped that these informants would spread the rumor in various large Negro communities across the land.

(quoted in Churchill and Wall 1988, 49)

Approved the next day, the proposal also contained a report on an earlier COINTELPRO directed at Carmichael:

> On 9/4/68, pretext phone call was placed to the residence of Stokely Carmichael and in absence of Carmichael his mother was told that a friend was calling who was fearful of the future safety of her son. It was explained to Mrs. Carmichael, the absolute necessity for Carmichael to "hide out" inasmuch as several BPP [Black Panther Party] members were out to kill him, and it was probably to be done sometime this week. Mrs. Carmichael appeared shocked upon hearing the news and stated she would tell Stokely when he came home.

One result of this malicious defamation of Carmichael's reputation may be detected in this statement of Minister of Defense of the Black Panther Party, Huey P. Newton, on September 5, 1970, that "We ... charge that Stokely Carmichael is operating as an agent of the CIA" (quoted in Churchill and Wall 1988, 49).

Hoover moved to initiate similar operations against the growing civil rights movements in the southeast, placing Martin Luther King's name in Section A of the Reserve Index (one step below the Security Index) on May 11, 1962. He directed the Atlanta field office of the Bureau that King should be added to their "pickup list for handling" under the provisions of the Detention Act in the event of a national emergency (Churchill and Wall 1988, 54). This alleged "state of emergency" also rationalized "a pickup list for handling" schoolboys' bodies.

V The Gender Politics of Curriculum Reform

> The body is ... a mirror of our hopes and fears, our needs and desires.
> —Robert L. Griswold (1998, 339)

In this section I report the research of Robert L. Griswold (1998), scholarship which makes clear the gender politics underwriting the national curriculum reform movement of the 1960s. In particular, Griswold's insightful review of the Kennedy administration's emphasis upon the body—especially, I argue, the young *white* male body—discloses how Cold War anxieties were grafted onto the bodies of the young. That "grafting" not only expressed a generalized worry over the fate of the nation. It expressed as well, through innuendo, that women—mothers and schoolteachers—were blameworthy in allowing American youth, specifically white male youth, to go "soft."

Such a characterization recalls centuries-long male anxieties over women's "threat" to boys' maturation into men, both in the school where, for instance, in the late 19th century, debates raged over coeducation animated by fears not only that boys would be softened, but that girls would be masculinized, threatening the "natural" order of gender and sexuality, and in the home where the absence of fathers and mothers' tendencies toward overprotection presumably risked producing feminized boys (see, for instance, Bederman 1995).

In the United States, this ongoing concern for manhood has been racialized as well. What historians—not without controversy (see Carnes and Griffen 1990)—have characterized as the "crisis of masculinity" has occurred, in part, in reaction to civil rights successes of African Americans (see Savran 1998). In 1960, with the Soviets in space and the fate of the nation at hand, once again "gender and race [would] conflate in a crisis" (Gates 1996, 84). These gendered and racialized conflations of mind and body, of physical and intellectual well-being, became focused in concerns for "rigorous" schooling: the 1960s national curriculum reform movement. While never explicitly racialized, as Griswold's account indicates, one can surmise that the Kennedy administration's campaign for physical fitness was not concerned over the physical condition of young black men's bodies. Those bodies—given the aggressivity of black student activism, not to mention the continuing white fantasies of black male rape—seemed to many European Americans "hard" enough.

Griswold (1998) cites John F. Kennedy's "The Soft American," which appeared in the December 26, 1960 issue of *Sports Illustrated*, as the beginning of the President-elect's campaign to persuade Americans to become physically vigorous. Christopher Lasch (1978, 101) found Kennedy's pronouncements on physical fitness "tiresome." Kennedy invoked standardized tests to "prove" the presumably dramatic decline of strength and fitness among American (especially white, male) youth. "Our growing softness, our increasing lack of physical fitness, is a menace to our security" (quoted in Lasch 1978, 101). Was the "our" gendered? Did he mean "psychological" as well as "national" security?

Kennedy praised the ancient Greeks' conviction (but not their sexual preferences) that physical excellence and athletic skill were "among the prime foundations of a vigorous state" and suggested that intellectual ability could not be separated from physical well-being (quoted in Griswold 1998, 323). This restatement of 19th-century "faculty psychology"—namely, that the mind was a muscle—left Kennedy worried over the state of young Americans' minds, as their bodies were, presumably, in terrible shape: "A single look at the packed parking lot of the average high school," wrote Kennedy, "will tell us what has happened to the traditional hike to school that helped to build young bodies" (quoted in Griswold 1998, 323). The future of America was imperiled by a military/space race in which the Soviets, by virtue of the 1957 Sputnik launching, had moved ahead. Intensifying the nation's crisis, Kennedy worried, was the flabby condition of American youth, especially American boys (Griswold 1998). Especially white boys.

With the *Sports Illustrated* article, Kennedy and his new administration launched a school-based program that soon had millions of children exercising the prescribed minimum of 15 minutes per day. Many took a battery of tests that stretched abdominals, flexed biceps, and challenged lung capacity in the 600-yard run. What was at stake? Was Kennedy only concerned about physical fitness? Griswold (1998) suggests that embedded in the fitness campaign were anxieties over morality, post-war consumerism, masculinity, and the survival of the nation itself. Griswold quotes Kennedy, who once again restates the conflation of mind and body:

> We are, all of us, as free to direct the activities of our bodies as we are to pursue the objects of our thought. But if we are to retain this freedom, for ourselves and for generations to come, then we must also be willing to work for the physical toughness on which the courage and intelligence and skill of man so largely depend.
>
> (quoted in Griswold 1998, 323)

The concepts—*freedom, toughness, courage*—are, Griswold notes, classic Kennedy rhetoric. Kennedy had molded his own body on the playing fields of Hyannisport, Choate, and Harvard, had tested it in World War II in the Solomon Islands. In his *Sports Illustrated* essay, Kennedy pointed out that young men in America had always been willing and able to fight for freedom but, he warned, the strength and stamina needed for battle did not come on their own: "These only come from bodies which have been conditioned by a lifetime of participation in sports and interest in physical activity." He warned that "our growing softness, our increasing lack of physical fitness, is a menace to our security" (quoted passages in Griswold 1998, 324). While Kennedy may have been thinking only of the Soviet "menace to our security," for especially white male southern listeners, that phrase—"menace to our security"— must have reverberated as a racial threat as well. The conflations of gender and race extend to religion in Ku Klux Klan leader Sam Bowers' pronouncement: "Communists, homosexuals, and Jews, fornicators and liberals and angry blacks—infidels all" (quoted passages in Howard 1999, 149)

In the fitness crusade of the Kennedy administration, the bodies of young white men—schoolboys specifically—became the "repository" (Griswold 1998, 352) for anxieties about the Cold War. The obsession with physical fitness, Griswold (1998, 235) argues, was about "redeeming manhood." Griswold focuses on manhood because, although the fitness campaign included both boys and girls, it emphasized boys. Why? The answer, Griswold suggests, has to do with the historical moment. He points out that the 1960s physical fitness movement occurred during a period of considerable (and, I would add, ongoing cultural) anxiety regarding the status and future of American manhood (Kimmel 1996). Psychiatric disorders associated with World War II, lingering anxieties about the absence of fathers during that war and the Korean conflict and post-war adjustment problems of veterans were all on the public mind, as they had been during the Weimar Republic. These anxieties became racialized in the mid-1960s in the Moynihan Report, which diagnosed racial disadvantage and educational underachievement specifically as functions of absent black fathers (see Moynihan 1965). Despite the "domestic revival" of the 1950s—in which father-led, mother-at-home families were, for many, the only option—many men worried about what they imagined to be overly protective mothers, who, they feared, were rendering American manhood impotent. Feminized boys and men seemed an imminent danger (Griswold 1998).

The 1948 Kinsey Report on male sexuality, Griswold reminds, had shocked many Americans with its report of widespread homosexuality. In the 1950s the homosexual "menace" horrified not only parents but politicians as well. The McCarthy witch-hunt for Communists targeted not only "gender inverts" but also "egg-sucking phony liberals," East Coast intellectuals, and emasculated "pinks, punks, and perverts." The United States government had been infiltrated, in the words of one of McCarthy's aides, had become "a veritable nest of Communists, fellow travelers, homosexuals, effete Ivy League intellectuals and traitors" (quoted phrases in Griswold 1998, 325). In the grip of such a gendered paranoia, a sex-crimes panic swept America in the late 1940s and early 1950s, reaching even into "the heartland" in the infamous "boys of Boise" scandal (Gerassi 1966). Even comic books—especially "Batman and Robin"—were presumed to pose a threat to young "red-blooded" American boys (see Torres 1996; Wertham 1953/1954).

Press reports were lurid and widespread. Outraged citizens and parents held mass meetings, security programs at schools were beefed-up, and in fifteen states government commissions were established to study the threat to children posed by "sexual degenerates" (Griswold 1998, 326). Many psychiatrists and government officials criticized overbearing mothers and passive fathers as the root of the problem and pleaded with teachers, clergymen, and police to watch for boys who were becoming effeminate. Conflating effeminacy with homosexuality and assuming that both were spread like STDs, suspicious boys should be directed to guidance centers for psychiatric counseling (Griswold 1998). Conservatives in America might have been surprised to learn that the Communist Fidel Castro was also worrying about the masculinity of young men, sending effeminate Cuban boys to "camps" for gender reprogramming (Leiner 1994, 28–29).

Animating this gendered paranoia, Griswold suggests, was the Cold War itself, specifically the fear that a military encounter with the Soviet

Union was inevitable. A series of gendered terms was commonly used to describe the crisis: "brinksmanship," "massive retaliation," and "flexible response" (quoted in Griswold 1998, 326). The fitness campaign occurred within this national anxiety; it was an effort to rescue manhood by rescuing the body; to teach boys, as one participant put it, to use the body in "forceful and space-occupying ways" (quoted in Griswold 1998, 326). It would also seem to offer a strategy for sublimating an evidently omnipresent homosexual desire, as "hard" bodies were imagined as prerequisites to the development of "normal" male identity (Griswold 1998). Programs of physical fitness conflated bodies with minds, and in so doing, would reinvigorate "manhood" so that "we" would defeat the Communist threat to national survival. The threat could not be met with "soft bodies" (Griswold 1998, 326).

The Cold War stimulated numerous anxieties, nearly all of which, Griswold (1998, 326) emphasizes, found their way onto the "bodies of the young." Among these were materialism, conformity, maternal overprotection, parental neglect, government paternalism, moral corruption, and sexual excess, most notoriously expressed in the appearance of the "beats," "rebels without a cause" (Savran 1998, 59; Young-Bruehl 1996, 337), even "the white negro" (Fabre 1991, 206; Mailer 1957). The consequence was an America "at risk," although that phrase would not be used for another thirty years, and then prompted by economic crisis and used to allege "malpractice" in the nation's public schools (National Commission on Excellence in Education 1983).

That national security was at stake was a point made by Attorney General Robert F. Kennedy in a speech in January 1961 at the "Coach of the Year Dinner" in Pittsburgh. Kennedy asserted that since the end of World War II—a war in which "we had proved we had the mental genius, the moral certitude and the physical strength to endure and conquer"—America had been on "a precipitous downward moral and physical slide" (quoted in Griswold 1998, 330). Like his brother, Robert Kennedy saw a direct correlation between this national decline and the softening of the (white male) body. Saving the nation, Kennedy seemed to imply, was up to the coaches. It was these older men who could "exert a tremendous influence for good in this country. ... You, who participate in football, who have played well and have trained others to play well, symbolize the needs of the Nation" (quoted in Griswold 1998, 330).

Robert Kennedy's reference to football was no accident, Griswold notes, as it disclosed the administration's focus upon the bodies of boys and young men. Given a pervasive fear about the state of American manhood throughout the post-war years, a rough sport like football—Oscar Wilde (quoted in Simpson 1994, 90) once quipped that "football is all very well as a game for rough girls, but it is hardly suitable for delicate boys"—reproduced a gendered hierarchy that elevated the muscular athlete over the limp-wristed sissy-boy, the (straight) stud linebacker over the gay artist (Griswold 1998). Physical force and toughness were combined to reproduce what gender theorists have termed "hegemonic masculinity" secured by "the heterosexual matrix" (Butler 1990, 1993; Disch and Kane 1996; Silverman 1992). In this gender system men presumably project strength, power, aggressiveness, morality, and superiority while "inferiorizing the other," that is, women and less manly men (Griswold 1998, 331).

Historically, American football has functioned to forge male solidarity around a beleaguered ideal of sovereign and powerful masculinity (see Lesko 2000; Pronger 1990). One hundred years ago masculinity was widely perceived to be in "crisis" (Carnes and Griffen 1990; Filene 1998). Michael Kimmel (1990, 57) has argued that the emergence of the sport in the late 19th century was prompted by a "perceived crisis of masculinity" among white middle-class males whose illusions of manly character and autonomy were compromised by profound political, economic, and gender shifts. Then the "crisis" was precipitated by the closing of the American frontier, by the mechanization and routinization of labor that erased economic individualism and autonomy (except for the so-called "robber barons"), by black political progress, by the rise of the women's movement (secular as well as Christian feminism [see Haynes 1998] and the campaign for women's suffrage [see, for instance, Du Bois 1987]), by the massive influx of immigrants into the industrial centers of the United States, by the end of "romantic" friendship and the appearance of "homosexuality." (In Europe a different set of causes precipitated a similar crisis of masculinity and at the same time: see Izenberg 2000.) In the United States of the 1960s, it was the Cold War from which radiated a multitude of gendered, racialized, and educational anxieties.

In the 1960s physical fitness crusades and the process of "inferiorizing the other" were expressed in gendered terms. Griswold points out that sports and exercise had different meanings for girls and boys, at least in the minds of fitness advocates. For boys, fitness leaders emphasized competition (i.e., winning the game, running the fastest, completing the most sit-ups). For girls, experts emphasized friendship, health, and becoming sexually appealing to boys. Griswold (1998, 331) cites Dr. Benjamin Spock's public doubts about the appropriateness of competitive sports for girls. Sports were "really invented by boys, for boys." If one added the modifier "straight," queer theorists would agree, if for different reasons: "It might be argued that with their homosexuality completely (or mostly) desublimated they have no need for them; for gay men team sports are experienced not as sexualized aggression, just aggression" (Simpson 1994, 90).

Fitness advocates emphasized the ways physical exercise enhanced girls' sexual attractiveness to young men. Some suggested that girls' "workouts" might also include watching the boys compete, thus enabling girls, as one writer put it, to "admire the boys for their [physical fitness] achievements" (quoted in Griswold 1998, 331). (Today, heterosexual girls might watch boys as sexual objects.) Girls could also use sports as a strategy to meet boys, a point made by *Seventeen* magazine when it suggested that walking a mile in eleven minutes would be made more palatable if accompanied by "a boy from the track team!" (quoted in Griswold 1998, 331).

A movie sponsored by the American Dairy Association and the President's Council on Physical Fitness made clear that fitness, drinking milk, and sexual attractiveness went hand in hand, a strategy replicated in the 1980s and 1990s by milk advertising campaigns in which nearly naked boys and girls swam across a lake, emerging from the lake with glistening bodies to the announcer's simple declaration: "milk!" In the 1960s, one newspaper publisher speculated that fitness "will make teen-age girls appear glamorous to teenage boys," and, later in life, support woman's "true destiny" (quoted in Griswold 1998, 331) by creating "healthful, vital, feminine women who can mother a vigorous generation" (quoted in Griswold 1998, 332).

Although the fitness crusaders publicly praised multiple forms of physical activity, it is clear, Griswold (1998, 332) notes, that many pinned their hopes on football, that manhood would be "reborn" on the nation's playing fields. "Rough sports" would make boys' bodies hard, capable of enduring pain, and restore masculinity itself. "Except for war," Robert Kennedy asserted, "there is nothing in American life which trains a boy better for life than football. There is no substitute for athletics—there can be no substitute for football" (quoted in Griswold 1998, 332). More than any other sport associated with the 1960s fitness movement, football engaged the imagination of politicians and the public alike. Here was a sport that turned boys into men (Griswold 1998).

In hardening his body, the young man's masculinity would, presumably, also be reinvigorated. Now his mind and body would be strong, resilient, tough; now both could be placed at the service of his country. Speaking to a New York City audience, Robert Kennedy emphasized that sport was central to the fate of the nation. Football was fun, but the patriotic significance of contact sports was that they built healthy bodies and promoted "stamina, courage, unselfishness, and most importantly, perhaps, the will to win." And without the will to win, added Kennedy, "we are lost" (quoted passages in Griswold 1998, 333).

Hot bodies and cold wars seemed to go together, at least in the mind of Robert Kennedy. Griswold tells us that he, his brother, and many others believed that physical fitness would prepare the male body for war. Nothing less than national survival was at stake in the bodies of young men; they constituted a flesh-and-blood barometer of national supremacy or decline. To make the young man's body strong and virile was to restore the nation's power and vitality. America could secure its future only if a vigorous fitness program could first transform the (white male) body. (Never mind that nuclear annihilation made the hardness or softness of bodies irrelevant.) If the soft, feminized bodies of boys could be hardened, Kennedy felt sure, then there was a chance to discipline their minds (Griswold 1998).

But bodies were foremost, or so it seemed, as Robert Kennedy pledged to physical education teachers that the administration was committed to fitness. Minds would come soon enough, as science and mathematics curriculum would be "toughened" as well in the national curriculum reform initiatives. (Mathematics and science functioned in the mid- and late-20th-century curriculum debates as Latin and ancient Greek had in 19th-century debates; like physical exercise, mental "discipline" also made the mind-as-muscle hard.) Robert Kennedy emphasized hard bodies, noting that mathematics and science curriculum reform would amount to little if American youth lacked the bodily strength to make use of their knowledge. After all, Kennedy asserted, even technological warfare requires American soldiers and technicians to walk to the silos to push the buttons: "If we are sick people; if we are people that have difficulty walking two or three blocks to the engineering laboratory, or four or five blocks to the missile launching site, we are not going to be able to meet the great problems that face us in the next ten years" (quoted in Griswold 1998, 336).

Robert Kennedy concluded his New York speech by praising Americans as a "tough, viable, industrious people" who do not "search for a fight" but are "prepared to meet our responsibilities." Evidently, as Griswold points out, pull-ups, sit-ups, and sprints in school gym classes constituted the first line of defense in the Cold War. "We cannot afford to be second in anything—certainly not in the matter of physical fitness," he insisted, using a logic that would be applied later to standardized test scores. Before the nation's strength was sapped further, Americans must implement a nationwide, systematic program that would make American youth strong, a "program that, in the defense of our freedoms, will enable them to pass any test, any time, any place in the world" (quoted passages in Griswold 1998, 336).

Griswold notes the echo here of late-19th-century efforts to resuscitate a masculinity perceived to be in "crisis." Then the causes were multiple, but in the 1950s, it was, above all, the Cold War that left youth in crisis, especially white male youth, now softened by the sins of indulgence and comfort. Presumably "[t]he future of manhood and of the nation itself hung in the balance" (Griswold 1998, 336). And while the Cold War dominated the rhetoric of fitness, it was not the only issue, Griswold reminds. Profound shifts in race, work, and community, all agitated by fears of male homosexuality and women's assertiveness, rendered the young man's body symbolic not only of continued male dominance, but of heterosexuality itself, linked—through U.S. Senator Joseph McCarthy's association of the Communist threat with homosexual traitors—to national supremacy. Like the nation's schools, by the late 1950s the young white male body seemed at risk. Like the public school curriculum, the young man's body required—so the nation's leaders insisted—a national response. Only such a massive intervention could restore the vigor and strength of both.

The Cold War came to represent, then, multiple issues. As Griswold (1998, 337) asserts, "boys' bodies" would be hardened not only to reassert the dominance of "men over women and less manly men," but to stand firm against the threats of the age. One threat of the age was military; another was politically ascendant African Americans, who, just, had gained legal access to previously all-white schools in the 1954 Supreme Court ruling in *Brown v. Board of Education*. Of course, actual access would come slowly, but the sense of threat, Griswold emphasizes, was then not only military, but gendered.

It was gendered and, specifically, masculinized. By lifting weights and participating in athletic competition, boys would, presumably, learn to become men, and only men could learn to become the fierce soldiers the Cold War presumably demanded. As Griswold notes, the re-masculinization of the American male body required the male body at war, and it would not be long after the Kennedy administration took office before American foreign policy would provide an opportunity. The Vietnam War would become a shattering experience, not only for American military hegemony, but for American manhood as well (Savran 1998).

As Nancy Lesko (2001, 178) has observed in another context, "schools are masculinizing institutions." While that has almost always been the case, since the politicization of public school reform in the 1960 Presidential election and its conflations of military, racial, and gendered anxieties, school reform and masculinization have been like twins in the same womb. Because they share the same "maternal body," their "birth" parallels the ontogeny of the individual boys in a patriarchal society, namely the repudiation of maternal identification and the overcompensating cultivation of separation, struggle, and competitiveness (Chodorow 1978; Gilmore 1990, 2001). The price for those who do not, or cannot, conform is high, as the disciplinary society becomes (almost) totalizing in its regulation of academic rites of passage. "In the United States," Lesko (2001, 151) points out, "the remasculinizing of schools includes a number of features: the spread of competitive sports; higher standards through increased testing; a more rigorous curriculum; zero-tolerance policies; and redoubled efforts in math, science, and technology." Such reactionary and racialized remasculinization, that is, school deform, comes at the cost of the cosmopolitan education the country so desperately needs.

Part III

The Progressive Moment
The Future in the Present

Chapter 5

The Dissolution of Subjectivity in Cyberculture

I Dream, Thought, Fantasy

> Always ambivalent, technologies project our emotions, intentions, and projects into the material world.
>
> —Pierre Lévy (2001, xv)

Those were two moments of the past in the present. What of the future? The progressive moment of *currere* may not elicit fantasies of the future in a literal sense, just as the regressive phase may not recall remembrances of the subject's personal past. As I have done here, one might focus on the professional and political past, a past shared, each in his or her own way, by us all. That collective past structures our present, as individuals and as a collectivity, as teachers. It foreshadows the future: "[I]t is the way in which we understand our past which determines how it determines us. But this understanding is itself intimately related to our orientation towards the future" (Sarup 1992, 38).

The progressive phase of *currere* is an exploration of what is imagined as futural. In one sense, by imagining the future, the future becomes the present. Each section in this chapter explores such a futural subject, a subject also present in the past, as we will see in chapter 6, examining Jeffrey Herf's scholarship on technology during Weimar Germany. The future is, then, not only "not-yet" but also "already was." By discerning the future in the past and present, we complicate temporally the moment we share together as contemporaries, dissolving what freezes us from finding futures not yet present. This is a present open to the not-yet, in Deleuzian terms, an inside folded into the outside. "In this way," Deleuze (1986, 89) explains, "the outside is always an opening on to a future: nothing ends, since nothing has begun, but everything is transformed." That promises too much but one proceeds as if cracks will reveal themselves.

Certainly the obsession with computers-in-the-classroom functions as a distraction from educationally engaging the cultural and political problems of the nation. In this sense, technology represents a concealment of reality. Oscar Wilde wrote to W. E. Henley: "Work never seems to me a reality, but a way of getting rid of reality" (quoted in Pine 1995, 193). Wilde's observation has a different, less dismal, point for us. Busywork may distract us from the facts we face, but serious educational work—academic study—can reconstruct the reality we experience. As Foucault once remarked to an interviewer: "One writes to become someone other than who one is. There is an attempt at modifying one's way of being through the act of writing" (quoted in Miller 1993, 33). So conceived, academic study and its articulation (including through writing) provides passage through the concealment of the present into the unraveled past. From there we can find the future.

For some only the future provides access to the present. Paolo Fabbri (1994, 79) asserts: "That is, you have to return to the present from the future." In the *Concept of Dread*, Kierkegaard had argued that "in a certain sense, the future signifies more than the present and the past; for the future is in a sense the whole of which the past is a part, and in a sense the future may signify the whole" (quoted in Taylor 1980, 177). Merleau-Ponty (1966, 441) felt the future like a storm coming one's way: "the future is not prepared behind the observer, it is a brooding presence moving to meet him like a storm." A generation later, Lyotard imagined the future itself as fictional, as disguising the compulsion to relive the past:

> Now this idea of a linear chronology is itself perfectly "modern ..." The very idea of modernity is closely correlated with the principle that it is both possible and necessary to break with tradition and institute absolutely new ways of living and thinking. We now suspect that this "rupture" is in fact a way of forgetting or repressing the past, that is, repeating it and not surpassing it.
>
> (Lyotard 1993, 76)

The most intimate acts of naming, knowing, and experiencing, Mark Ledbetter (1996) appreciated, occur through the body, itself structured by memory and fantasy. Norman O. Brown (1959, 163) elaborates:

> The more specific and concrete mechanism whereby the body-ego becomes a soul is fantasy. Fantasy may be defined as a hallucination which cathects the memory of gratification; it is of the same structure as the dream, and has the same relation to the id and to instinctual reality as the dream.

And what can we say about the relations among dreams, fantasy, and thought? In his astonishing study of Flaubert, Sartre (1981, 214) tells us: "The time is not far off when Gustave will say, 'My life is a thought'." Is this the project of the early Sartre, in which the individual—I am thinking of Roquentin in *Nausea*—creates a life through aesthetic engagement in the world? Or does "thought" mean something less materializing and more imaginary, closer to "hallucination"?

Dream, thought, fantasy: these are modes of releasing the imagination, as the legendary Maxine Greene (1995) depicted the process of education. Releasing the imagination means moving into the future, at least as the contents of dream, thought, and fantasy are discerned as split-off fragments of self and society that, in their dissociation from what is, function to conceal the present. Like the regressive, the progressive phase or moment in the method of *currere* is an effort to sidestep the ego and its present preoccupations, to dislodge material the ego has covered up, denied, evaded or misplaced in the "technostructure" in which many of us are now embedded (Kroker 1984, 57).

Fantasy serves us in many ways. It can "negate" what is by symbolizing the literal, by pointing allegorically to a mythic as well as idiosyncratic future. As Brown (1959, 167) observed: "Fantasy, as a hallucination of what is not there dialectically negating what is there, confers on reality a hidden level of meaning, and lends a symbolical quality to all experience." While it can seem fragmentary, ambiguous, illusory, fantasy can confer upon everyday events allegorical significance. Pasolini understood the political and psychological potential of thinking mythically in an age when meaningless materialism renders individual lives pointless.

Against audience expectations, Pasolini rendered the mythic (by definition "unreal") centerpiece of *Oedipus* Rex in a realistic fashion. Yet, as Naomi Greene (1990, 156) points out, the lyrical, silent prologue in that film is "wraithlike and hallucinatory ... a remembered dream." "The intense lush green of the meadow," Pasolini explained, was presented as "an aestheticizing and fantastic element" (quoted in Greene 1990, 156). The progressive phase of *currere* is in this Pasolinian sense "hallucinatory," rendering the futural present. The progressive is like a "remembered dream," wherein the future seems cast as already past, as Weimar threatening to become present again. Brown (1959, 166) suggested: "[T]hey [fantasies] do not exist in memory or in the past, but only as hallucinations in the present, which has no meaning except as negations of the present." In terms of text as well as time, Roland Barthes imagined text as an intertext, that is, a space to be perceived simultaneously forwards and backwards, without progressional assumptions (see, e.g., Barthes 1981; Hasebe-Ludt and Hurren 2003). If progression is hallucination, perhaps it is true that "[p]resence [itself] is hallucinatory" (Deleuze 1993, 125).

Fantasy is private but it can be public; it is through ideas expressed in specific traditions that one can engage the private fantasies of others: our students, for instance. Brown (1959, 7) asserts: "[I]t would be more correct to say that repression deals with the emotions, but these are comprehensible to us only in their tie-up with ideas." Richard Rorty (1991, 121) understood the role of fantasy in culture, specifically in intellectual culture: "[M]any transfigurations of the tradition … begin in private fantasies. Think, for example, of Plato's or St. Paul's private fantasies—fantasies so original and utopian that they became the common sense of later times."

Making fantasies "common sense" is not the point of the progressive phase of *currere*, a phrase in which the movement of fantasy enacted through sublimation into culture is reversed back into oneself, to the subjective processes of self-formation: at first self-shattering and later, during the synthetical phase, self-mobilizing. One writes for oneself, not for "culture," more precisely, in Ronell's (1992a, 107) phrasing, for "no one. Still, writing for no one at no address counts for something; it is the writer's common lot." There may be no concrete other when one writes, but there is an Other to whom one is speaking; it is the other that is oneself denied, repressed, split off, for instance the "bad parent" as public school teacher. It is a self that can only be imagined; it is culture not yet conceived; it is, for Paul Wapner (2010, 163), precisely the otherness of nature that "offers us the chance to shake off our habitual ways of being in the world and experience things anew."

In fantasies of the future there are "fear and trembling"—fueled by prospects of political polarization, economic crisis, ecological catastrophe—as well as hope and determination. Pasolini understood that one's fondest dreams and dreaded nightmares were both derived from the same fabric: "In my films, barbarism is always symbolic: it represents the ideal moment of mankind" (quoted in Greene 1990, 129). Fantasy can be "barbaric," as it reinscribes the violence of subjectivity's structuration. "[T]he essence of society is repression of the individual and the essence of the individual is repression of himself," Brown wrote (1959, 3) too simply perhaps, but understandably, given that that he was working toward the end of Eisenhower's second term. In re-experiencing the intrapsychic violence structuring subjectivity—what Wapner (2010, 158) calls "the dream of mastery"—one might experience what is affirmative, in Nietzschean terms what is noble, what (in Pasolini's anti-modernist symbolism) is barbaric, what is for Marla Morris (2001) dystopian.

Not only the thematic content of fantasy is noteworthy; so is its narrative structure, including its sequence, character, and tone. Discussing Pasolini's *Oedipus Rex*, Naomi Greene specifies a number of that film's qualities which also specify the character of the fantasy one might experience during the progressive phase of *currere*:

> In this atmosphere of baroque instability, narrative divisions take the shape of striking ruptures and sudden metamorphoses. The abrupt cuts Pasolini had always favored—as he went, without transition,

from close-ups to long shots, or from one close-up to another—
fragment the narrative itself as it slashes across time and space, the
known and the unknown, legend and imagination. By virtue of a
cut, a baby born in Fascist Italy becomes the mythical Oedipus.

(Greene 1990, 150)

In this sense, the progressive phase of *currere* is like working on the
cutting-room floor, after the event, in the face of the future's demands.
"After this hallucinating process, which is quite simply called experience" (Sartre 1981, 252), one stitches the frames together, perhaps (after
Pasolini) in abrupt, transition-less moves, a montage. Such a composition of juxtapositions might suggest the structure of futural fantasy,
might encourage in the student something akin to self-conscious hallucination and dream. The progressive phase of *currere* is like Pasolini's
"cinema" which references as it restructures the psychic–historical–
social substrata of everyday life. "Releasing the imagination" (Greene
1995) can provide opportunities to become clear about the intellectual
"objects" and those intrapsychic—inevitably also intersubjective—processes of identification and disidentification that constitutes complicated
conversation (Butler 1997; Munoz 1996).

Robert Musil understood the temporal complexity of what is "not
yet." He would dislike my making a method of it, its "splitting off"
(he would also eschew psychoanalytic language) into a stage or phase
of educational experience. I am a teacher (certainly in the conventional
sense of always working to make an esoteric subject accessible); but
that is not the only motive for constructing "steps" to take in a temporally sequential method. I realize, as Musil reminds, that the regressive-
progressive–analytic–synthetic does not occur in a discrete temporal or
conceptual sequence, but simultaneously:

[W]hat in the distance seems so great and mysterious comes up to
us always as something plain and undistorted, in natural, everyday
proportions. It is as if there were an invisible frontier round every
man. ... What originates outside and approaches from a long way
off is like a misty sea of gigantic, ever-changing forms; what comes
right up to any man, and becomes action, and collides with his life,
is clear and small, human in its dimensions and human in its outlines. And between the life one lives and the life one feels, the life
one only has inklings and glimpses of, seeing it only from afar, there
lies that invisible frontier.

(Musil 1955 [1905], 159–160)

For Musil the process of education is also a form of self-revelation, a
process in which outer events provoke inner transformations one cannot

easily perceive, certainly not initially. Only in retrospect do the movement, texture, and meaning of experience become evident. Writing about the young Torless (as noted earlier, a student at a *fin-de-siecle* residential Prussian military academy), Musil tells us:

> There was within him now something definite, a certainty that he had never known in himself before. It was something mysterious, almost like a dream. It must, he thought, have been very quietly developing under the various influences he had been exposed to in these last weeks, and now suddenly it was like imperious knuckles rapping at a door within him. His mood was that of a woman who for the first time feels the assertive stirring of the growing child within her.
>
> (Musil 1955 [1905], 116)

"Her" presence is not only metaphoric, either. Torless feels "girlish," and not only emotionally, but bodily:

> Today for the first time he felt something similar again—again that longing, that tingling under the skin. It was something that seemed to partake simultaneously of body and soul. It was a multifold racing and hurrying of something beating against his body, like the velvety antennae of butterflies. And mingled with it there was that defiance with which little girls run away when they feel that the grown-ups simply do not understand them. ... Torless laughed quietly to himself, and once again he stretched luxuriously under the bed-clothes.
>
> (Musil 1955 [1905], 129)

Butterflies, bed-clothes, body, and soul: the series reiterates a dream sequence, and perhaps not only for young Torless. When we dream of the future (provided we do not disappear into cyberspace), might we climb out of "bed" and go "outside"?

II "Let Them Eat Data"

> Environmentalism is unpopular, in part, because it rejects the frontier psychology and the dream of unlimited expansion.
>
> —Christopher Lasch (1984, 86–87)

For many—especially politicians and profiteers—the future of education hinges on technology, specifically the computer but also scientific breakthroughs—like the so-called "learning sciences" (Taubman 2009,

161)—that technology makes possible. "The synergy between computer scientists, information processors, and cognitive psychologists," Taubman (2009, 167) explains, "not only generated new metaphors to describe thinking and behavior but also resulted in conceptualizing knowledge as information." C. A. Bowers (1995, 4) understands: "This myth is predicated on an anthropocentric view of the universe and the further assumption that our rationally based technology will always enable us to overcome the breakdowns and shortages connected with the natural world." More specifically, Bowers (1995, 12) explains "that the cultural orientations amplified through educational computing are the very same cultural orientations that have contributed to destroying the environment in the name of progress." This is this same fantasy of "mastery," Wapner (2010, 189) notes, that "brought us the nightmare of climate change."

In his important book *Let Them Eat Data*, Bowers (2000, 22) questions "whether computers lead us to substitute decontextualized ways of thinking about the world for the sensory encounters with the natural world that intertwine our lives." Probably that "substitution" occurred several hundred years ago, but probably it is intensified by "cyberspace" and standardized testing. If he and other eco-analysts are right, the "point of no return" approaches. Prior to the Industrial Revolution, the concentration of CO_2 in the atmosphere was 280 parts per million (ppm); today it is approximately 390 ppm (Flannery 2009, 56). The tipping point, many agree, is 450 ppm of carbon dioxide: "once we cross that threshold, climate catastrophe is all but certain" (Wapner 2010, 174).

Bowers is surely right to criticize those policymakers who spend enormous sums on computerizing the schools while neglecting teachers' work conditions (among them salary, class size, and scheduling), those who naively accept "Western myths that represent change as linear, progressive, and evolutionary" (Bowers 2000, 8). But it seems to me he overstates his case when he asserts "the inescapable reality is that computerization commodifies whatever activities fall under its domain" (Bowers 2000, 8). Commodification is pervasive in capitalism and cannot be ascribed causally only or even primarily to "computerization." In terms of the struggle for ecological sustainability, computers might, in fact, be helpful, at least in the dissemination of information regarding the crisis. While "computers provide us a window (information) for recognizing the early warning signs of over stressed ecosystems," Bowers (1995, 13) allows, "they also [he warns] mesmerize us into thinking this is the primary form of knowledge we need for correcting the problem." Wapner (2010, 154) also appreciates this problem:

> Extreme confidence in human ingenuity and technological prowess, and the faith that humanity is the be all and end all of life on earth,

suggests that, if we want, we can bioengineer new species and someday even bring back extinct ones.

Complementing delusions of mastery, Wapner (2010, 147) suggests, is the "dream of naturalism that places nature on a pedestal and calls on humanity to align itself with the natural way of things." That, too, is a discredited dream; Wapner (2010, 157) wants "a middle way." That middle way seems missing in Bowers' brilliant analysis. In his conceptualization of the "biosphere" (Bowers 1995, 1) even individuality disappears, as Lasch (1984, 19) knew: "The minimal or narcissistic self is, above all, a self uncertain of its own outlines, longing either to remake the world in its own image or to merge into its environment in blissful union." Bowers (2000, 58) acknowledges "the breakdown in the distinction between our private and public lives," but appears to reinscribe this immobilizing state of affairs in his embrace of "the biosphere."

For me, Bowers' (2000, 12) strongest point is that "our ecological crisis is essentially a crisis of cultural beliefs and values," as such, it is a problem of education. It is culture—including American culture—that must be reconstructed. Bowers (2000, 56) saw little reason for hope in the institution of schooling, as it remains embedded in capitalism and Enlightenment mythology. Bowers is alarmed that computers represent the lynchpin in the ongoing cultural crisis that threatens to destroy the very conditions of sustainability of the species. His summary of these conditions rings true still today:

> the subjectivity of cyberspace expresses all the attributes of the individualism of the Industrial Revolution: a natural attitude toward being a rational, self-determining individual who looks on both past and present in terms of immediate self-interest; a view of the environment as a technological and economic opportunity; an expectation that change leads to a personal enlargement of material well-being; and a view of the world's other cultures as evolving toward the rootless individualism that can easily adapt to the rapidly changing routines of technologically intensive modes of production.
> (Bowers 2000, 41; see also Bowers 2000, 106)

Cyberspace threatens to disperse subjectivity, creating caricatures of "individualism," rendering rationality sensate, even unrecognizable in its modernist manifestations, as we see in the next section.

Certainly Bowers (2000, 177) is right in expressing skepticism toward the current obsession—he terms it "addiction"—with computers in schools, with what, in a different context, Lasch (1978, 217) termed a "grandiose vision of a technological utopia." Likewise, Ted Aoki (2005 [1983], 114, 128) speaks of the contemporary "intoxication" with technology and science. Lasch (1984, 33) worries that: "By holding out a vision of limitless technological possibilities—space travel, biological engineering, mass destruction—it removes the last obstacle to wishful thinking. It brings reality into conformity with our dreams, or rather with our nightmares." In bringing reality into conformity with our dreams, reality disappears.

III The Death of the Subject?

[T]echnology is the grammar of capitalism.
—Arthur Kroker (1984, 119)

While some of us have been skeptical for decades regarding the promise of technology for education, many school deformers maintain their faith despite the data. Data are what Jacob Vigdor and Helen Ladd of Duke's Stanford School of Public Policy provide. Vigdor and Ladd studied computer use among a half-million fifth through eighth graders in North Carolina. They found that the "spread of home computers and high-speed Internet access was associated with significant declines in math and reading scores" (Brooks 2010, A17). While scores on standardized tests are not interesting to me (as they measure nothing significant), the deleterious effects of computer use—specifically the Internet—do demand one's attention. David Brooks (2010, A17) references research that indicates that the Internet is creating a "short-attention-span culture." While this hardly a new development—decades ago Lasch (1978) had associated presentism with narcissism—it is newsworthy that recent research indicates that the "multi-distraction, hyperlink world degrades people's abilities to engage in deep thought or serious contemplation" (Brooks 2010, A17). Note how standardized tests are suited to such a culture. No need to remember anything; just figure out the puzzle before you. Standardized exams become a kind of computer game, requiring the same "cognitive skills" and to the same "virtual" end. Brooks (2010, A17) acknowledges the view—promoted by technology companies and their "charitable" foundations—that playing computer games and performing Internet searches actually improve a person's ability to process information and focus attention. The Internet, these self-interested parties predictably claim, is a boon to schooling, not a threat. But as curriculum theory appreciates, construing academic knowledge as "information" erases remembrance as it converts contemplation into test-controlled attention (Crary 1990, 2002).

On occasion the enthusiasm for computer technology has rendered the book an archaic artifact bound for extinction. In one such uncritical report, Julie Bosman (2010, C1) lauds developments in e-books that "go beyond the simple black-and-white e-book that digitally mirrors its ink-and-paper predecessor." New multimedia books integrate video with text and, Bosman suggests, they are best read—and watched—on an iPad. Ignored is the simple fact that vapid prose—print or video—is, well, vapid, but somehow now the notion is that the medium is all that matters. Despite this obviously false assumption, it is true that the digitalization of the world's books—so that they can be downloaded by title anywhere Internet access exists—would be a remarkable development. But like Jason Epstein (2010, 4), I too decode digitalization as a strong argument for the continued production of physical books, given that one click could conceivably obliterate all accumulated knowledge. Given the elimination of inventory expense, shipping, and returns, readers may pay less when buying e-books, but I do not share Epstein's confidence that authors will earn more, nor that book publishers, stripped of much of their physical infrastructure, will "survive and may prosper" (2010, 4). We'll see.

We'll also see whether reading on a machine will replace reading from books. Sue Halpern (2010, 22) allows that "there is something deeply satisfying about a 'real' book," with "pages bound between hard or soft covers, into which you can slip a bookmark, whose pages you can fan, whose binding you can crack and fold as you move from beginning to end." In contrast, e-books seem to her "ephemeral" (2010, 22). Moreover, the iPad encourages "mental roving," as it makes easy—while reading or trying to read—checking e-mail, listening to the radio, watching a film, playing poker, scanning the headlines, editing photos, composing a song, shopping for shoes, counting calories, checking receipts. You could even write a book. Reading in any serious sense seems seriously imperiled.

Despite this (at best) mixed picture, enthusiasm for technology in education continues unabated, entirely unscathed by the facts. "Textbooks have not gone the way of the scroll yet," Tamar Lewin (2009, August 8, 1–2) begins (in millennial fashion), "but many educators say that it will not be long before they are replaced by a digital version—or supplanted altogether by lessons assembled from the wealth of free courseware, educational games, videos and projects on the Web." That would be a loss, as textbooks play a primary role in organizing knowledge. Complaints about textbooks continue—that teachers depend on them too much, that they present a distorted picture of knowledge as linear—but in an era in which information flows helter-skelter, such ordering might prove pivotal in any project of sustained and self-conscious understanding. Information may be free, but knowledge is not democratic (Cohen 2010, A3).

David Brooks makes this important point. Brooks regards the Internet-versus-books debate as derived from Marshall McLuhan's assertion that the medium is the message. "But sometimes," he (2010, A17) notes, "the medium is just the medium." Thank you. Brooks overdraws the distinction between high and popular culture in this piece, but he reminds readers that judgment—aesthetic, ethical, political—is at the center of studying literature. In light reading (Brooks thinks of beach reading) entertainment may be the sole criterion of value. Brooks (2010, A17) appreciates that serious literature is "better at helping you become cultivated, mastering significant things of lasting import. To learn these sorts of things, you have to defer to greater minds than your own."

Teachers do not demand deference, but intellectual engagement. Intellectual authority derives from the argument (Nussbaum 2010, 51) and more broadly, the conversation itself. The teacher's knowledge and capacity for engaging students are crucial in that endeavor, but it is students who must aspire to understand matters of more than momentary significance. The point of the Internet, Brooks concludes, is not to settle the books–Internet debate, but to draw people to serious literature. Indeed. The Internet's virtuality is interesting only insofar as it is juxtaposed to the world of materiality, yes the world of *Realpolitik* but also and especially the natural world. Serious literature—to which I would append academic knowledge generally—helps us understand both.

Rather than enabling students to study serious literature, the Internet often undermines such efforts. At Rhode Island College, a freshman copied and pasted from a Website's "frequently asked questions" (FAQ) page to complete an assignment about homelessness. When confronted, the student explained that he did not think he needed to reference the source because the Webpage did not include information about the author. That's like repeating a line in a conversation but failing to acknowledge someone else just said it because she didn't introduce herself. At DePaul University, another student's plagiarism was indicated by the purple color of several paragraphs he had lifted from the Web; when confronted, he thought he'd done nothing wrong, but he was curious to know how, in the future, he could change purple text to black (Gabriel 2010, August 2, A1).

A senior at the Rutgers University campus in Camden, N.J., Susan Brookover, admitted that many of her classmates plagiarized. A student-worker in the library, Brookover linked plagiarism with the Internet: "Because you're not walking into a library, you're not physically holding the article, which takes you closer to 'this doesn't belong to me'," she said. Online, "everything can belong to you really easily" (quoted in Gabriel 2010, August 2, A10). Faculty have always been alert to the possibility of plagiarism, but now more than a few force their students to submit their papers through turnitin.com, a plagiarism search engine (Furchgott 2010). Is the prospect of plagiarism now the rule, not the exception?

Trip Gabriel (2010, August 2, A1) suggests so, reporting that such stories are "typical" and that many students "simply do not grasp" that plagiarism is a serious infraction. In surveys conducted from 2006 to 2010 by Donald L. McCabe, co-founder of the Center for Academic Integrity and a business professor at Rutgers University, almost *40 percent* of 14,000 undergraduates admitted to plagiarizing a few sentences in their written assignments. The number who appreciate that copying from the Web constitutes "serious cheating" has declined from 34 to 29 percent during the last decade. Researchers who study plagiarism suggest this lapse may be attributable to the "unbridled exchange of online information," one consequence of which is the erosion of long-standing concepts of intellectual property, copyright, and originality (Gabriel 2010, A1).

Originality is associated with an Enlightenment conception of the individual; it is expressed in intellectual property rights (such as copyright law), University of Notre Dame anthropologist Susan D. Blum explained in an interview. Blum studied 234 Notre Dame undergraduates who told her they were less interested in cultivating a "unique and authentic identity" than in experimenting with many different personas, something social networking sites on the Web encourage. Summarizing students' views, Blum said:

> If you are not so worried about presenting yourself as absolutely unique then it's O.K. If you say other people's words, it's O.K. If you say things you don't believe, it's O.K. If you write papers you couldn't care less about because they accomplish the task, which is turning something in and getting a grade, it's O.K.
> (quoted passages in Gabriel 2010, August 2, A10)

The suggestion that integrity, originality, and responsibility are passing historical fashions is alarming, to say the least. Also alarming is the suggestion that many now feel free, even entitled, to take whatever suits them from the vast "vortex of information" (2010, A10) on the Web and present it as their own. Such theft and deception reenact ethically and intellectually the imperialism many associate with the Enlightenment, when Europeans—representing nation and church—were emboldened to take whatever they discovered, murdering millions of indigenous peoples in the process. Gabriel reports the controversy associated with Helen Hegemann, a German teenager whose best-selling novel about Berlin club life turned out to include plagiarized passages. Refusing to apologize, Hegemann asserted that "there's no such thing as originality anyway, just authenticity" (quoted in 2010, A10). And I thought the two were reciprocally related.

Neither did the plagiarist's defense persuade Sarah Wilensky, a senior at Indiana University, who told Gabriel that plagiarism "does not foster creativity, it fosters laziness. … It may be increasingly accepted, but there are still plenty of creative people—authors and artists and scholars—who are doing original work" (quoted passages in 2010, A10). Wilensky blames the proliferation of plagiarism not on the Internet but on—you guessed it—the schools, specifically inadequate writing instruction in high schools. No corroborating data were offered.

When academic knowledge—representing years of research, considered intellectual judgment, threaded through the scholar's subjectivity and disciplinary commitments—devolves into a "vast vortex of information," curriculum is no longer a complicated conversation in which it is only courtesy to acknowledge the interlocutors whose conversation you have joined, or are attempting to join, or attempting to understand. It would appear that the Internet encourages the imperialism critics have before identified only with the nation-state and with global capitalism; its blurring of ego boundaries through online experimentation with various personae—avatars—encourages the fantasy that your land (or body or mind) is actually mine. Is the Age of Information a new Age of Discovery in which the death of the subject—initially a theoretical criticism of the self-made man—becomes a subjectively literal, specifically historical, culturally catastrophic, fact? In the present instance, however, it is not the indigenous who die, but the victors, and by their own (technological) hand. Unless …

IV Avatars

> The pursuit of technological advance is what constitutes human excellence in our age and therefore it is our morality.
> —George Grant (1966, iv)

In the most popular movie made thus far—James Cameron's *Avatar*—the subject does survive. As on the Internet (Chun 2006, 54), it is the body that dies. As in the world, in the movie the natural world is under attack, evidently by "ourselves," as the soldier-scientists (to revise a concept by Jünger: see chapter 6) engage in "resource recovery" on a planet peopled by sentient creatures remarkably reminiscent of indigenous peoples, specifically as these have been imagined as pre-agricultural hunter-gatherers who survive in total attunement to nature. Threatened with destruction by aggressive and greedy Americans, the indigenous people—the Na'vi—are led in their efforts to survive the U.S. onslaught by one renegade soldier named Jake. Operating his avatar from within his computerized pod, Jake enables the Na'vi to triumph. But he is fatally injured in the combat. The natives bring his dying body to the Tree of Souls where, in a sacred ceremony, his consciousness is transferred to his Na'vi avatar (Mendelsohn 2010, 13).

Aside from the visual beauty of the film, what drew so many viewers? Is there a pedagogical point? "Like the message of so much else in mass culture just now," Daniel Mendelsohn (2010, 13) explains, the message in *Avatar* is that reality is "dispensable ... provided you have the right gadgets." There is no need to confront the ugliness of our own civilization or to sacrifice one's pleasure in order to stay the civilizational course. "Whatever its futurist setting, and whatever its debt to the past," Mendelsohn (2010, 13) concludes, "*Avatar* is very much a movie for our time." That future time—as Mendelsohn's insightful commentary makes clear—is, like past times, a contradictory time in which democracy has devolved, through capitalism, into imperialism and colonialism. In this futural fantasy, Mendelsohn suggests, we are rescued by a primitivist reappropriation of the very technology that is the medium of such destruction.

Can the violence and aggression of technology—as portrayed in the film—be redeemed by incorporating culturally disclaimed elements associated with the indigenous? What does the disappearance of the embodied civic subject portend for civil society? Is social networking creating new models of social exchange in which the individual—as an ongoing project of originality and social responsibility—disappears? Is this disappearance of the subjectively coherent subject accelerating with younger generations? A survey by Nielsen Online, entitled "What Americans Do Online," reported on Internet use in the United States. Nearly one-third of the time Americans spend online is devoted to social networks like Facebook and online games; the time allocated to e-mail and portals such as Yahoo is decreasing (Harris 2010, A1). "The Internet is not a database," Wendy Hui Kyong Chun (2006, 107) points out. Whatever else it is, to some it has seemed one vast porn site (see Chun 2006, 108–127).

Technology has apparently become so embedded in college students' "often frantic" lives that many students fear they would be even more "frazzled" without it. An Associated Press–mtvU Poll found that 57 percent of students said that life without computers and cellphones would leave them even "more stressed," but a significant number—25 percent—thought that life without technology might turn out to be a "relief." A significant majority of students reported feeling "pressured" to reply "instantly" to texts or voice mails, and most felt "nervous" if someone failed to reply "immediately" to their messages. Nearly half wondered if the texts they receive are sincere or at all truthful (all quoted passages in Fram and Tompson 2010, A4). "Despite the mix of promise and peril," Lan Fram and Trevor Tompson (2010, A4) conclude, technology was judged favorably. Eight-five percent of students surveyed reported that social networking sites leave them feeling "more connected" rather than less. Some 54 percent believe that "increased" use of technology enables them to feel "close" to others. But 28 percent reported that technology makes intimacy "tougher" (Fram and Tompson 2010, A4).

Such statistics hide horror stories. Each evening Kim Yung-jeong and her husband, Kim Jae-beom, 41, left their one-room apartment for an all-night Internet café where they role-played until dawn. Online each raised a virtual daughter, daughters who followed them everywhere and whom they fed, dressed, and cuddled. Parenting was conducted through quick clicks of the mouse. On the morning of September 24, 2009, the couple returned home after a twelve-hour game session to find their actual daughter, a 3-month-old named Sa-rang—"love" in Korean— dead due to malnutrition. The parents fled for six months, but in March 2010 they were apprehended and charged with negligent homicide. They were sentenced to two years in prison, but the judge suspended Ms. Kim's sentence because she was seven months pregnant; he thought she required "mental stability" (Sang-Hun 2010, A4).

The Kims are, apparently, no isolated case. In February 2010, a 22-year-old man was arrested for the murder of his mother after she had confronted him about his Internet dependency. In the same month, a 32-year-old man dropped dead from exhaustion in an Internet café after playing through the five-day Lunar New Year holiday (Sang-Hun 2010, A4). Among the most technologically sophisticated people in the world, South Koreans have also suffered the highest rates of Internet addiction. The government has responded with counseling programs. According to the Korean Ministry of Public Administration and Safety, the estimated number of teenagers diagnosed with Internet addiction has declined from more than one million in 2007 to 938,000 in 2009. But the number of addicts in their 20s and 30s has been increasing, to 975,000 last year (Sang-Hun 2010, A4).

A 2010 New York Times/CBS News poll found that most Americans believe that devices like smartphones, cellphones, and personal computers have made their lives better and their jobs easier. But they also admit that these devices can be "intrusive, [and have in fact] increased their levels of stress and made it difficult to concentrate" (Connelly 2010, A12). What the poll found has been confirmed by scientists investigating these new technologies' impact on the brain. University of Kansas professor Paul Atchley concluded that "heavy technology use can inhibit deep thought" and can "cause anxiety," but that spending time in "nature can help" (Richtel 2010, August 16, A10). He found that users' realization that new messages and other information were waiting for them if only they would only log-on instilled a "false sense of urgency" that undermined the ability to "focus" (Richtel 2010, August 16, A10).

Others, invoking a mind-as-muscle metaphor common in 19th-century curriculum theory to rationalize the teaching of Latin and ancient Greek, question these conclusions, predicting instead that heavy use will turn "users" into "multi-taskers" (Richtel 2010, August 16, A10). Does the fragmentation of experience that multi-tasking requires disperse subjectivity into an ongoing instrumentalizing immediacy intensified by an interminable sense of urgency? Does that "state of emergency" become pleasurable, even addictive? "Users are *created*," Chun (2006, 249) points out in her discussion of electronic interactions, "by 'using' in a similar manner to the way drug users are created by the drugs they (ab) use." There are scientists who warn that "when people keep their brains busy with digital input, they are forfeiting downtime that could allow them to better learn and remember information, or come up with new ideas" (Richtel 2010, August 25, B1). Solitude may be required to even remember the difference between old and new ideas, between others' ideas and one's own.

Except for their gadgets, many feel alone. Is that solitude? Can contemplation occur while being pummeled with data? By 2008, Americans consumed three times as much information each day as they had in 1960. The sheer volume of information required them to constantly shift their attention rather than concentrate at length on a single idea or problem. Computer users at work report changing windows and/or checking e-mail or other sites some thirty-seven times an hour. Does such restlessness constitute increased productivity? At home, people consume twelve hours of media a day, more than double the five hours they did in 1960, reported researchers at the University of California, San Diego. In their study, computer users visited an average of forty Web sites a day. Research conducted at Stanford University showed that multitaskers tended to scan for new sites rather than dwell on older, possibly more valuable information (Richtel 2010, August 16, A10). "Why exactly is Internet *access* valuable?" Chun (2006, 147) asks. "Indeed," she continues:

> narratives of the digital divide and digital empowerment form a circle that circumvents questions about the value of information, or the value of access alone, since the Internet—redefined through issues of social justice—becomes inherently valuable and desirable.

Does commercialization convert psychic lack into the compulsion to consume?

In a world of compulsory consumption, "disadvantage" might prove advantageous. There is now research, Matt Richtel (2010, August 16, A10) reports, that suggests that technology use may be eroding the capacity of the brain to control behavior, including the capacity to focus and to prioritize tasks. What scientists characterize as the more "primitive" or sensory parts of the brain demand that we attend to whatever seems new. Being glued to the screen may provide sensory satisfaction but it undermines judgment. The concern that information overload causes not only distraction but subjective dissolution is supported by more and more research, admitted Melina Uncapher, a neurobiologist at Stanford University. Others in the same physical space no longer represent distractions, as Stanford researchers found that heavy technology use "diminishes empathy" by limiting interpersonal engagement, including when in the same room with others. "We are at an inflection point," one researcher worries. "A significant fraction of people's experiences are now fragmented" (quoted in Richtel 2010, August 16, A10). Not only empathy is at risk, evidently so is memory, at least short-term memory, according to research reported by Gary Small, a psychiatrist at the University of California, Los Angeles (Richtel 2010, August 16, A10). Like authenticity and originality, are memory and empathy also reciprocally related?

Other researchers report additional dangers of heavy technology use, including deterioration of the personality, evidenced by increased impatience, impulsivity, and narcissism, all signaling an inability to distinguish between self and other. As a model for dialogical encounter, complicated conversation—requiring careful consideration of others' often dissonant ideas—is replaced by chat rooms. "More and more life is resembling the chat room," concludes Dr. Elias Aboujaoude, director of the Impulse Control Disorders Clinic at Stanford University. "We're paying a price in terms of our cognitive life because of this virtual lifestyle" (quoted in Pope 2010, A13). That price includes subjective stasis, according to Dr. Aboujaoude, who worries that being frozen to the screen disables us from "letting go, causing us to retain many old and unnecessary memories at the expense of making new ones" (Pope 2010, A13). Stasis may prove preferable to the more pervasive memory loss—and the subjective dissolution it signifies—that the presentistic obsession with the "new" incurs.

Other researchers are less apocalyptic, although still worried. In Australia, for instance, one study showed that technology use structured students' daily lives. While rejecting "addiction" as too strong a word to describe what she observed, Nicki Dowling, a clinical psychologist who directed a study of students at the University of Melbourne, termed the problem one of "Internet dependence" (quoted in Pope 2010, A13). Others, like Dr. Kimberly Young, a professor at St. Bonaventure University in New York, who directed research on the addictive nature of online technology, likened being online to suffering from eating disorders (Pope 2010, A13).

Steven Pinker will have none of this. If the new media were "hazardous to intelligence," he (2010, A27) retorts, the "quality of science would be plummeting." Quite aside from the astonishing scale of casualty he assumes, do we know that science is not "plummeting"? Pinker (2010,

A27) reassures readers that the "effects" of the new information technologies are likely to be "more limited" than the "panic implies." Why am I not reassured? Is it because the scientist's assertion is made without evidence? It doesn't help that Pinker denies transfer effects generally, insisting that the "effects of experience are highly specific to the experience themselves" (2010, A27). This generalization—were it indisputable fact—would discredit standardized tests entirely, as these depend on the faith that the "cognitive skills" they "measure" apply to a wide range of academic, vocational, and real-life settings. Nor does it reassure that Pinker (2010, A27) admits that the "constant arrival" of bits of information can be "distracting or addictive"—potentially a catastrophic admission—"especially" (as that word implies, "not exclusively") to people with attention deficit disorder. The "solution," he (2010, A17) suggests, is not to fear technology but to develop "strategies of self-control," as one must vis-à-vis other "temptations." But if online living erodes that part of the brain that "controls"—see above—how can "self-control" succeed? Perhaps sensing that his case has unraveled, Pinker (2010, A27) returns from self-dissolution to the simplistic assertion of certainty: "Far from making us stupid, these technologies are the only things that will keep us smart." The *only* things? In decades past other media asserted that same salvational pretension.

V Breaking News

News is not information but drama.

—James W. Carey (1992, 21)

In the First Edition (Pinar 2004, 175, 256) I referenced journalism's significance to public deliberation that is not confined to economic calculations. In this edition I keep this issue—associated with the famous Dewey–Lippmann debate—with its ongoing significance for reconstructing the public sphere (see chapter 8). If in historical terms print created the public sphere, and if newspapers hold a special responsibility for reporting diversity of point of view in public deliberation, with intensifying economism—the assumption that all that matters is the economy—it is any wonder newspapers themselves are struggling? Add to economism the supposed democratization of information flowing freely on the Web and journalism—a profession, with that concept's positioning of informed judgment as central—fades, as now whatever happens demands attention, even if it's not news.

The plunges in newspaper circulation, the fall-off in advertising revenues, the increasing debt and mounting losses are all matched by corporate buyouts and layoffs. According to the blog PaperCuts, newspapers lost 15,974 jobs in 2008 and another 10,000 in the first half of 2009. That's 26,000 fewer reporters, editors, photographers, and columnists, Michael Massing (2009, 29) points out, who can "analyze political and economic affairs, root out corruption and abuse, and write about culture, entertainment, and sports." Like teachers', journalists' judgment and professional knowledge are indispensable to determining what even counts as news (or knowledge in the comparison) but somehow Americans imagine that reality reveals itself automatically, transparently, falling like snow.

Not only a site for free-flowing information, the Internet is, Michael Massing (2009, 29) points out, parasitic. It depends on professional newsgathering undertaken by professional journalists employed at established institutions; without such professional journalism ("dirt" research in Harold Innis' earthy phrase), many Web sites would vanish. Massing (2009, 29) does allow that considerable "original, exciting, and creative (if also chaotic and maddening) material" does show up on the Web, and this material requires newspaper editors and executives to "take note." But he (2009, 31) also acknowledges the "polemical excesses" found especially on blogs, and their parasitic interconnectivity: according to one study, 85 percent of blog links were to other blogs of the same political inclination. (As we will see momentarily, such self-enclosure is reflected in patterns of mobile communication as well.) Massing (2009, 31–32) admits that the Internet remains a "hot-house" for "rumors, distortions, and fabrications." Despite these problems, Massing (2009, 31) reminds that "the Web is home to all kinds of intriguing experiments." You roam the Web; I'll stay with *The New York Times*, however disappointing its uncritical coverage of education has often been.

Even first-rate newspapers—like *The New York Times*—are under pressure to align their reports with consumers' preferences, troubling to those who appreciate the significance of editorial judgment to all journalism. "Rather than corrupting such judgment by causing editors to pander to the most base reader interests," Jeremy Peters (2010, B4) reports, "the availability of this technology so far seems to be leading to a more surgical decision about how to cover a topic so it becomes more appealing to an online audience." While the risks here—primarily pandering—are obvious, such "interactivity" is not unlike teachers' engagement with their students in classrooms; it enables both journalists and teachers to make more precise decisions about what questions need to be asked, what points need to be pursued, and when to move on.

For Harold Innis, however, the newspaper could be an "addictive drug" that destroyed individuals' critical faculties (Watson 2007, 383). Innis was working during the decades before television, when radio was new, and newspapers in large metropolitan areas appeared more than once a day. The ersatz urgency that "breaking news" creates today is not, then, a new ploy, but Innis was even more concerned over newspapers' capacity to promote their ideological agendas, concerned that people's reliance on news for their increasingly mediated experience of the world would eventually disengage their capacities for experience and judgment.

Brainwashing was not political only: Innis knew that advertising would slowly alter readers' perception, functioning like constant "news" to encourage a constant sense of expectation, a "permanent sense of excitement" in anticipation of "change" (Watson 2007, 384). For Innis, Watson (2007, 384) explains:

> The same basic mechanism applies in such widely separated fields as fashion and politics. It is as if we have gone full circle and returned to the ecstatic basis of social education characterizing pre-literate societies. Unfortunately, the new ecstasy created by the newspaper is oriented towards fueling the most banal forms of consumerism.

Because it is necessarily close to the vernacular, the newspaper—surely the recent versions of information technologies are closer, even supplanting the vernacular with neologisms like "tweeting"—penetrates the senses, Innis felt sure. Recall that the same leveling tendencies of radio worried many Weimar intellectuals, and not only those on the right.

Marshall McLuhan would take this realization regarding technology's penetration of the senses even further, proclaiming not long after Innis died that the pervasiveness of technology was creating a hypnotic environment, a "technological sensorium" (Kroker 1984, 58). The consequences of such interpenetration, Innis had believed, were deeply deleterious, as they only threatened to intensify "social hysteria, irrationalism, and the appeal to force at the expense of [the] rational, [the] contemplative" (Watson 2007, 385). Because the technological sensorium is an extension of our psyche but becomes an independent social field, and because the social, then, mirrors back to us our psychic preoccupations, the narcissistic pleasure of self-recognition can quickly turn to horror—and specifically paranoia—when self-difference, internal alterity, becomes projected as socially disturbing (Chun 2006, 270–271; Watson 2007, 386).

Especially the political history of the United States demonstrates such self-enclosing, even circular, relations among information technologies, narcissism, and politics. In the United States, Innis argued, the commercially driven development of mass communication technologies undermined the democratic ideal of the rational, individual citizen through their perfection of techniques for manipulating public opinion. The consequence was, over time, to strengthen the executive branch of government and specifically the office of the President—thereby reinstating in that office the power of the monarchy the American Revolution had deposed—who could manipulate the mass media to activate public sentiment, often through demonizing adversaries. Not limited to domestic political campaigns, this series of developments—all, Innis insisted, aggravated by information technologies—spelled an "inconsistent, force-oriented foreign policy that was subservient to short-term domestic politics" (Watson 2007, 387). While Innis died in 1952, his analysis proved prescient, as the history of U.S. foreign policy in Afghanistan—in the 1980s it was pro-Taliban against the Soviets—flip-flops as enemies change according to domestic political priorities: first Communism, now terrorism, as the September 11 attacks made "terrorists, particularly Muslim zealots, the 'communists' of the day"—(see Hetherington and Weiler 2009, 56). These threats may have been—are in fact—real, but the foreign policies planned and implemented to contest them change not according to rational assessment of the threat, but according to calculations of short-term domestic political gain.

Richard Hofstadter—that great American historian whose lapse of judgment in his 1962 *Anti-Intellectualism in American Life* helped to set the stage for fifty years of school deform (and whose work, Hirsch [2010, 19] feels sure, is never studied in education courses)—understood that "politics can be a projective area for feelings and impulses that are only marginally related to the manifest issues" (1996 [1965], ix). This psychic vulnerability enables, Hofstadter (1996 [1965], 3) appreciated, a politics that can only be called "paranoid" given "the heated exaggeration, suspiciousness, and conspiratorial fantasy" it evokes and manipulates. Such manipulation by information technologies makes the "enemy" vivid precisely because—while real—"this enemy seems to be on many counts a projection of the self: both the ideal and the unacceptable aspects of the self are attributed to him. A fundamental paradox of the paranoid is the imitation of the enemy" (Hofstadter 1996 [1965], 32). Preemptive strikes, Chun (2006, 302) points out, cause the events they were designed to prevent.

Information technologies blur the boundaries between subjectivity and sociality, thereby disabling the self from making the sometimes subtle, sometimes sharp, distinctions necessary for rational deliberative judgment to proceed, and not only politically. For Innis, the tragedy of mass culture in America followed from the "intrinsic tendencies of both printing press and electronic media to reduce space and time to the service of a calculus of commercialism and expansionism" (Carey 1992, 133). In such a calculus, increased "centralization and imperialism in matters of culture and politics" (1992, 136) are inevitable as only the present moment matters. With Americans' subjectivities splintered, economically obsessed, and politically paranoid, "permanent war" would follow, Innis worried (Watson 2007, 387). The "war on terror"—with

its projection of enemies everywhere, including inside the "homeland"—
is just such a war.

Such fear is only fueled by the right-wing media. Frightening people,
Mark Lilla (2010, 56) points out, is hardly new in American political
life, often animated (as it was the 1950s and 1960s) by fear of a hidden
enemy. What is different now is that right-wing demagogues have at their
disposal a variety of technologies permitting them to target "cocksure
individualists" who want to be addressed and heard directly, and without leaving the comforts of home (2010, 56). Because these permanently
enraged, often paranoid, socially insulated, self-enclosed "cocksure individualists" never have to venture outside the house, never have face the
unfamiliar except as mediated through the prism of like-minded ideologues (like Rush Limbaugh, who likened the Obama administration's
health care logo to a Nazi symbol: see Urbina 2009, 3), an "increasingly segmented audience absorbs what it wants from its trusted sources,
embellishes it in their own voices on blogs and websites and chatrooms,
then hears their views echoed back as 'news'" (2010, 56). This is a self-
enclosed system of political narcissism in which one's prejudices are mir-
rored back as "fact," as, in fact, "the news."

It is this narcissistic dissolution of the public sphere, rendering it real
only as a displaced fragment of one's own psychic preoccupations, that the
new technologies intensify. Innis was horrified by the politically manipu-
lative potential of these technologies. For Innis, Watson (2007, 410) tells
us, the political press of the United States and the Nazi loudspeaker had
the same consequence: they destroyed human beings' capacity to think
critically, reducing the citizenry to "mere automatons in a chain of command." Today one can witness just such manipulation on Fox News,
where even mainline, professional news organizations are demonized as
"liberal." Even more ominous in the acceleration of technological developments since Inniss death some sixty years ago is the blurring of boundaries between self and other, subjectivity and sociality. Consider, for
instance, that innocent and helpful device, the mobile phone.

VI Intimacy and Abjection

The death of God has left us with a lot of appliances.
—Avital Ronell (1992b, 5)

"Mobile communication," Rich Ling (2008, 3) observes, "seems to
strengthen communication within the circle of friends and family." He
suggests that mobile communication "supports better contact within
the personal sphere," if, however, "sometimes at the expense of interaction with those who are co-present" (2008, 3). This acknowledgment
that mobile communications technologies increase exchanges within

the "personal sphere" contradicts Ling's larger argument that mobile communication—because it represents a ritualistic affirmation of social cohesion—in fact strengthens social bonds (see 2008, 3, 7, 43–49, 83). As his argument proceeds, what becomes clear is that the preeminence of the personal *prohibits* social bonds. Ling (2008, 5) does acknowledge that many researchers have concluded that interactive technology is "straining the social structure and causing a drift toward individualism." As is the case in so many sociology-inspired studies, "individualism" is used here too broadly; I suspect it refers to narcissism and social atomism. (Each eclipses individuality, which is in fact associated with authenticity, originality, and creativity.) No longer is a simple opposition between the individual and the social defensible, as the social (like the public sphere) dissolves into an extension of the personal, and that latter domain itself often dissolves, no longer individual, but a dispersed series of sensory excitations.

How does mobile communication contribute to this accelerating culture of narcissism? First, let us acknowledge that the trend has been already under way for decades, as Christopher Lasch has famously documented (1978). The rapid expansion of television in the 1950s (which accompanied suburbanization) reduced radically opportunities for social interaction, especially with strangers (and then only strangers in commercial encounters, such as the grocery store and other such sites of consumer services). Now, Ling (2008, 32) notes, various electronic-based activities further isolate people from each other during leisure time. Surfing the Internet and the use of gaming machines such as Nintendo, Xbox, Wii, and Game Boy also isolate many of us from others. Email, chatting, Web-based gaming, and email represent relative exceptions, he suggests, but I regard these as compromised by the use of avatars and other forms of social deception.

In his analysis Ling positions sociality and individualization at opposite ends of the spectrum (see, for instance, 2008, 16, 37). They are, instead, mutually constitutive and inevitably interwoven. True, this mutually constitutive reciprocity is not structurally stable nor independent of circumstance or historical moment. Moreover, mobile communication may well be further destabilizing subjectivity, as Ling's analysis (inadvertently) suggests. If subjectivity requires ongoing engagement with alterity, then the ritualized intimacy of mobile communication dissolves subjectivity. Ling (2008, 37) admits that mobile phones put very few people in touch with very few people: most calls are directed to a circle of fewer than six intimates. Mobile communication, he (2008, 37) continues, "strengthens small groups" so that they become, in effect, "cliques." This finding mirrors the more general conclusion that for decades Americans have been withdrawing into "communities of like-mindedness" (Lilla 2010, 54).

At one point (2008, 56) Ling admits that mobile communication technology "probably will result in new forms of anomie," but he quickly supplements that prediction with another: "they will also provide new channels for making and cultivating social contact." Left unspecified in this optimism, given the patterns he has described, is that such "social contact" will be carefully circumscribed. As Ling (2008, 159–160) appreciates:

> In a situation where there otherwise might have been the opportunity for talking with a stranger (e.g., waiting for a bus or standing in a checkout line), we can instead gossip, flirt, or joke with friends, intimates, or family members.

Exactly: mobile communication eviscerates the public sphere by converting it into an extended private "space" where one chats with intimates not strangers. In its ritualistic repetitiveness such self-enclosed encounters undermine actual individuality as it erodes ego boundaries that only alterity can strengthen. If sociality is an extension of intimacy, the ego dissolves or, more specifically, regresses into its primary process, into the discontinuity and irrationality of psychic life.

Not only does such self-enclosed "communication" ritualize withdrawal from the public sphere, surveys report that mobile phones "encroach" on what's left of it (Ling 2008, 93). Anyone reading or trying to experience solitude in a cafe knows that cellphone talk destroys solitude as it converts the public sphere into a public forum for the speakers' preoccupations *du jour*. (Ling [2008, 163] will only concede that the mobile phone "produces some turbulence with regard to co-present activities.") Not only are such calls an assault on the privacy of others "co-present"—that last word an irritating piece of jargon that renders presence somehow supplementary—their content can be injurious to the interlocutors themselves. Ling (2008, 92) allows that with mobile communication "we get the small-scale talk and the embroidery of everyday events ... the stuff of routine life." This ritualistic reporting of trivia does not challenge one to rethink one's assumptions, reconsider the past, to imagine more satisfying futures, or to critique current events. Instead, we stay submerged in a steady stream of sensory excitation without subjective restructuring. After all, intimacy involves the illusion of self-acceptance, being loved for who one is. The "big questions" go, as the minutia of sensory experience preoccupy, even comfort in their familiarity and repetition. Difference is kept at bay, in part through mechanisms of disavowal like gossip. As Ling (2008, 154) allows, the "use of a mobile phone may actually enhance the ability to gossip." Worse, the mobile phone makes more likely that "this kind of interaction takes place on a nearly continual basis" (2008, 162). Mobile "communication," then, encourages a self-referential present-mindedness that, as Innis feared and Lasch has documented, instantiates a pervasive culture of evidently intensifying narcissism. Submerged in what is, the past and future become absorbed by the present. They simply disappear.

Not only the temporal complexity of our lives becomes flattened, its spatiality becomes smaller, as where the "now" takes place recedes as it concerns fewer others and can occur anywhere (there is reception). Ling (2008, 163) reports research that documents the decreasing number of those in whom we can confide confidential matters. (Chatting is not necessarily confession.) In this "tightening" of one's social network—excluding those who are marginal to our circle of friends and family—is, Ling (2008, 176) suggests, "the development of bounded solidarity." Such "bounded solidarity" also risks group-think, already a danger not limited to adolescents, with whom it is often associated. As patterns of mobile communication shrink the size of one's world they also render it more urgent and compelling. The intensity of daily life—punctuated by the cellphone ringing (or the ever-present possibility of its doing so)—hampers callers' capacities to engage in intellectually and emotionally extended discussions and debates. Instead, we retreat from the dissonance of the public sphere into the coziness of intimates (Ling 2008, 180–181). Some research suggests that this overemphasis upon small groups risks "the exclusion of outsiders, excessive claims on group membership, restrictions on individual freedom, and downward leveling of norms" (Ling 2008, 182). Ling (2008, 185) is unconvinced, but his counterexample—that we "pick up on ideas and trends in other locations and groups" (2008, 186) seems not especially cosmopolitan. Certainly that is the case when we "pick" on vulnerable others.

Being online leaves one vulnerable not only to surveillance (Vega 2010), a problem not only for those who prize what's left of privacy (Rosen 2000), but also because being online evidently facilitates social aggression. Cyberbullying may not have replaced the old-fashioned in-person kind, but it seems to have intensified its effects, as images become available to any who choose to witness them. As Jan Hoffman (2010, A1) notes, cyberbullying is an "imprecise" concept referencing a wide range of online activities, ranging from textual assaults to outright sexual harassment. While its incidence is difficult to quantify, the Cyberbullying Research Center sets the figure as involving some *20 percent* of all middle-school students in the United States (Hoffman 2010, A1).

Late in September 2010, Seth Walsh retreated into the backyard of his home in the desert town of Tehachapi, California. There the gay teenager—aged 13—hanged himself, apparently unable to bear a "relentless barrage" of "taunting, bullying and other abuse" from his peers. After a little more than a week on life support, Walsh died. Earlier the same month, Billy Lucas, a 15-year-old from Greensburg, Indiana hanged himself after suffering a "constant stream of invective" at school. Also during September, Asher Brown, a 13-year-old from the Houston suburbs who had just "come out" to his peers, shot himself after being taunted at his middle school (McKinley 2010, October 4, A9).

Defenders of the Internet insist nothing is new here. Kids used the telephone and before that whispering campaigns to defame former friends and vulnerable targets. That is the argument advanced by Susan Engel and Marlene Sandstrom (2010, A19), who insist that children are "no meaner" than they ever were. Children have, they suggest, "always victimized" each other, have often ignored the rights and feelings of others, and have rarely defended victims (2010, A19). Engel and Sandstrom do acknowledge that cellphones and the Internet have made bullying more "anonymous and unsupervised" (2010, A19), a point they evidently deem incidental but which seems to me key to understanding the difference between then and now. Whatever would make bullying more "anonymous" and "unsupervised" would also lead to its proliferation and intensification, as the absence of adult authority is, presumably, one prerequisite for peer violence.

Predictably the Internet is left uncriticized; it is—how did you guess?—the *schools* that are to blame. At least Engel and Sandstrom (2010, A19) realize that the contemporary obsession with standardized test scores has eliminated an "essential" marker of the well-educated person: a sense of "responsibility for the well-being of others." This acknowledgment of the relation of academic study to sensibility recalls Nussbaum's (2010, 101) rationale for the arts and playfulness generally, as we will review in chapter 8 (section I). Referencing not Nussbaum but research on child development, Engel and Sandstrom (2010, A19) believe there is "only one way" to confront bullying:

> As an essential part of the school curriculum, we have to teach children how to be good to one another, how to cooperate, how to defend someone who is being picked on and how to stand up for what is right.

While such social engineering has never worked before—it would be horrifying if we could enforce complete conformity through the curriculum—surely it is right for schools to offer courses that enable students to understand what is happening to them, specifically, how their beloved gadgets increase those dangers the inexperience and psychological instability of youth precipitates. The study of bullying—even workshops on what to do when bullied—could form teachers' thoughtful response to the basic curriculum question: *what knowledge is of most worth?*

Study is insufficient when the new technologies intensify the effects of assault. Law and its enforcement are required. In early summer 2010, in Washington state, a new anti-bullying law came into effect. State education officials report that nearly 15,000 students had been suspended for bullying during the 2008–2009 school year and that 442 had been expelled (Associated Press 2010). When technology disintegrates that subjective coherence and social responsibility central to civic society, social violence and psychic vulnerability follow. Are we caught by surprise because we were sure the future would always be different from the past?

Chapter 6

The Future in the Past

I The Technology of Cultural Crisis

> To be able to name a catastrophe and to see the future of its becoming links unintelligibility with prophecy, irony with pathos.
> —Avital Ronell (2003, 157)

Weimar Germany, Eric Weitz (2007, 247) tells us, underwent the "greatest transformation of media culture" since Johannes Gutenberg's invention of the movable-type printing press in the late 15th century. Prominent in this transformation was the appearance of the radio. As early as 1922, Kaes, Jay, and Dimendberg (1995, 594) note, in order to maintain the new medium in the public interest, radio in Germany became state controlled, housed in the postal ministry. Public ownership was to provide protection of German culture from the threat of its trivialization by commercialization, so obviously underway in the United States. There were Germans who worried that the new technological medium would violate the private sphere and that it would result in the collectivization of experience, that it would in fact destroy the individual. As decades later Pierre Lévy imagined for the Internet (see Pinar 2004, 152–154), many Germans during the 1920s regarded radio as a "great force for democratization," certain that it would break down the barriers between classes and even between nations, or, among members of the Communist Party of Germany (KDP), that it would turn out to be a medium that would construct an "alternative" to bourgeois culture, that is, a proudly proletarian culture (Weitz 2007, 241).

Under the directorship of Hans Flesch and (from 1929 to 1933) Ernst Schoen, Radio Frankfurt emphasized high not proletarian culture, broadcasting music by Hindemith and Krenek, lectures by Adorno, radio plays by Brecht and Walter Benjamin; these were, however, punctuated by live coverage of sports events by Paul Laven (Kaes et al. 1995, 595). Like Weimar cinema, radio was "wildly popular" (Weitz 2007, 238–239). Like the movies, radio was also popular in the United States, where by 1922 there were over two hundred radio stations, all privately owned and supported by advertising. Kaes et al. note the irony: made public to protect the public, under the Nazis state-controlled radio broadcast propaganda. Those Germans who had embraced radio as a "freewheeling, democratic medium ... in which virtually anyone could broadcast [and] that would serve as an avenue for the radical critique of capitalist society" were, to say the least, disappointed (Weitz 2007, 241–242). Commercialization has provided no protection from right-wing propaganda in the United States, however, as Rush Limbaugh now reaches some fifteen million listeners each week (McKibben 2010, 44).

As is the case in the United States today, Germany's obsession with constant technological innovation became intertwined with its very national identity (Herf 1984, 10). By Weimar's end, technology had been embraced even by those cultural conservatives who had before associated German nationalism with a simpler, preindustrial pastoral life, *contra* urbanization and modernization (Herf 1984, 6). These two threats—urbanization and modernization—to German culture represented cultural invasions by its former enemy in World War I; it was from America, with its uncontrolled technological dynamism, that, conservatives argued, Germany needed protection (Herf 1984, 12).

The public debate over "America" in Weimar Germany was, Peukert (1992, 178) points out, a debate about Germany itself. It focused on the challenge that American dynamism presumably posed to it. Associated with technology, consumption, and mass media, Kaes (2009, 182) explains, America had become a "powerful" influence in the "economic" and "cultural modernization" of Weimar Germany. It was just such "Americanism" that alarmed many Germans: what was the future of humane values in such an unregulated and increasingly technological society? For many Germans, Peukert (1992, 181) tells us, "freedom" and "human dignity" had only been desecrated if "European traditionalism" had been exchanged for the "new conformity" of a "rationalized, modular-built American future." Soviet-style Bolshevism appealed to many (but never a majority of) Germans, as it threatened, Stefan Zweig ([1925], in Kaes et al. 1995, 399) complained, "the same will to monotony pressed ominously in a different form: the will to the compartmentalization of the individual, to uniformity in worldviews, the same dreadful will to monotony." Germans began to search for a third cultural and political path between these two threats: America and the Soviet Union.

By the mid-1920s, Kaes (2009, 183) tells us, while "America" represented an alluring mass culture of jazz, sports, and cinema, it had also become associated with an "inhuman" emphasis upon technological development with its industrialized social efficiency. Above all, Americanism meant economism—accented by "efficiency, discipline, and control"—and both the political right and the left became critical of what they considered the "encroachment" of "instrumental rationality" (and specifically "cost effectiveness": sound familiar?) into all areas of life, including culture, which educated Germans had always realized was "antithetical" to the business world (Kaes 2009, 183). While there remained futuristic associations of an America where economic productivity, technology, and democracy were interwoven in positive fashion, increasingly Germans began to focus on a "nightmarish" America: a "materialistic, mechanized society ruled by exploitation, commercialism, and a lowbrow mass culture cynically catering to the largest possible audience" (Kaes 2009, 184). After the stock market crash of 1929, this view of America became the predominant German view.

If America and the Soviet Union represented different but equally ruinous alternatives, surely there must be a third, specifically German, way? Martin Heidegger—who would later collude with the Nazis (see, for instance, Gay 2001 [1968], 83), a complicity, however brief, that still reverberates among historians (see, for instance, Herf 1984, 110–111; LaCapra 2009, 125–139; Weitz 2007, 284) and curriculum theorists (Morris 2002, 228)—attempted to specify such a path between American capitalism and Soviet Communism. The crisis of German culture was conveyed, Heidegger asserted, through the conformity modernization demanded, de-individuating the self by emphasizing "surface appearances and shallow hyperactivity" (Weitz 2007, 280). This was the modern dehumanized world of technology that American democracy encouraged. German culture, Heidegger asserted, offered the possibility of a "spiritual" revolution that could transcend both capitalism and Communism (Herf 1984, 114; LaCapra 2004, 198). While this "confrontation" between technology and culture did not start during Weimar, Herf (1984, 8) reports that "it certainly came to a head in those years."

Right-wing thinkers emphasized Germany's special role in world history as the liberator of a humanity debased most conspicuously (if differently) in the United States and the Soviet Union. It was a special role that forefronted technology (Herf 1984, 12). Technology became crucial not only for the realization of Germany's world-historical destiny, it was deemed indispensable for the restoration of the German soul. Technology, not nature, provided passage to cultural rejuvenation. But, these right-wing thinkers insisted, Germany's technological potential could be realized *only after* technology was freed from the Weimar Republic's regulations and restrictions (1984, 32). Like "free market" enthusiasts today, right-wing Germans during the 1920s also saw regulation as only inhibiting—rather than providing rational institutional support for— that spontaneous creativity and innovation that would lead to the rapid development of new technology and with it, economic prosperity.

"Whatever this program may have meant for German industry," Herf (1984, 32) explains, "for right-wing intellectuals it meant the resolution of a cultural crisis." Herf (1984, 32) emphasizes that this conjoining of technology, history, and culture was itself an intellectual innovation: "The idea that *economic advance could overcome a cultural crisis* was new, at least for Germany's nontechnical intellectuals." No longer new, this is the view that recirculates in contemporary America, especially among school deform zealots, for whom the installation of computers in every classroom promises to correct for the socio-economic disadvantages of certain students and the alleged ineptitude of many teachers. Curriculum theorists have long known that the intellectual and affective labor of understanding cannot be accomplished by a machine. Nor can teachers perform the labor of academic study for their students, however helpful teachers can be to those students who want to learn. But for many Americans, as for many Weimar Germans, it is technology that can provide safe passage through the cultural trauma of historical injury, avoiding the pain associated with "working-through" (LaCapra 2009, 25).

Prominent among 1920s German right-wing intellectuals who came to think so was Ernst Jünger. Herf tells us Jünger—famous for his glorification of masculine camaraderie and heroism on the World War I front—was from the start less critical of technology than was Martin Heidegger. (The two were friends.) Still, at first Jünger was also less enthusiastic about its promise than fellow rightists who proclaimed, in Herf's (1984, 43) words, a "fusion of technology and soul." Not unlike contemporary assertions of computers as prostheses (rendering us as cyborgs), the unlimited, including spiritual, potential of technology was more strongly asserted by other right-wing thinkers, notably Hans Freyer and Carl Schmitt.

Recall (from chapter 3, section II) that Schmitt was a respected political scientist remembered for his now chilling argument—made in his *The Concept of the Political* (1932)—that (in Herf's [1984, 44] gloss) the "actual situation creates its own legality, that emergencies obviate normative law, and that he is sovereign who makes the decision regulating the emergency situation," a view now informing the work of contemporary theorist Giorgio Agamben (2005; LaCapra 2004, 166). A student of Max Weber (Herf 1984, 45) and a close friend of Jünger's (1984, 115), Schmitt suggested that political dynamism—deadened, he thought, by bureaucratization—could be restored by forefronting technology under the aegis of an authoritarian state.

The error—associated with 19th-century romanticism—that German culture had allegedly committed was withdrawal from the public sphere into a subjectivity celebrated for its potentiality. Such subjectivism, Schmitt insisted, had resulted in German impotence. It had, he explained, countenanced a twofold withdrawal from the world:

backward into a mythic past and *inward* into the private self, substituting "unmanly passivity" and an "amoral helplessness" for political activism and social responsibility (1984, 117). For Schmitt, the "endless talk" associated with "democracy" was thus gendered (Herf 1984, 118; Jay 1993a, 60). As with Spengler and Jünger, Herf (1984, 118) explains:

> a masculine cult of action and will permeates Schmitt's protest against the rationalization of political conflict and is meant to distinguish this cult from nineteenth-century German romanticism, which it viewed as effeminate and hence passive and apolitical.

We saw a similar gendered bifurcation in 1960s America (chapter 4, section V).

Herf (1984, 45) names Werner Sombart as another key figure in the right wing's appropriation of technology in its determination to destroy democracy in Germany. Sombart's *Jews and Economic Life* (1911) had associated Jews with the "market rationality" and "commercial greed," and Germans (as if Germans were not also Jews) with "productive labor" and "technology" (1984, 45). Sombart's diatribe, Herf (1984, 45) explains, redirected resentment against capitalism and the market away from critiques of technology and onto liberalism, Marxism, and the Jews, intertwining categories in many conservative Germans' imagination (see also Herf 1984, 129–134), as they remain in the minds of many authoritarian Americans today (see Hetherington and Weiler 2009, 4).

Because neither Jünger or Sombart joined the Nazi party and because Heidegger and Schmitt joined for a short time only, scholars have stressed the differences between their views and those associated with National Socialism. For Herf (1984, 47), however, the continuities are more striking than the differences; he points out that Hitler shared with these thinkers a view of politics as aesthetic spectacle and moral struggle against the sickening sense that Germany was "sinking into a state of hopeless degeneration." For Hitler, such degeneration became focused exclusively on Jews: if Germans could eliminate this source of their decline, they could restore the nation to its inherent greatness. Hitler's "genius," Herf (1984, 47), suggests, lay in convincing millions (but never a majority: Herf 1984, 198; Peukert 1992, 265) that he could achieve the latter.

II The Degradation of the Present

> Since the end of the war the technologization of life has proceeded with bewildering speed.
> —M. M. Gehrke ([1930], in Kaes et al. 1995, 613)

What was the situation elsewhere in Europe? In Italy, France, and England, Herf (1984, 47) tells us, many avant-gardists associated technology with a "masculine violence and eros," with a "new aesthetics," and with "creativity rather than commercial parasitism." Technology intensified lived experience, promising a "full life lived to the emotional limit" (1984, 47). Herf (1984, 47) lists Marinetti and the futurists in Italy, Wyndham Lewis and Ezra Pound in England, Sorel, Drieu la Rochelle, and Maurras in France; all, he (1984, 47) explains, were drawn to rightwing politics *because* they were drawn to technology.

Herf (1984, 48) underscores the specificity of the German situation in the early 20th century. Nowhere else, he informs us, had industrialization occurred so quickly; nowhere else had modernization clashed more violently with a traditional agrarian culture. And nowhere else had skepticism toward the Enlightenment—the elevation of reason over faith, the centrality of science to economic progress—become so pronounced as it had become in Weimar Germany. To illustrate these points, Herf (1984, 49) turns to Oswald Spengler's *The Decline of the West (1918, 1923)*, one of the best-known expressions of such skepticism toward modernity. At the same time, Herf stresses, this widely read work managed to reconcile anti-modernism, romanticism, and irrationalism with enthusiasm for technological advancement. Spengler's hope, Herf (1984, 49) summarizes, was that *The Decline of the West* would turn young people *away* from poetry and philosophy (the traditional domains of German high culture) and *toward* technology and politics, a shift already well along in the United States.

Spengler drew a series of contrasts, Herf (1984, 55) explains, prominent among them the creative concreteness of technology versus the "parasitic," "unproductive" and abstract character of "cosmopolitan" finance. In Spengler's analysis, it had been (this is Herf [1984, 57] paraphrasing) democracy and liberalism that had enabled the "triumph of money" over the legacies of ancestry and instinct. In the struggle that Spengler felt certain would ensue, Herf (1984, 57) continues, it would be "politics, not economics" that would prove to be the "decisive force" in the "battle of blood and tradition against mind and money." Power rather than dialogical deliberation, ancestry not egalitarianism, and instinct not rationality and erudition: these were the binaries posed by right-wing thinkers during Weimar. These choices were all substitutes for stereotypes. Cultural degradation, demanded by democracy and the soulless world of finance that democracy promoted, could only be reversed by targeting the group who embodied these threats: the Jews (Herf 1984, 60).

Often overlooked by students of Spengler's call to arms, Herf (1984, 55) suggests, was his embrace of technology as central to cultural rejuvenation. Spengler positions technology at the center of a national insurrection against "political liberalism" and "rootless international finance" (1984, 63). For Spengler, technology symbolized the "heroic ascent," Herf (1984, 65) explains, the "creative emancipation of the species from its natural limits." While neither a Nazi nor aligned with Italian and French fascism, Spengler nonetheless articulated concepts animating each of these movements. Primary among them, Herf (1984, 64) emphasizes, was culture, which was positioned as primary: religion, politics, art, and even technology were all derivative, intelligible only within culture. (Such a cultural reductionism is risked today by cultural studies and identity politics.) Cultural renewal, however, depended upon technology, itself somehow split from rationality and democratic deliberation. Herf (1984, 66) notes that Spengler celebrated a "virile anti-intellectualism" by linking technology with feudal images of nobles, soldiers, and adventurers. In this contradictory but at the time convincing association we see the right wing's fusion of backward-looking conservatism with forward-looking liberalism, for Spengler's metaphors, Herf (1984, 66) continues, are "feudal *and* industrial, anti-bourgeois *and* militarist, illiberal *and* orientated to a technological future." Through Spengler one could have it both ways, past and future, fused in the present.

This fusion was also achieved by the gendering of technology that was evident in the work of Jünger. Jünger drew upon the *Fronterlebnis*, or the direct experience of war, to "reconcile" backward-looking conservatism with forward-looking liberalism, both of which were materialized in technology (Herf 1984, 70). Like Heidegger, Jünger claimed to discern what lay behind the world of appearance; he identified technology as the dominant dynamic of human life (Herf 1984, 71). Like Spengler, Jünger presented the choice between what was "lifeless and mechanized" and that "animated ... instrument of human will that is modern technology" (1984, 72). Not only cultural renewal could be achieved through technological development, so would be "intoxication" (1984, 72). In *The Worker* (1932), Jünger drew upon his memory of World War I as "exciting," surrounded by "sudden danger, death, masculine energy, and exotic and elemental forces" that, Herf (1984, 72) explains, "reminded him of his prewar travels to Africa." This racial association with masculine mastery was hardly original, dating back to the so-called curse of Ham (Haynes 2002).

Homoeroticism, racialization, and political aggressivity became fused in Jünger's image of the "new man," the "worker-solider" who would occupy center stage in the future authoritarian state mobilized for industrial productivity and military aggression (Herf 1984, 72). For Jünger, Herf (1984, 73) explains, action was a welcome "relief" from the "restrictions" of rationality. For Jünger (see Herf 1984, 76), violence was the means to genuine self-realization, a simplistic formula echoed in (masculinized) athletics today (Messner 1992; Pronger 1990; Simpson 1994). As in sport, in war and in technology there could be an "active assertion of self [as well as] an actual surrender to forces beyond one's control" (Herf 1984, 77). While never joining the party, Herf (1984, 81) reports, Jünger nonetheless praised both the "living energy" and "willingness to sacrifice" he saw in the Nazis.

A bifurcation between appearance and reality—drawn from wartime experience in which horror had morphed into heroism, camaraderie, even the sublime—also structured Jünger's conception of technology. Like masculinized aggression in war, technology represents, Jünger imagined, "what lies inside us," and, like militarism, brings the body closer to the "flawless functioning" of the machine (Herf 1984, 79). Jünger was certain that "everything transitory is only a mirror" separating the surface from the deep "moving power" beneath it (quoted in Herf 1984, 82). Even individuality is transitory, and it is technology that eclipses it, Jünger affirmed (Herf 1984, 87). Compensating for such anonymity and "voluntary uniformity" (Jünger, quoted in Herf 1984, 100) would be technological innovation and national solidarity, both under a "halo of heroism" (1984, 89), generating a new "life feeling" (1984, 91). Jünger's image of the worker-soldier, Herf (1984, 92) emphasizes, fused German cultural traditionalism with technological modernism, providing a powerful theme for the Third Reich.

Unlike Spengler, Jünger, Freyer, Schmitt, and Heidegger, Herf (1984, 150) reports, Sombart declined any philosophy of technology that attributed to technology any inherent power, insisting instead that technology was "culturally neutral, morally indifferent, and could be placed in the service of both good and evil." It was the fact of technology's neutrality in human affairs that made mandatory its rescue from capitalism, something achievable only by a strong nation-state. Critics accused Sombart of being an "enemy of technology," but he countered by accusing his critics of deifying technology, according it the "highest and most elevated value" (quoted in Herf 1984, 150). Promoting what he termed a "technopolitics" that would replace the free market, Sombart asserted that technology would then serve the common welfare, enforcing the National Socialist assertion that "common good comes before self-interest" (quoted in Herf 1984, 150). While the continuing commercialization of technology, and of the Internet in particular, remains a contentious issue today (Flichy 2007, 162), any likewise nationalist solution to the cultural problems technology poses is not credible. Replacing control by corporations with control by the state remains control, even when it is justified by terrorist threats to the "homeland." Freedom is not security (Chun 2006, 291).

III A Philosophy of Technology

> Whatever most Germans hungered for, evidently it was not reason,
> whether in its conciliatory or its critical form.
> —Peter Gay (2001 [1968], 45)

Whereas the social sciences in France, England, and the United States were straining for scientific legitimacy, in Germany, Herf (1984, 157) reports, the cultural balance of power between the humanities and the sciences was "reversed." It was incumbent upon engineers to demonstrate a theoretical sophistication associated with the humanities not, as is the case in the United States today, the other way round. To press for progress through quantitative research and/or primarily logical or conceptual analysis, Herf (1984, 157) explains, would have left German scientists vulnerable to charges of materialism, a menace associated with France, England, and, especially, the United States. Herf notes that however paradoxical the concept of a philosophy of technology seemed in those countries, in Germany it was considered almost obligatory.

These interdisciplinary demands were circulating in Germany before the establishment of the Weimar Republic. Herf (1984, 158) references Edward Mayer's 1906 *Technik und Kultur* as naming a theme that would be repeated over and over again. Rather than representing the soulless organization of human labor for the maximization of profit, technology should express the personalities of the scientists who devised it. That assertion captures my view of teaching, but we part company when Mayer argues that technology itself emanates from an "instinct to re-form," a basic form of the "human essence" that seeks to master nature (quoted in Herf 1984, 158). As Herf (1984, 158) summarizes: "Technological mastery over nature combines inwardness and creativity with order and organization." As it had for Jünger and other right-wing intellectuals, World War I—even though it had ended disastrously for Germany—provided encouragement for those who saw unlimited potential when technological development could be supported by a strong nation-state.

The coordinated mobilization of state, business, labor, and technical expertise during World War I left in place a model many Germans sought to make permanent. Just as Jünger had drawn upon memories of masculine camaraderie in the trenches in his construction of the "worker-citizen," many engineers, Herf (1984, 160) reports, drew upon their experience of wartime mobilization to imagine a post-Weimar future in which technology predominated. These ideological dispositions were intensified by the ongoing economic crisis of the Weimar period: by 1932, Herf (1984, 160) notes, only 20 percent of engineering graduates of German universities could find employment. Nazism's appeal for German engineers followed from its promise to unleash technology from the commercial constraints imposed upon it by parliamentary democracy (Herf 1984, 161).

But, Herf (1984, 162) emphasizes, economic self-interest was not the main motivation for engineers' seduction by National Socialism. In contrast to their English, French, or U.S. counterparts, German engineers devoted considerable time and energy to cultural politics. It was Germany's unique nature, many believed, to combine "idealism and exact thinking" (Herf 1984, 166). It was destiny, then, that the nation that had produced so many of the world's great philosophers and poets should also produce the world's greatest scientists and engineers. Moreover, technology for some was "inherently" associated with national service, not with private profit (Herf 1984, 171). Others, as do many enthusiasts today, emphasized that technology was no abstract sterile enterprise, but, instead, was a vibrantly intellectual undertaking that incorporated both fantasy and the imagination (Herf 1984, 175).

In this convergence of culture and civilization, the humanities and the sciences, a nationalist philosophy of technology made sense to many German scientists and engineers (Herf 1984, 177, 211). *Die Tat*, the major journal of right-wing radicalism, served as the "institutional bridge" between anti-democratic conservatism and the growing ranks of unemployed engineers (Herf 1984, 179). One of the most prominent to write on the relationship between technology and culture was Heinrich Hardensett, who likened the labor of engineers to that of artists and architects (1984, 181). Hardensett claimed that capitalists profited from the distribution of depersonalized products for a mass market, and in so doing sacrificed quality for quantity. In instrumentalizing what should fundamentally be an aesthetic undertaking, capitalism destroyed "all bonds of feeling, blood and spirit" (quoted in Herf 1984, 182). Instead of a nation of artists and creative scientists, capitalism constructs a nation dominated by "finance men" who inhabit a "world of numbers," a "colorless, abstract world, an artificial world, a world of money" (quoted in Herf 1984, 183).

In Hardensett's judgment, the consequences were catastrophic. Imported from the United States, the economic efficiency movement of the 1920s installed the "soulless demonism of labor" that erased from the workplace all "comradely playful transcendence, all joyful, plastic sensuality" (quoted in Herf 1984, 183). Because capitalism is organized around manufacture and monetary exchange, it vitiates technology's aesthetic metaphysic (Herf 1984, 183). Rightly understood, then, technology creates—not just sells—objects and is imbued with the "ethic of the master builder"; as an aesthetic process it has an intrinsic "service value" (Hardensett, quoted in Herf 1984, 183). Herf (1984, 184) characterizes Hardensett's philosophy of technology as "radically subjectivist," as technology is above all the creation of individuals. I would add, however, that such subjectivism seems entirely in the service of the nation. Herf (1984, 187) himself acknowledges this fact—which renders Hardensett's philosophy collectivist, not subjectivist—when he points out that the "central ideal" of National Socialism, that is, the superiority of the common interest over self-interest, was "inherent in technology itself." As in the concept of *Bildung* (see chapter 3, section VII), self-realization could not be imagined outside devotion to the nation.

That the point of individual labor was service to the nation-state was a philosophy that could be readily appropriated by the Nazis. For the Nazis politics was a struggle in which the strongest survived; technologically weak nations and impotent peoples deserved their fates. The first political leader to use the airplane extensively, Herf (1984, 194) notes, Hitler saw technology less as an extension of his subjectivity than of the Aryan will-to-power. His propaganda minister, Joseph Goebbels, directed a considerable part of his campaign to proclaiming that the German soul and modern technology were in fact inseparable. For Goebbels, the war years had been a period "overflowing with deeds," in sharp contrast to the "exaggerated intellectualism" of the Weimar Republic (Herf 1984, 197). In 1944, Goebbels promised that the combination of Hitler's leadership, the spirit of the German people, and the V-1 and V-2 rockets would reverse the course of the war (Herf 1984, 197).

During the first four years of Nazi rule, Herf (1984, 201) reminds, Nazi economic policy was formulated to ensure recovery from the Depression, in part by reducing German dependence on the world economy through technological innovation. The prospects for the latter had been severely reduced by the exile of Germany's most important scientists, many of them repelled or directly threatened by the Nazis' anti-Semitism. Many fled to the United States, where they became indispensable to the war effort (Herf 1984, 214). Herf points out that politicization eliminated the expertise of scapegoated communities that would have proved prerequisite to a German victory in World War II. "In a totalitarian system lacking in free public discussion," Herf (1984, 222) reminds, "ideology need not test itself against reality or at least opposing interpretations of reality." Political zealotry—accented by demonization and scapegoating—ensured technological underdevelopment *and* strategic ineptitude (Hastings 2009, 55). It will also do so today.

The philosophy of technology that right-wing intellectuals devised during the Weimar Republic played a crucial role in reconciling technological development with the anti-capitalism of National Socialism. Rescued from its commercialization, technology became the means of national development, consonant with earlier conceptions of the *Volk*, celebrating "immediacy, experience, the self, soul, feeling, blood, permanence, will, instinct, and finally the [German] race" (Herf 1984, 224). By associating technology with creative (masculinized) labor and disassociating it from "parasitic (Jewish and effeminate) finance capital" (Herf 1984, 224), right-wing thinkers showed that technological development *required* the demise of democracy. Once an ugly concomitant of capitalism, in right-wing thinking technology became a "beautiful alternative" (1984, 224), one that demanded a strong state for its realization.

In this right-wing reformulation, then, technology became an externalization of the German will-to-power, with its masculine domination of nature. Remaining traces of 19th-century German anti-technological naturalism were discredited as "effeminate and escapist" (1984, 224–225). Moreover, right-wing thinkers succeeded in construing technology as "indispensable" to the rejuvenation of the German nation in which the state, not the economy, was the crucial institution. The "dictatorship of money" would be destroyed, Herf (1984, 225) summarizes, and a new "mastery of blood" established. By associating technology with soldiers' camaraderie during World War I—the *Fronterlebnis*—right-wing thinkers ensured its association with virility and patriotism. Moreover, right-wing zealots claimed technology as a "uniquely German project" bearing no relation to the "financial swindles of the Jews" (1984, 225). Finally, the right wing positioned Germany as the country located *between* East and West, with a unique and world-historical mission. Both the Americans and the Soviets were mired in materialism; only the Germans could integrate technology and soul (Herf 1984, 225).

IV Technology and Soul

> Canada's principal contribution to North American thought consists of a highly original, comprehensive, and eloquent discourse on technology.
>
> —Arthur Kroker (1984, 7)

Marshall McLuhan, Arthur Kroker reminds, emphasized how technology affects our experience. Those effects are subliminal and continuous. In fact, in McLuhan's view technology infiltrates the body, affecting how we move, on what we focus, how we feel. It infiltrates us like a disease (Kroker 1984, 72). Like disease, technology alters our very being, affecting us "not from outside, but from within" (Kroker 1984, 69). Moreover, distinctions between inside and outside blur, as our "environment" becomes a technological "extension" of the human body and our senses (Kroker 1984, 60). The world becomes a "technostructure" that is the "lens" through which we perceive the world; indeed, it becomes that with which, Kroker (1984, 60) explains, "human experience has become imperceptibly, almost subliminally, merged." But it not only the blurring of boundaries—crystallized in the concept of the cyborg—that follows the prosthetic status of the computer, time itself flat-lines, as the past and the future disappear into an endless present. McLuhan attributed the "anxiety" of our age to our unmediated exposure to the "instantaneous world" created by the information technologies, requiring him, Kroker (1984, 62) continues, to speak of technology in "highly ambivalent terms as, simultaneously, containing possibilities for emancipation and domination." Those poles sharpen in associations of information technologies with increased productivity, economic development (Brynjolfsson and Saunders 2010, 22), and democratization (Flichy 2010, 1) on the one hand, and with an ever-expanding surveillance and control on the other (Chun 2006; Rosen 2000; Vega 2010, A1).

These bipolar possibilities were of profound concern to McLuhan's contemporary, the great Canadian public intellectual George Grant. What concerned Grant, Kroker (1984, 48–49) points out, was the consequences of technology on subjectivity specifically, and of technological society for Western civilization generally. Grant advocated an "ethics of charity" to contest the hegemony of "calculation" capitalism installs in the public sphere; in his *Philosophy in the Mass Age* (1959), "mythic consciousness" is contrasted to "instrumental activism" (quoted in Kroker 1984, 49). Recall that allegory attempts to teach through articulating the mythological significance of historical particularity.

For Grant, historical remembrance was primary, but for McLuhan what was compelling was charting the cultural geography of the new media (Kroker 1984, 53). Countering Grant's horrific image of humanity splintered into "half-flesh/half-metal," McLuhan seemed mesmerized by technological extensions of humanity, imagining that these will make humanity "more cosmopolitan" (Kroker 1984, 53). Whereas Grant dwelled on the devolution of subjectivity through technology, McLuhan insisted that technology was now the "locus of a 'redeemed' human civilization" (Kroker 1984, 53). *Locus* is the key concept here, for it was less the content and more the medium that marked the novelty of the new media: the medium becomes, famously, the message. In teacher education during the same period we can see an analogous privileging of *process* over *product*: what matters is not *what* you know but *how* you teach. Curriculum theory contests the bifurcation, critiquing instrumental rationality (Macdonald 1995, 162) as it devises new languages for understanding education non-technologically (obvious in the important work of Huebner and Aoki), and, most recently, reasserting the primacy of academic knowledge (Ravitch 2010, 29).

Before the onset of the Great Depression, Harold Innis noticed that accelerating advances in technology in Canada had left the population "myopic and intellectually exhausted" (Watson 2007, 162). From the outset, Innis discerned technology's tendency to restructure the mental as well as material conditions of human existence (2007, 163). The increasing frequency and intensifying instrumentalism of interpersonal exchange threatened to destroy the oral tradition, which Innis associated not with *behavior* but with *intersubjective understanding*; orality represented the "very possibility of public life" (Carey 1992, 164). The proliferation of "talk"—Aoki (2005 [1991], 180) calls it "chit-chat"—was replacing opportunities for testimony, debate, and contemplation. In such a degraded public sphere, Watson (2007, 182) explains, "Innis ironically associated the silence of reading, writing, and thought, far more than the sound of public debates and pronouncements, with the oral tradition." *Contra* common sense, orality in its behavioral forms—speech that amounted to distracting chatter and/or instrumental calculation—rendered silence the site wherein communication could still occur. At one point Innis went so far as to conclude that "discussion has become a menace rather than a solvent to the problems of a complex society ... the tyranny of talk has ominous possibilities" (quoted in Watson 2007, 191). Nowhere was this more obvious, Innis thought, than in the University.

Innis attributed the decline of the University, Watson (2007, 243) explains, "directly" to the ever-increasing size and aggressivity of the university's administrative apparatus. Its encroachment into domains that had formerly been under the faculty's jurisdiction threatened, Innis thought, not just faculty governance but, much more importantly, the very quality of that research and scholarship conducted at universities. One such encroachment was a tendency toward an administrative prioritizing of research according to the administration's agenda:

> Scholars can only be judged by their peers. Scholarship is a tough activity and involves unremitting toil over a long period with no prospect of immediate recognition—indeed with the prospect of decreasing recognition as the university is attracted to publicity stunts or becomes concerned with media such as radio and television which are impossible for scholars.
>
> (quoted in Watson 2007, 243)

The more public schools become aligned with the ceaseless chatter of contemporary culture (e.g. cyberspace mistaken for the real world), the more academic curriculum becomes intellectually eviscerated. And Innis' first point also speaks to the profession's degradation today: teachers themselves should be the primary judges of teachers' teaching. Of course, students' and parents' assessments must be solicited, but these are best expressed in face-to-face discussions where context and nuance figure prominently. A former teacher in one-room schools in Ontario and Alberta (Watson 2007, 16), Innis would have appreciated that the least relevant indicator of a teacher's acumen is how her or his students fare on standardized exams.

Innis was trained in political economy at the University of Chicago; during his early years—the 1920s—as a faculty member at the University of Toronto he conducted extensive fieldwork (what he called "dirt" research) to provide first-hand testimony and knowledge of the history of political economy in Canada. In the final phase of his now legendary career, working on the interrelations among communication, power, and cultural change, Innis worked as theorists always work: reading, taking notes, reassembling these into paragraphs structured by subjective insight and intellectual judgment. Insofar as such intellectual work is crafted as an oral (as Innis defined the concept) engagement in an ongoing classroom-based conversation, it becomes a form of curriculum development. Insofar as such engagement is primarily disciplinary, it becomes research attempting to advance collective understanding of the field's questions. In both, loosely analogous, domains, acknowledging who said what when is always necessary. For Innis, Watson (2007, 282) concludes, that apparently straightforward referencing process anticipated future extensions of the very technological-communicative capacities he was in fact studying:

> In mining the work of hundreds of authors, paraphrasing and juxtaposing their most profound thoughts, and creating new works at the end of the process, was Innis not anticipating the most profound cultural change that would occur in the generations following his death: I am referring to the switchover from the biological storage of information in the brain and in non-interactive physical records banks such as libraries and archives to the storage of far greater amounts of information in digital form and its interactive retrieval and manipulation through software and search engines.

Watson (2007, 283) argues that in this methodology (it is both pedagogical and disciplinary), Innis was "rediscovering the technological underpinning of the oral tradition—the ancient art of memory—and attempting to revive it." Orality is not, finally, behavior, as much as it is an ongoing process of self-conscious intertextuality, acknowledging and (in one sense) performing the palimpsest that is reality. Its political strength, in Innis' view, was that it could not be easily "monopolized" (Carey 1992, 166). Such orality, as conversation, includes self-excavation, as it focuses on finding one's way, a social (re)search inspired by Innis' "belief in the primacy of the individual" and "driven by the sense of deep personal responsibility" (Watson 2007, 53). These are the dual domains of "soul" and subjectivity, themselves restructured by technological development.

Watson (2007, 78–80) locates the genesis of Innis' research on technology and communications in his experience of 1914–1918. As was the case for so many Weimar intellectuals, World War I was an utterly imprinting experience on which Innis drew for the rest of his life. "The sacred force to which the novices of the Great War were exposed," Watson (2007, 89) recalls, "was, above all, technology, but technological in a diabolical rather than its traditionally benevolent guise." This contradictory character of technology—we have seen contemporary examples of that fact earlier in chapter 5—would, Watson (2007, 89) notes, "mark Innis' work profoundly," contrasting it to McLuhan's at times celebratory embrace of technology. Not only the death and destruction technology demonstrated during the Great War haunted Innis, so did technology's intensifying devastation of the natural world. Innis' history of Canada's political economy, Watson (2007, 89) points out, was focused mostly on the "exhaustion of resources that follows the application of new technologies to virgin materials." Finally, World War I had also informed Innis' sense of the ongoing devaluation of public dialogue, as he appreciated that the war "devalued oratory by reducing it to propaganda" (Watson 2007, 84). Technology not only altered human communication and thereby human history, Innis was arguing, technology altered human nature itself (Kroker 1984, 91–92; Watson 2007, 157). In their ongoing presentistic immediacy, do the new information technologies create a subjective state of emergency?

For Kroker (1984, 101) Harold Innis mediates between two poles of Canadian intellectual life and its preoccupation with technology, power, and survival. At one pole is the "technological dependency" Kroker associates with George Grant and at the other is that "technological humanism" he associates with McLuhan. In his belief that technology has potential for the recovery, in civic life, of an ancient orality, Innis is, Kroker (1984, 1010) suggests, "midway between the tragic perspective of George Grant and the utopian imagination of Marshall McLuhan." Like Grant, Innis positioned as primary "historical remembrance" (Kroker 1984, 110), and like McLuhan, he reasserted the centrality of orality and the auditory in human culture, against print culture and the triumph of ocularcentrism, against the devaluation of the poetic by the logocentric (Kroker 1984, 114). This cultural analysis was, Innis knew, profoundly political, as the very concept "political" had achieved its historical meaning through the collective and "oral" research undertaken by communities of citizens. That research—by definition both "personal" and "social"—was conducted through open dialogue of individual members for the "good" in a community (Watson 2007, 11). No technology of subjectivity or sociality, such research enabled Innis to invoke intellect in matters of soul (see chapter 1, section III). Whether in the academic disciplines or school classrooms, intellectual advancement is to be conducted as a complicated, "inspirited" (Aoki 2005 [1990], 374), conversation that expressses Innis' affirmation of orality.

Part IV

The Analytic Moment
Understanding the Present

Chapter 7

Anti-Intellectualism and Complicated Conversation

I Anti-Intellectualism

> To what extent able students stayed out of teaching because of its poor rewards and to what extent because of the nonsense that figured so prominently in teacher education, it is difficult to say.
> —Richard Hofstadter (1962, 318)

In the regressive moment we saw how public education became racialized and gendered in the American popular imagination. We saw how public schools become screens onto which national crises were projected, their causes relocated and avenged through "school reform." Now we understand that teachers' positions of "gracious submission" to anti-intellectual, often ideologically driven, politicians are in fact covert racialized and gendered positionings in which the academic—intellectual—freedom to develop the curriculum and devise the means of its assessment has been usurped by those same politicians in the name of "accountability." As Linda McNeil (2000, 7) has pointed out, the "conservative transformation of American public education [has occurred] through the use of technicist forms of power." Such "accountability" is one face of fascism in America today.

Using a business model, politicians and others have made the commonsensical (if anti-educational) argument that all that matters is "the bottom line"—scores on standardized tests—and in the process converted the school into a business, a cram school, but a business—not an educational institution—nonetheless. Again, McNeil understands these issues precisely. Speaking of Texas school reform, an antecedent for (former Texas Governor) George W. Bush's presidential educational agenda, McNeil (2000, xxiv) points out that "incipient in [these] reforms was the shifting of control over public schooling away from 'the public,' and away from the profession, toward business-controlled management accountability systems." As the financial crisis of 2008 made clear, business accountability is an illusory exclusively rhetorical "ideal" that businesses themselves fail to realize. What the privatization of education has meant is not greater competitiveness or efficiency but a plundering of public budgets for corporate gain.

Employing a classic "blame-the-victim" tactic, politicians have insisted that educators are to blame, and not just for what they judge to be low test scores. In the 1950s and early 1960s teachers were blamed for jeopardizing the American military position vis-à-vis the Soviet Union and, in the early 1980s, for U.S. currency devaluation. Now teachers are held "accountable" for America's economic performance in the "new millennium," distracting the public from the unethical and unprofitable practices of many American businesses, among the most spectacular instances of which were Enron, WorldCom, Countrywide, Lehman Brothers. As it turns out, "accountability" is nothing more than a "projection" onto educators of that ethical responsibility to the public many businessmen and politicians themselves so profoundly lack.

Much of school deform is simple scapegoating, but it has occurred and succeeded as a tactic in the "conservative" restoration of the last forty years. And this is a political phenomenon that could not have occurred without aggressive participation of the racially reactionary white South (Black and Black 1992). First in the 1964 Goldwater campaign, conservatives discovered they could draw upon reactionary (white) southern resistance to (especially) racial justice to animate their broader causes of cultural authoritarianism and economic elitism. In allegiance with "conservatives" in the Midwest and the Far West, conservatives first contained, then repudiated the progressive political potential unleashed during the 1960s civil rights and anti-Vietnam War movements. Without the reactionary white South, right-wing politicians, business executives, and religious fundamentalists (often intersecting categories) could not have forced their elitist agenda on an increasingly polarized American electorate (Hetherington and Weiler 2009, 39, 68).

This coalition of business, religious, and cultural reactionaries has distracted attention away from itself and focused public attention on the schools, where its political representatives have forced teachers— through so-called "school reform" initiatives—to do their bidding. It had been students and professors who had animated the 1960s revolt against racial injustice and U.S. imperialism abroad, and it would be educational institutions where right-wing fanatics would focus their attention in the decades following, at first complaining about liberal indoctrination of university students, precipitating the so-called "culture wars." Once these skirmishes were lost, and except in Texas and those local school districts where right-wing majorities allowed naked power plays to proceed, right-wing zealots switched tactics. By tying the curriculum to student performance on standardized test, teachers were forced to abandon their (relative) intellectual freedom to choose what they teach, how they teach, and how they assess student learning. By tying the curriculum to standardized tests and assessing not only students' but teachers' performance according to scores on those tests, right-wing zealots and their profiteering collaborators have gained control of the U.S. school curriculum.

While historically public school teachers have not taken advantage of their academic freedom to the extent their colleagues in the university have, now they have little opportunity to do so. Curriculum theory is that interdisciplinary field in which teacher education is conceived as the professionalization of intellectual freedom, forefronting teachers' and students' individuality, that is to say their originality, their creativity, protecting their opportunities to dissent, engaged in ongoing if complicated conversation informed by a self-reflexive, interdisciplinary erudition. The marginalization of curriculum theory in U.S. teacher education is in part a reflection of the anti-intellectual vocationalism of mainstream teacher education. Too often teacher educators have colluded in preparing teachers to accept their positions of gracious submission in the school. While victims of anti-intellectualism in government and of anti-intellectualism in the culture at large, the academic field of education too has embedded within it destructive anti-intellectual tendencies, in large part *due* to these external influences.

That there is in American culture—in which U.S. curriculum studies is thoroughly embedded—a profound and persistent anti-intellectualism has been documented by, among others, Richard Hofstadter (1962). Anti-intellectualism, enforced by the hegemonies of business and religion, disables democracy and its medium of maintenance and regeneration: communication. In his summary of the intellectual history of U.S. communications studies, Carey (1992, 144) points out that communication is no simple exchange of information; it is, in fact, that complex and ongoing process "whereby a culture is brought into existence, maintained in time, and sedimented into institutions." The culture communication creates, then, includes "art, architecture, custom and ritual, and, above all, politics," the latter domain of which requires us to maintain an "intense concern" with public life, considering those conditions that support "rational and critical discourse and action" (Carey 1992, 144).

Despite (and also due to its) constant change, American culture tends toward the conservative, as various groups contest the pace and cultural content capitalism encourages. This tendency positions intellectuals (and artists), often dedicated to cultural experimentation and progress, oppositionally in those local cultures in which they live and work. For Americans, this anti-intellectualism is historic and specific; Hofstadter (1962) associates it with business and religious zealotry. Christopher Lasch (1978, 52) points out that, in America, the two intersect: "According to the myth of capitalist enterprise, thrift and industry held the key to material success and spiritual fulfillment." In America, business becomes a secular religion, as the two domains fuse.

In addition to business and religion, Hofstadter also associates anti-intellectualism with teachers and, especially, teachers' teachers, the education professoriate. In his *Anti-Intellectualism in American Life*, Hofstadter's main target is life adjustment education, that post-World War II amalgamation of earlier progressive and social efficiency movements in education. Hofstadter (1962, 343) declares that the life-adjustment movement "was an attempt on the part of educational leaders and the United States Office of Education to make completely dominant the values of the crusade against intellectualism that had been going on since 1910," a "crusade" he associates with the child-centered wing of progressivism. Hofstadter appears to hold John Dewey responsible for this crusade, which he describes in the following terms:

> the central idea of the new educational thought [was] that the school should base its studies not on the demands of society, nor any conception of what an educated person should be, but on the developing needs and interests of the child.
>
> (Hofstadter 1962, 369)

Probably only a minority of child-centered progressives ever held this extreme view, a view which was never the "central ideal of the new educational thought." As for Dewey, he insisted that education and society were inextricably linked, not only with each other but with the psycho-social and intellectual growth of children as well (Dewey 1916, 1938).

As a professional historian, did Hofstadter mistake the project of professional education—the point of which is to train, in his case, competent historians—for what gets called "general education," in which the interdisciplinary study of important ideas is to be linked to society and to students' self-formation? Is that why he was so quick to judge the life-adjustment movement as "anti-intellectual"? Note his response to a passage he quotes from *Life Adjustment Education for Every Youth*, which defines life adjustment as "a philosophy of education which places life values above acquisition of knowledge" (quoted in Hofstadter 1962, 345). Hofstadter (1962, 345) comments: "Repeatedly, life adjustment educators were to insist that intellectual training is of no use in solving the 'real life problems' of ordinary youth."

Now there were, in all likelihood, life-adjustment educators who held such an anti-intellectual view, but his claim does not follow, as Hofstadter implies, from the statement he has quoted. From that quoted sentence there is no reason to believe that those who formulated the idea of life-adjustment education devalued the acquisition of knowledge except, possibly, for its own sake. Knowledge acquisition, it is asserted

in the passage Hofstadter quotes, must be in the service of "life values."
Knowledge is obviously valued; it is to be sought, as the passage makes
clear, in the service of "life values."

There *were* excesses in the life-adjustment movement, and Christopher Lasch—who, like Hofstadter, provides a caricature, rather than a
history, of progressive education—is eager to reference them. Quoting
Joel Spring (1976, 18–21), Lasch (1978, 137) provides surely the most
questionable examples of "life adjustment." In Illinois, advocates of life
adjustment urged schools to give curricular attention to such "problems
of high school youth" as "improving one's personal appearance," "select-
ing a family dentist," and "developing and maintaining wholesome boy–
girl relationships." Such socialization into consumption and society as
spectacle—Lasch's point—could, however, have become educational
were these subjects taught from a critical and intellectual point of view.
But like Hofstader, Lasch makes no argument, supplies no evidence; he
only makes declarations in his condemnation of the "democratization of
education" (Lasch 1978, 125). Such education, he judges:

> has neither improved popular understanding of modern society,
> raised the quality of popular culture, nor reduced the gap between
> wealth and poverty, which remains as wide as ever. On the other
> hand, it has contributed to the decline of critical thought and the ero-
> sion of intellectual standards, forcing us to consider the possibility
> that mass education, as conservatives have argued all along, is intrin-
> sically incompatible with the maintenance of educational quality.
>
> (Lasch 1978, 125)

Who *could* argue that public education has significantly improved critical thought, intellectual standards, and the quality of American popular
culture, certainly not after forty years of school deform? But it is also
obvious that schooling is not specifically or only to blame for the under-
developed state of American popular culture.

Lasch's allegations contradict his broader argument, in which the
school, like the family, like sport, like politics, and even aging, all
become degraded in the American "culture of narcissism." He writes:
"Institutions of cultural transmission (school, church, family), which
might have been expected to counter the narcissistic trend of our culture, have instead been shaped in its image" (Lasch 1978, 141). While
he is disinclined to trace this crisis of American culture to one cause, at
least in the 1978 book, capitalism seems a likely suspect. In the 1984
book, historical events, among them the Holocaust and the Cold War,
join capitalism as contributing to the dissolution of both the public and
private spheres.

In his last book, Lasch seems to resolve this ambiguity. No longer does he target the school, but, instead, acknowledges that:

> most of the shortcomings of our educational system can be traced ... to the growing inability to believe in the reality either of the inner world or of the public world, either in a stable core personal identity or in a politics that rises above the level of platitudes and propaganda.
>
> (1995, 186–187)

I wonder if this shift, evident too in his generally favorable treatment of Dewey, can be attributed, in part, to the addition to the University of Rochester History Department (now relegated to history by arrogant administrators; see Moses 1999) of Robert Westbrook, whose important book on Dewey and the politics of progressivism (see Westbrook 1991) may have had influence. Lasch's 1995 book is dedicated to Westbrook.

Hofstadter (of whom Lasch is sometimes critical) is more focused in his complaints, targeting progressive education and, specifically, the life-adjustment movement. Drawing on Lawrence Cremin (1961), Hofstadter draws a throughline from Dewey's *Democracy and Education* to life-adjustment education (see Hofstadter 1962, 361). While he focuses on "the limitations and the misuse of these [Dewey's] ideas," Hofstadter (1962, 359) asks us not to read his account as a "blanket condemnation of progressive education." "Although its reputation suffered unwarranted damage from extremists on its periphery," he judges, "progressivism had at its core something sound and important" (1962, 359). Hofstadter makes a list:

> The value of progressivism rested on its experimentalism and in its work with younger children; its weakness lay in its effects to promulgate doctrine, to generalize, in its inability to assess the practical limits of its own program, above all in its tendency to dissolve the curriculum. This tendency became most serious in the education of older children, and especially at the secondary level, where, as the need arises to pursue a complex, organized program of studies, the question of the curriculum becomes acute.
>
> (Hofstadter 1962, 360)

Was it was the progressives' commitment to the public school curriculum as a public sphere, that is, linked to society and to students' interests ("life values" in life-adjustment movement rhetoric) that distressed Hofstadter most?

Hofstadter's book was widely read and has been enormously influential, except in mass culture, where the anti-intellectualism of the American preoccupations with business and religion have continued, even intensified, since the book's publication fifty years ago. Probably few present-day university arts and science faculty remember Hofstadter's condemnation of the "life-adjustment" movement, which he associated with progressivism (regarding which, despite his claim to find "something sound and important" at its "core," he is mostly negative). But his association of academic vocationalism with "traditional education" (Hofstadter 1962, 355)—that is, mistaking professional for general education—serves the political and institutional interests of many arts and science faculty. What remains most of all, I suspect, is Hofstadter's *ad hominem* hostility to teacher education, uncomfortably evident in this gendered and classed diatribe:

> The more humdrum the task the educationists have to undertake, the nobler and more exalted their music grows. When they see a chance to introduce a new course in family living or home economics, they begin to tune the fiddles of their idealism. When they feel they are about to establish the school janitor's right to be treated with respect, they grow starry-eyed and increase their tempo. And when they are trying to assure that the location of the school toilets will be so clearly marked that the dullest child can find them, they grow dizzy with exaltation and launch into wild cadenzas about democracy and self-realization.
>
> (Hofstadter 1962, 340)

And this fantasy in a book awarded the 1964 Pulitzer Prize in *nonfiction*! True, this passage is one of the few pieces of nonsense in the book. Overall, Hofstadter's argument is carefully crafted, perhaps why the anti-intellectualism of his diatribe passed for considered and scholarly judgment.

To his credit, Hofstadter understood that, in America, serious intellectual work makes sense only when it leads to wealth, spiritual or material. In America, intellectual work tends to be for, well, eccentrics. Not surprisingly, more than a few Americans consider intellectuals (and artists) as eccentric, or worse. And so our calling as teachers—dedicated, perhaps, to "life values"—tends to position us in tension with, sometimes in opposition to, many, perhaps most, of our fellow citizens, and to not a few of their children. Despite these unfavorable, profoundly anti-intellectual, conditions, we teachers must find ways to initiate complicated conversation with students. As Michael Oakeshott knew, the curriculum is itself an ongoing complicated conversation.

II An *Unrehearsed* Intellectual Adventure

> In a conversation participants are not engaged in an enquiry or a
> debate; there is no "truth" to be discovered, no proposition to be
> proved, no conclusion sought.
>
> —Michael Oakeshott (1959, 10)

For many practicing teachers, "curriculum" is understood as what the
district office requires them to teach, what the state education department publishes in scope and sequence guides. For many prospective
teachers, curriculum denotes a course syllabus, perhaps only a list of
books to read. A highly symbolic concept, school curriculum is what
older generations choose to tell younger generations. Whatever the
school subject, the curriculum is historical, political, racial, gendered,
phenomenological, autobiographical, aesthetic, theological, and international. It is the symbolic character of curriculum that renders debates
over the canon struggles over the American identity itself (Castenell and
Pinar 1993).

Because the curriculum has become the tail on the dog that is testing,
it may not be obvious how we might conceive of curriculum as "conversation," as this term is usually employed to refer to more open-ended,
sometimes personal and interest-driven, events in which we dialogically
encounter each other (Freire 1968). That curriculum has become so
often distant from the everyday sense of conversation signals how profoundly the process of education has been deformed by school reform.
Instead of employing school knowledge to complicate our understanding
of ourselves and the society in which we live, teachers are forced to prep
students for standardized exams, ensuring that countless classrooms are
filled with forms of ventriloquism rather than intellectual exploration,
wonder, and awe (Huebner 1999).

Imagining that the best is behind us, "conservatives" have indeed
managed to turn back the clock, and with a vengeance, so that the "crisis
of the classroom" identified by Charles Silberman at the end of a decade
of national school reform has only intensified. Thirty years of "back to
the basics" and "accountability" render Silberman's dated description
chillingly current: "It is not possible to spend any prolonged period visit-
ing public school classrooms without being appalled by the mutilation
visible everywhere—mutilation of spontaneity, of the joy of learning, of
pleasure in creating, of sense of self " (Silberman 1970, 10).

The dissociation between school curriculum and public life, between
school curriculum and students' self-formation, that the current cult of
cram school only aggravates, creates profound social alienation that is
marked, on occasion, by spectacular school violence (Webber 2003). In
Japan, it has been self-violence that has followed from the pressures of

testing. Beginning in 2000 (and then contested by political conservatives: see Asanuma 2003, 438), a progressive policy was promoted by the Japanese Ministry of Education: the New Course of Studies (NCS). NCS employed the phrase *ikiru chikara* (living power; passion for life) to designate a shift in curricular emphasis. Instead of focusing only on the improvement of test scores, mindful of proliferating problems of student bullying and an increasing number of student suicides, the Ministry declared that the most critical issue faced by Japanese children was the struggle to live everyday life (see Asanuma 2003, 436). Was that a Japanese form of "life-adjustment" education?

In sharp contrast to Western reform focused on constant testing, in Japan *yutori* (relaxation or slowing down) was named as the national curricular aspiration (Asanuma 2003, 437). The most prominent point in this reform, Asanuma (2003, 437) reports, was the project method. Associated with the 1920s U.S. progressive William Heard Kilpatrick who was, for decades, maligned by conservative critics in the U.S. (see Ravitch 2000, 182), the organization of the curriculum after students' projects was installed at all elementary and middle school levels for two or three hours each week. Ninth graders were permitted to decide what they want to learn for approximately one hundred hours each school year. In addition to the cognitive gains that were presumed to accrue, psychological benefits were also promised (see Asanuma 2003, 438). This shift in curricular policy seems primarily organizational, however, as it did not include curricular acknowledgment of past atrocities, among them the Nanking Massacre and importation of "comfort" women from Korea (see Asanuma 2003, 435). Such censorship occurs in countries where nationalism precludes the accurate and candid curricular treatment of the nation's history. It also occurs in countries where standardized tests stress "cognitive skills" bleached of historical memory and cultural knowledge.

As Dwayne Huebner once remarked to me, school violence is a curricular issue. Is it not strange that the sometimes violent aggression of secondary school students (often boys) is not the pretext for interdisciplinary courses on the history and/or gender of violence, including bullying? Why are teachers not permitted, indeed, encouraged, to show students that academic knowledge is not (like standardized tests) self-contained, that it reaches out toward and back from life as human beings live it? Not life "adjustment" but life "reconstruction" can follow from academic study. How can the school curriculum not be conceived as a provocation for students to reflect on and to think critically about themselves and the world they will inherit?

Conversation is not "chit-chat," Ted Aoki (2005 [1991], 180) reminds, nor is it the simple exchange of messages or only the transmission of information. None of these, he suggests, requires "true human presence," what Harold Innis might characterize as the oral tradition. Nor is language only a tool by means of which thoughts are recoded into words conveying information. Curriculum as conversation is no conveyor belt. It is a matter of attunement, an auditory rather than visual conception, in which the sound of music—for Aoki (2005 [1990], 367), jazz specifically—being improvised is an apt example. Given the poetic quality of Aoki's theorization, poetry provides another example of the sound of complicated conversation.

The *educational* point of the public school curriculum is *understanding*, understanding the relations among academic knowledge, the state of society, processes of self-formation, and the character of the historical moment in which we live, in which others have lived, and in which our descendants will someday live. It is *understanding* that informs the ethical obligation to care for ourselves and our fellow human beings, that enables us to think and act with intelligence, sensitivity, and courage in both the public sphere—as citizens aspiring to establish a democratic society—and in the private sphere, as individuals committed to other individuals. As feminist theory has shown, the two spheres are not, finally, separable (Grumet 1988).

"Conversation," Oakeshott (1959, 9, 10) explains, is the "meeting-place" where "the diverse idioms of utterance which make up current human intercourse" converge. "Conversation is not an enterprise designed to yield an extrinsic profit," he is clear; nor is it "a contest where a winner gets a prize" (1959, 10). Surely he overstates his case when he insists it is not exegesis or inquiry, and when he insists (1959, 11) "it is an *unrehearsed* intellectual adventure." Surely it can be prepared for, it can provoke or be the consequence of study, and, of course, it can be spontaneous, perhaps playful. Oakeshott is not guilty of overstatement when he observes that conversation "is impossible in the absence of a diversity of voices: in it different universes of discourse meet, acknowledge each other and enjoy an oblique relationship which neither requires nor forecasts their being assimilated to one another" (1959, 11). Alterity structures and animates complicated conversation.

Oakeshott cannot escape his time or place, and his situatedness in time and place is evident when he asserts that conversation is the appropriate image of human intercourse because it recognizes the qualities, the diversities, and "the proper" (1959, 11) relationships of human utterances. "As civilized human beings," he continues, echoing 19th-century assumptions of civilization and progress that legitimated Empire, "we are the inheritors, neither of an enquiry about ourselves and the world, nor of an accumulating body of information, but of a conversation, begun in the primeval forests and made more articulate in the course of centuries." There are English shades of the German mythology of the *Volk* here (Hannaford 1996). But I can accept his acknowledgment that this conversation is one "which goes on both in public and within each of ourselves" (Oakeshott 1959, 11). As the emphasis upon allegory in this formulation of curriculum theory testifies, the two are inextricably interrelated.

Oakeshott seems to acknowledge his earlier overstatement, admitting that "of course there is argument and enquiry and information" (1959, 11), but he nicely conceives of these as "passages" in conversation, complaining quickly, as if to honor his ongoing ambivalence regarding the point, these are not the most "captivating" (1959, 11) of passages. Once again the Empire and the Great Chain of Being echo, innocently perhaps, in Oakshott's thinking, as he insists that: "It is the ability to participate in this conversation, and not the ability to reason cogently, to make discoveries about the world, or to contrive a better world, which distinguishes the human being from the animal and the civilized man from the barbarian" (1959, 11). The distinctions are not so obvious now (LaCapra 2009, 127; Santner 2006, 12).

Oakeshott appreciates the significance of the concept of conversation to understanding education, at least in the Anglo-American tradition: "Education, properly speaking, is an initiation into the skill and partnership of this conversation in which we learn to recognize the voices, to distinguish the proper occasions of utterance, and in which we acquire the intellectual and moral habits appropriate to conversation" (Oakeshott 1959, 11). He appreciates as well the importance of interdisciplinarity to such educational conversation: "[t]he final measure of intellectual achievement is in terms of its contribution to the conversation in which all universes of discourse meet" (1959, 11). In conversation, that judgment is both immediate and deferred, present and displaced.

Oakeshott is astonished that conversation has survived as a concept and practice in education, given how "remote" (1959, 12) our ideas of education have become from the concept. Oakeshott (1959, 15) hopes to "rescue" "conversation," by which he means "to restore to it some of its lost freedom of movement," and while he suspects "rescue" is too ambitious an aspiration, he proposes something "more modest." He proposes that we reconsider the "voice of poetry; to consider it as it speaks in the conversation." To do so he considers the nature of the "self." This is evocative of the "oral tradition" that Innis wants to resuscitate, that contemplative encounter with the Other that reconstructs subjectivity and society.

As Oakeshott understands it, "the real world is a world of experience within which self and not-self divulge themselves to reflection." He acknowledges that the distinction is "ambiguous and unstable." Even so, it allows him to characterize the work of the self as "separating itself from a present not-self: self and not-self generate one another" (Oakeshott 1959, 17). It is difficult not to think of object-relations theory here, and the primal "object" from which, especially, the male child separates itself is the maternal body (Chodorow 1978). This fundamental separation, with its inauguration of language and the symbolic, inspires allegory as well, with its juxtaposition of the abstract universality of mythology and the concrete specificity of historical experience (Rauch 2000, 85–86).

"The self appears as activity," Oakeshott (1959, 17) reminds. Sounding like the Jean-Paul Sartre of *Nausea* and *Being and Nothingness*, Oakeshott (1959, 17) asserts that the "self is not a 'thing' or a 'substance' capable of being active; it is activity." His ontology of the self sounds Sartrean—"this activity is primordial; there is nothing antecedent to it" (1959, 17)—but curiously devoid of history, culture, and the moment as lived, all aspects of the "situation" in which, for Sartre, the "self-as-activity" finds itself and takes form. The situatedness of the self may be what, by different semantic means, Oakeshott (1959, 17) is describing when he acknowledges that "[o]n every occasion this activity is a specific mode of activity; to be active but with no activity in particular, to be skillful but to have no particular skill, is as impossible to the self as not to be active at all." One must acknowledge that this ceaseless activity may be altered by various technologies of the self, among them psychotherapies, bodywork, meditation, and other religious regimens, as well as drugs.

Given the multidimensional complexity of the self-as-activity, it is curious that Oakeshott (1959, 17) decides to settle on one aspect as definitive: "imagining," by which he means the self "making and recognizing images," and "moving among them." Whatever the modality of experience—Oakeshott lists sensing, perceiving, feeling, desiring, thinking, believing, contemplating, supposing, knowing, preferring, approving, laughing, crying, dancing, loving, singing, making hay, devising mathematical demonstrations, and, I would add, making love—each, he asserts, is engaged in the experience of imagination.

There is a powerful literature on visuality and, especially, its complex role in "modernity" (see, for instance, Brennan and Jay 1996; Crary 2002; Jay 1993b; Levin 1993; Mitchell 1994). Given that he would not have known this scholarship, Oakshott's apparent participation in the "hegemony of the vision" (Levin 1993, 5) seems unself-conscious. For Oakeshott (1959, 18), "the not-self, then, is composed of images." But not all images are located outside the self: "the self is constituted in the activity of making and moving among images" (1959, 18). Oakeshott's reliance on the image underscores the centrality of the imagination to educational experience (Eisner 1979; Greene 1995; Rugg 1963). Conversation is, Oakeshott (1959, 19) explains, "the meeting-place of various modes of imagining; and in this conversation there is, therefore, no voice without an idiom of its own: the voices are not divergences from some ideal, non-idiomatic manner of speaking, they diverge only from one another."

Oakeshott's characterization of conversation as not conforming to a predetermined end enables us to understand how the aggressive use of standardized examinations cannot countenance a curricular conversation. Classroom conversation requires curricular innovation and experimentation, opportunities for students and faculty to articulate, in their own terms, informed by the subjects they are studying, their lived experience. It is not, as Jerome Bruner (1977, ix) summarized the academic vocationalism of the 1959 Woods Hole Conference (which he chaired), learning to "talk physics" with students rather than "talk about" it to them. (Of the thirty-four Conference participants, only three were education specialists; no school teachers were present [see Bruner 1977 [1960], xix].)

Michael Oakeshott accomplishes much more in his essay on "the conversation of mankind," and I recommend that the essay be read in its entirety. For now, however, let us acknowledge the danger of relegating "conversation" to "classroom discourse." Even as sophisticated a scholar as Arthur Applebee succumbs to that temptation.

III Curriculum as Complicated Conversation Is Not (Only) Classroom Discourse

> [A] curriculum is like an animated conversation on a topic that can never be fully defined.
>
> —Jerome Bruner (1996, 116)

It is true that one sense in which the curriculum is a complicated conversation is that the school subjects, often introductions to the academic disciplines as they are organized and advanced at the university, are themselves conversations. While highly regulated and bureaucratized, the academic disciplines "represent ... an ongoing debate about significant aspects of human knowledge and experience" (Applebee 1996, 10). While this statement is accurate, Arthur Applebee's formulation is here a bit too voluntarist, too rationalistic, especially given that sectors of the academic disciplines—especially the natural and social sciences—are built in response to foundations' initiatives and public funding, that is, to politics (Kuhn 1962; Shapin 2010). More recent work in the cultural study of science punctures completely the fantasy of self-disinterested and high-minded scholars who are immune to social rewards and influence and only rationally research "significant aspects of human knowledge and experience" (Weaver, Appelbaum, and Morris 2001; see also Gough 1998).

It is true, as Applebee (1996, 10) tells us, "the disciplines exist because thoughtful people care about the traditions of knowing and doing that they represent," but they also exist due to governmental priorities, business interests, and political lobbyists. As a longtime student of autobiography, I cannot quarrel with Applebee's (1996, 11) citing of Michael Polanyi (1958) to remind us that even the most "scientific" ways of knowing are finally "grounded in the tacit knowledge of participants in the dialogue out of which the field is constituted." Michael Oakeshott (1959, 27) makes a different but related point, namely that science too is "a universe of discourse," a discipline of the imagination, distinguished by its process (the scientific method) as much as its product (scientific knowledge). Science too, Oakeshott (1959, 28) insists, is a "conversable voice." That is, science is no sacrosanct discourse apart from everyday human affairs, but, rather, a disciplinary form of participation in those affairs.

For Oakeshott (1959, 10) those affairs—what he terms "the diverse idioms of utterance which make up current human intercourse"—are discussed in what he thinks of as a "meeting-place." He adds: "this meeting-place is not an enquiry or an argument, but a conversation" (1959, 10). Surely Oakeshott overstates his case when, in the sentence quoted earlier, he asserts that conversation is not debate or inquiry—surely it is also both—but his point is a strong one, namely that scholarly discourses, even scientific ones, must be situated in human affairs and discourse, and that the "meeting-place" for this complex cacophony is "conversation."

When we understand curriculum as conversation, it means, as Applebee (1996, 20) is right to observe, that the academic disciplines are "living traditions," although this characterization does not address the problem of their educational significance, the problem for curriculum theory. What does Applebee mean by "living traditions"? He suggests the matter can be "put simply," that such traditions are of "knowledge-in-action." By that he means such traditions are "dynamic" and "changing," learned through "participation" and focused on the "present and future rather than the past" (1996, 20). In contrast, schools too often organize "knowledge-out-of-context," which casts curriculum "in terms of what students should learn about, and in the process they strip knowledge of its most vital contexts" (1996, 20). "Action" evidently refers to "classroom discourse," which plays a "critical mediating role between broader traditions and schooled knowledge" (1996, 35). But classroom discourse is a means to another, usually predetermined, destination, as "the process of schooling must be a process of actually entering into particular traditions of knowing and doing"(1996, 36).

It is this positioning of classroom discourse as mediating between "broader cultural traditions and schooled knowledge" that leads

Applebee to think about curriculum as conversation. "Through such conversations," he writes:

> students will be helped to enter into culturally significant traditions of knowledge-in-action. In most schools, these traditions will reflect the major academic disciplines—language, history, literature, science, the arts—though they can just as easily be interdisciplinary or cross-disciplinary, or be based on the traditions of home, community, or workplace.
>
> (Applebee 1996, 37)

While he allows the possibility of inter- and cross-disciplinary "traditions," in general Applebee seems willing to leave the curriculum as organized after the academic disciplines unquestioned. What's "new"— as he suggests his approach is (1996, 37)—is that kids will talk more in class. Even when he acknowledges that the school subjects are "domains for conversation" (1996, 37), he seems to limit classroom discourse to the school subjects as they mirror the academic disciplines. I want them informed, indeed inspired, by those disciplines, but not limited to a vocationalistic competence in them, although that is without question preferable to curriculum as standardized test preparation.

Neither does Applebee, or so it seems sometimes, as in the notion that education represents an "entry into ongoing cultural conversations about their lives and the world in which they live" (1996, 39), but he quotes Gerald Graff (1992, 77; in Applebee 1996, 39): "In short, reading books with comprehension, making arguments, writing papers, and making comments in a class discussion are social activities. They involve entering into a cultural or disciplinary conversation, a process not unlike initiation into a social club." Doesn't Graff mean "country club"? Such a sentence is not surprising coming from a sophisticated player in an academic discipline at the university level, and for higher education (especially at the graduate level), the notion makes a certain, if self-serving, sense.

But for a public school curriculum, such "entering" amounts to academic vocationalism, a self-interested self-perpetuation of institutionalized, indeed, bureaucratized, conceptions of the school subjects' educational significance as primarily preparing students to become disciplinary specialists in the academic disciplines. It is *not* a conception of curriculum that directs school knowledge to individuals' lived experience, experience understood as subjective *and* social, that is, as gendered, racialized, classed participants in understanding and living through the historical moment. Referring to Graff's conception of the academic disciplines as "social clubs," Applebee confirms my suspicion that his sense of "conversation" is limited to classroom talk: "Curricular conversations are similarly constructed by their participants. The knowledge that evolves is knowledge that is socially negotiated through the process of conversation itself; it is knowledge-in-action" (Applebee 1996, 39–40).

Confined to classroom discourse, curriculum becomes a "domain for conversation" (Applebee 1996, 42), not the conversation itself. These "domains" turn out to resemble the conventional curricular organization of separate school subjects: "domains would represent 'culturally significant' traditions of knowing and doing. ... [A]ny curriculum is a selection that represents what a community believes is worthwhile" (1996, 42). Having reinscribed the conventional curriculum, Applebee (1996, 44) construes "the problem of curriculum planning, then, [as] the problem of establishing a conversational domain and fostering relevant conversations within it. In a general sense, the conversational domains that are most important in American schools begin with the traditions of science, mathematics." Here he reiterates the taken-for-granted positioning of science and mathematics as central, in the 1960s a military, and now an economic, reiteration of 19th-century classical curriculum theory, founded on faculty psychology: The mind is a muscle, and the weightier subjects produce muscles that bulge, minds that are rigorous and disciplined. We glimpsed the gendered politics of 1960s curriculum reform in chapter 4.

Having paid homage to mathematics and science, Applebee (1996, 46) turns to the humanities for an example: "Creating a New Conversational Domain in an Introductory American Literature Course." Here it is again clear that he leaves the conventional curricular structure intact. "Conversation" has now become relegated to teaching and technique, not content. Applebee acknowledges that teachers have little control over what they teach, but rather than complain about this fact—it is devastating to curriculum-as-conversation—he de-emphasizes the educational significance of "content" in general, declaring that "[i]nstitutional constraints on subjects and materials may be less critical than the teacher's decisions about the conversations in which students will be asked to engage" (Applebee 1996, 50). Of course, the two are inextricably interrelated, but his emphasis upon teacher decision making risks elevating "how" over "what" gets taught.

By Applebee's chapter 5, we are working exclusively within a bureaucratic logic, a statement of social engineering, and, predictably, he tells us he can name the "characteristics of effective curricula" (Applebee 1996, 51). He is not speaking of the overall curriculum, but rather "the curriculum of the individual course, which is the level at which curriculum planning and debate usually take place in American middle and high schools" (Applebee 1996, 51). That is true given that the larger curriculum questions have been answered by politicians, bureaucrats, and profiteers. He acknowledges that "at the college level, course content is more likely to be the prerogative of the individual professor, and debates about curriculum structure are cast more broadly, about what courses to teach and what relationships, if any, there should be among them" (Applebee 1996, 51), but he fails to see the educational significance of such professional prerogatives, and how damaging to the project of public education the absence of these prerogatives for public school educators is.

Given the erasure of academic—intellectual—freedom for schoolteachers, it is true that "curriculum planning is usually approached as an exercise in domain specification and task analysis" (Applebee 1996, 51). Rather than focusing on inventories of the structure of the subject matter, Applebee (1996, 52) advises that "we begin with a consideration of the conversations that matter—with traditions and the debates within them that enliven contemporary civilization." He appears on the verge of taking the curriculum question seriously, but quickly—as do too many professors of education today—he retreats from curriculum to teaching: "The question then becomes, how we can orchestrate these conversations so that students can enter into them?" (Applebee 1996, 52). Orchestration means arranging a piece of music for a particular orchestra, an analogy for arranging subject matter for one's students. This very quickly becomes an emphasis on technique (although later he asserts that a "curriculum of conversation is more than just part of a pedagogy in support of knowledge-in-action" [1996, 127]). The point is to change the official curriculum so that students' entry into intellectually engaged conversation is made more likely by making the academic content more compelling.

Applebee (1996, 52) quotes Grice, a philosopher of language, to help him name the features of "an engaging and well-orchestrated curricular conversation." Grice notes that effective conversations are guided by "a common purpose or set of purposes, or at least a mutually accepted direction. This purpose or direction may be fixed from the start (e.g., by an initiation proposal of a question for discussion), or it may evolve during the exchange" (Grice 1975, 45; quoted in Applebee 1996, 52). Applebee is now ready to make his list: "A curriculum that is cooperative and effective in a Gricean sense has four important characteristics. ... [These include] quality, quantity, and relatedness of the topics of the conversations, and the manner in which the conversation is carried forward" (Applebee 1996, 52–53). So curriculum as conversation, for Applebee, is another formula, and one that is too commonsensical to represent an intellectually vibrant experience. If we are determined to list characteristics, I much prefer Bill Doll's (1993, 2002), as they are grounded not in bureaucratization but in curriculum history and theory.

There are issues on which I can agree with Applebee, namely his criticism of the contemporary obsession with testing (1996, 116), his praise of Ted Sizer (1996, 116), his criticism of the melting-pot metaphor and advocacy of a notion of "common culture in which diversity yields rich-ness rather than chaos" (Applebee 1996, 127), and his commitment to conceive classrooms that are more "interesting" (Applebee 1996, 128). But by focusing on classroom conversation on state-mandated school subjects aligned, more or less, with post-elementary and secondary school destinations, whether those be the workplace or the university, Applebee trivializes the concept of conversation and leaves undisturbed the official curriculum.

Until educators—in collaboration with university faculty (and not only in education but in the arts, humanities, and sciences), and in con-versation with parents and students—exercise greater control over what they teach, and until what they teach permits ongoing curricular experi-mentation according to student concerns and faculty interest and exper-tise, school "conversation" will be scripted, disconnected from students' lived experience and from the intellectual lives of the faculty. Under-stood as the education of the public, complicated conversation *is* our professional practice. William Wraga (2002, 17) reiterates a discredited dualism when he asserts: "But curriculum is more than a conversation; curriculum is a realm of action." In the profession of education, con-versation *is* action. Or, as Ted Aoki (2005 [1984], 133) appreciated, in teaching "competence" is "communicative action and reflection."

How do we—school teachers and the education professors who teach them—find ourselves in this strange situation in which we have so little influence over what we teach, when politicians and others feel entitled to insult us by suggesting that schoolteachers have not before had "stan-dards" or that education professors have not worried about "outcomes" or that either concept adequately communicates the complexity of edu-cation? How is it that politicians can speak openly about and pass leg-islation to "end the ed. school monopoly on teacher education"? The present political situation is a complex confluence of many factors and forces, among them (as we saw in chapter 4), the displaced and deferred repudiation of the 1960s. What does the defection of long-time school reformer Diane Ravitch portend? Has she joined the struggle to save the schools too late?

IV Is it Too Late?

> I hope it is not too late.
>
> —Diane Ravitch (2010, 14)

As my phrase makes explicit, school "reform" has been, in fact, school *deform*, converting academic institutions into businesses the "profitabil-ity" of which is determined by scores on standardized examinations.

One of the major participants in this ideological sacrifice of schools has been Diane Ravitch. Given her centrality to school deform, Ravitch's recent conversion from ideologue to critic is noteworthy. While her analysis is curiously ahistorical and avowedly revisionist—she attempts to salvage her earlier involvements in school reform while disavowing the last ten years—it is well worth reading in the original. Here I gloss the main points.

Despite a professed "skepticism' toward "movements" (2010, 2), Ravitch (2010, 3) begins by admitting what any observer of school reform knows all too well, that she had "jumped aboard a bandwagon, one festooned with banners celebrating the power of accountability, incentives, and markets." As assistant secretary of education under U.S. President George Walker Herbert Bush, Ravitch (2010, 7) had promoted "voluntary national standards" for every academic subject, a stance implying the inadequacy of local standards.

Central to her (past) thinking, Ravitch (2010, 8) acknowledges, were "choice, charters, merit pay, and accountability," all of which rationalized shifts in the organization of schools that would force teachers to be judged by their "performance ... a basic principle in the business world." As Martha Nussbaum (2010, 53) has pointed out, such simplistic misrepresentations of "the business world"—never mind the profoundly mistaken assumption of equivalence between business and education—can only deform the academic character of educational institutions. Now, Ravitch (2010, 11) realizes that "corporate reformers betray their weak comprehension of education by drawing false analogies between education and business." Now, Ravitch (2010, 12) understands that "curriculum and instruction [are] far more important than choice and accountability." Curriculum studies scholars have been making this point for decades. School deform could proceed not only by silencing school teachers but by discrediting progressive professors of education as well. In the past Ravitch (2000) participated in both.

Ravitch (2010, 13) wants to emphasize the "essentials of education." Like the public schooling I experienced in suburban Columbus Ohio during the 1950s and early 1960s (before, evidently, schools had standards), today's schools should have, she (2010, 13) asserts, a "strong, coherent, explicit curriculum that is grounded in the liberal arts and sciences." As an effort to undo the effects of school deform, Ravitch's recommendation is welcomed. By its emphasis upon "skills"—the attainment of which can presumably be "measured" by standardized tests—school deform denudes the curriculum, in part by stripping away any efforts at intimacy with university research in the arts, humanities, and sciences. Supplementing the national curriculum she envisions, Ravitch adds, should be "plenty of opportunity for children to engage in activities and projects that make learning lively" (2010, 13). Has the historian overlooked her earlier (see Ravitch 2000, 182) criticism of this idea, advocated over ninety years ago by William Heard Kilpatrick? The final "plank" of Ravitch's revised platform is teacher education, insisting that "our teachers are well educated, not just well trained" (2010, 13). This acknowledgment of the centrality of a liberal arts education is a tacit criticism of school deform's insistence that teachers are to be assessed not by what they know but only by their capacity to improve their students' test scores.

The turning point for Ravitch, she reports, was 1994, when Lynne V. Cheney—wife of George W. Bush's Vice President, Richard Cheney—attacked the secondary-school history standards, charging them with political bias. Recall that conservatives, led by House Speaker Newt Gingrich (still a player in right-wing politics), had just decisively defeated the Democrats in the 1994 mid-term elections. Ravitch (2010, 18) reports that she, too, was "disappointed" with the standards, but she felt sure (unlike Cheney) that "they could be fixed by editing." It is not obvious how such "editing" would not amount to ideological intervention. Questions of intellectual independence and academic integrity—central to the profession of teaching at all levels—do not seem to concern Ravitch.

Indeed, the point for Ravitch about the 1994 national controversy over the U.S. history curriculum is not the egregious violation of academic freedom by right-wing politicians. In her revisionist history, the point about the controversy was, in her (2010, 20) judgment, that it signaled that the standards movement had "died." What she regards as "substitutes" for national standards—state standards—"steered clear of curriculum content" (2010, 20). That governments have a powerful role in curriculum content would seem to contradict conservatives' alleged preference for minimal government. As the case of Canada indicates, however, government-endorsed guidelines are not inevitably threatening to teachers' intellectual independence (see Tomkins 2008 [1986]).

While she does not specify the racial and gendered drivers of school deform, Ravitch (2010, 23) does acknowledge that the 1983 A Nation at Risk was a "response to the radical school reforms of the late 1960s and early 1970s." A Nation at Risk's politically reactionary function—as a "response" to, in fact a repudiation of, 1960s initiatives—quickly fades in Ravitch's narrative as she emphasizes instead declines in SAT scores and cites, remarkably, even anecdotal complaints (2010, 23). In alleging that public schools had lost their way, the rhetoric of A Nation at Risk was—Ravitch (2010, 24) admits—"flamboyant," but she justifies the means by the end, namely, "that's how a report about education gets public attention." That evidently causal admission should disqualify Ravitch as a reliable critic on ethical grounds alone, as she is admitting that the report inflated its assessment—in bald terms that its authors lied—but she defends the distortion on instrumental grounds.

In acknowledging that the assessment of public education in the United States (i.e., that the nation is "at risk") was inaccurate, Ravitch is conceding that the allegations made against America's schools were in fact false. I have never understood why U.S. teachers' representatives—the National Educational Association (NEA) and the American Federation of Teachers (AFT)—did not sue the Commission for libel. They can still—should—sue newspaper reporters who casually reference America's "failing schools," as if such slander did not require empirical evidence, which test scores, in and of themselves, do not provide.

For Ravitch, the importance of A Nation at Risk was what it did not say but implied, namely that schools should relinquish their social obligations and concentrate instead on their academic mission (2010, 25). As curriculum theory makes clear, the two domains are not finally distinguishable. Ravitch adds that the report was insisting that schools "live up to our nation's ideal" (2010, 25). This would seem to be a social obligation, would it not? U.S. progressives have long insisted that education is central to social reconstruction. Now right-wing zealots claim the same, implying that academic underachievement—and its presumed social consequences, among them poverty, crime, and decreased international economic competitiveness—is solely the function of "failing schools." By lying, it is school deform zealots who have placed the nation at risk.

While serving a reactionary political purpose and slandering America's teachers, A Nation at Risk did—as Ravitch (2010, 25) points out—focus on the curriculum. That is laudable. The report was critical of curricular diffusion—the so-called "cafeteria-style" curriculum—and of student choice. (Later "choice" becomes acceptable when limited to parents, now recoded as consumers of educational services.) Micromanaging, A Nation at Risk was also critical of teachers' decreasing assignment of homework. It bemoaned insufficient enrollments in mathematics and sciences, the long-time curricular preferences for school deform fanatics since Sputnik. Martha Nussbaum will comment forcefully on the short-sightedness of this curricular obsession, as we see in the next chapter. Near the end of her book, Ravitch does acknowledge that the other subjects—including art—are indispensable to a "comprehensive liberal arts education" (2010, 226).

According no academic freedom for teachers or curricular choice for students, the Reagan-era Commission proclaimed The Five New Basics. These consisted of four years of English, three years of mathematics, three years of science, three years of social studies, and one-half year of computer science. The college-preparatory curriculum was to include two years of a foreign language; the arts and vocational education were endorsed (Ravitch 2010, 26). "It was right," Ravitch (2010, 27) asserts, "to point to the curriculum as the heart of the matter, the definition of what students are expected to learn." While the curriculum is indeed the heart of the matter, it hardly coincides with "the definition of what students are expected to learn." Ravitch deflects concerns for the intellectual quality of the curriculum by accenting expectations for student learning, a preoccupation that plays into the hands of performance-based evaluation schemers.

Curiously (given that she is a historian), Ravitch fails to situate *A Nation at Risk* in historical context. It appeared during the early Reagan years, an administration committed to dismantling liberal social welfare reforms from the New Deal era of Franklin Roosevelt on. By emphasizing the "five new basics," Commission members were discrediting claims for curricular relevance, including the incorporation of marginalized subjects, for example, academic knowledge associated with Women's Studies, African American Studies, and other "area" studies. Ignoring history, Ravitch denies the report's political subtext and its powerful role in the further destruction (including through privatization) of the U.S. school system (see 2010, 28). Instead Ravitch (2010, 104) links the "demolition" of public education in the United States only to *No Child Left Behind*, of which she admits she was "initially supportive" (2010, 15). She succinctly summarizes NCLB as "measure" and "punish" (2010, 93). To her credit Ravitch is clear that the academic curriculum disappears in NCLB, that the Bush-era legislation was a:

> technocratic approach to school reform that measured "success" only in relation to standardized test scores in two skill-based subjects, with the expectation that this limited training would strengthen our nation's economic competitiveness with other nations. This was misguided. ... It produced mountains of data, not educated citizens. It ignored the importance of knowledge ... [I]n the age of NCLB, knowledge was irrelevant.
>
> (Ravitch 2010, 29)

Knowledge remains irrelevant, replaced by "skills" measured by test scores. But determined to separate "standards" from "accountability," Ravitch asserts that, in NCLB, school reform had been "hijacked" (2010, 30).

This is revisionist history, as the continuities between *A Nation at Risk* and NCLB are pronounced. Each displaced federal government policy failures onto the public schools, and specifically onto teachers (2010, 110). Each positioned schools symbolically as the site wherein the future of the nation unfolds, flattering but false. Just as scientific and military failure was ignored in the aftermath of the 1957 Sputnik incident, the economic ineptitude of right-wing politicians—cutting taxes for the wealthy would, they assured, "trickle down" to the rest of us—

was ignored in both 1983 and 2010. Despite her ahistorical analysis, Ravitch's appreciation of the centrality of curriculum and its displacement through a regime of standardized testing is important. The test-driven curriculum *is* dysfunctional, as Ravitch now appreciates:

> Its [NCLB] remedies did not work. Its sanctions were ineffective. It did not bring about high standards or high accomplishment. The gains in test scores at the state level were typically the result of teaching students test-taking skills and strategies, rather than broadening and deepening their knowledge of the world to understand what they have learned.
>
> (Ravitch 2010, 110)

Exactly. The obsession with "skills" guarantees misunderstanding of the world, as their emphasis denudes cognitive functioning of its worldliness, a fact test-makers are now evidently hustling to correct (Dillon 2010, September 3, A11).

In her review of Davis Guggenheim's "propagandistic" *Waiting for "Superman,"* Ravitch (2010, November 11, 22) reminds readers of the facts that movie ignores. Fewer than 17 percent of charter schools succeed in raising student test scores, she points out, and many fail to raise scores at all. Guggenheim repeats the demonizing falsehood that it is teachers who are responsible for student failure. Research shows that less than 10 percent of student test score gains are attributable to teachers' efforts; some 60 percent of achievement is associated with non-school factors, such as family income. The movie also ignores the fact that charter schools' internal budgets can make public school budgets seem tiny. Geoffrey Canada's Harlem Children's Zone has assets of over $200 million, Ravitch (2010, November 11, 24) notes, and the SEED charter boarding school in Washington, D.C. spends $35,000 per pupil, more than three times the typical expenditure for public school students. Guggenheim praises these generously financed schools while insisting that *public* schools need no more money. "Bizarre," Ravitch (2010, November 11, 24) muses. A different sense of "bizarre" also describes the defection of Diane Ravitch. It is not "bizarre" in the sense of dissociation from the facts or as another (indirect) word for lying. Ravitch's realization that school reform is school *deform* is "bizarre" in the sense of astonishing. Never mind her revisionism: the hour is late. With Diane Ravitch joining the struggle, perhaps it is not too late after all?

Part V

The Synthetical Moment
Reactivating the Past,
Understanding the Present,
Finding the Future

Chapter 8

Subjective and Social Reconstruction

I A Struggle within Each Person

> [T]he political struggle for freedom and equality must first of all be a struggle within each person.
> —Martha C. Nussbaum (2010, 29)

This significant insight Martha Nussbaum (2010, 2) associates with Mahatma Gandhi. It is also an insight long embraced in curriculum theory. Working subjectively—from within—toward a free and democratic nation, as Gandhi understood, is never only formalistically political. It is simultaneously psychological and spiritual. Avarice and narcissism undermine democracy as they deform the public sphere to an extension of private preoccupations. This deformation of the public sphere takes not only social but gendered forms, as Nussbaum (see 2010, 39) appreciates. Nor is it limited to the U.S., as Nussbaum spends considerable time commenting on the situation in India (see 2010, 1, 6, 19, 29). As we have seen, U.S. school deform is decidedly gendered and racialized. As social and political processes, gender and race are by definition de-individuating, always informed by stereotypes, and reproduced by ritual. They are pervasive phenomena that invite subjective and social reconstruction.

Those who accept gender and race as always determinative, whether due to genetics or ordained by God, that is, those who do not appreciate their historical and cultural variability as well as their metamorphoses into apparently unrelated realms (such as militarism, nationalism, and school deform) forfeit opportunities for self-reflection and social understanding. As Nussbaum (2010, 50) notes: "Another problem with people who fail to examine themselves is that they often prove all too easily influenced." An uncritical culture of acceptance can characterize U.S. business, itself gendered and racialized. The anti-democratic character of corporate culture becomes yet another and definitive statement of its non-equivalence with education. The point of being in the world is not to exploit its resources and peoples for profit.

Thoughtful business educators, Nussbaum (2010, 53) reports, trace several spectacular business disasters—including Enron and WorldCom (see Pinar 2004, 164)—to a corporate culture of "yes-people, where authority and peer pressure preclude criticism, including self-criticism." The financial crisis of 2008 and British Petroleum's (BP) 2010 oil spill in the Gulf of Mexico must be added to these. In the former, tens of thousands of businesses engaged in Ponzi-like schemes that could only lead to catastrophe, misrepresenting what was at stake all along the way (Morgenson 2010, B1, B2). In the latter, a history of risk-taking for the sake of maximizing profit cost not only incalculable ecological damage but human lives as well. Yet consistently politicians hold up business as a model for education!

What is valuable in business could be accented by academic study. For instance, innovation—often reduced to a self-promoting concept of "entrepreneur" that obscures the supportive roles of government and collegial collaboration—is considered central to success in American business. Innovation's roots in liberal arts education—in the cultivation of the imagination and intellectual independence (Nussbaum 2010, 53)—are rarely acknowledged by self-aggrandizing entrepeneurs who often claim all the credit for themselves. Subservience to authority and the power of peer pressure—not limited to business but too often promulgated there—undermine innovation. A specialist in ancient Greek philosophy, Nussbaum (2010, 51) reminds us that "what Socrates brought to Athens was an example of truly democratic vulnerability and humility. Class, fame, and prestige count for nothing, and the argument counts for all." She (2010, 51) adds: "Nor does the peer group count," a problem also in the education research community where almost a cult of "collaboration" rules the roost, threatening to reduce academic specializations to social clubs.

Fidelity to the argument is not self-aggrandizement but, Nussbaum (2010, 54) argues, a "social practice ... important in any democracy." While self-disinterested—in the sense of scrupulously declining to conform the argument to advance one's self-interest—such (for Nussbaum it is Socratic) thinking cultivates individuality, as it invites self-reflection, self-critique, and creative articulation of what one experiences. These are among the dynamics of subjective reconstruction. Like Ted Sizer, Nussbaum (2010, 55) cites class size as one organizational prerequisite to self-expression through dialogical encounter. Recall that Sizer insisted that no teacher work with more than seventy students. Politicians howl when educators make this obvious point, insisting disingenuously that public education is already overfunded. When their own pet projects are "earmarked," however, budgets are increased dramatically and class size is held minimal (Urbina 2010). The sheer hypocrisy of many school deform zealots is matched only by their ignorance and aggression.

The self-reflection and dialogical encounter that characterize curriculum as complicated conversation become meaningful only when threaded through academic knowledge, as Nussbaum's impressive erudition itself demonstrates. A cosmopolitan curriculum—what Nussbaum (2010, 89) associates with "world citizenship"—takes specific curriculum forms. While I argue it is imperative to allow individual teachers to answer the classic curriculum question *what knowledge is of most worth?*—animated by the historical moment, their own intellectual passions, and the particular, irreplaceable individuals they teach—Nussbaum (like Ravitch) specifies curriculum content in advance. But who could argue with Nussbaum's assertion of world history as central in understanding? Nussbaum (2010, 89) emphasizes social, economic, and political history, while I would emphasize intellectual history, but this is no serious disagreement. She adds to these key subjects "a rich and non-stereotyped understanding of the major world religions" (2010, 89), another obviously central subject, but not one I would require for every student. In addition to the breadth—what used to be called in curriculum terminology "scope"—of world history, Nussbaum (2010, 89) recommends specialization, that is, studying topics in "more depth" and, additionally, "at least one unfamiliar tradition," sensible recommendations I endorse but again would not require for every student. I do share Nussbaum's enthusiasm (2010, 91) for multicultural understanding, although what that aspiration means differs according to national history, culture, and politics. Acknowledging autobiographical referents for her current curricular preferences, Nussbaum (2010, 89) recalls appreciatively opportunities to study (during her fifth and sixth grades) Uruguay and Austria, each in depth.

Like Maxine Greene (1995), although emphasizing (through the choice of gerunds) the agency of teaching, Nussbaum (2010, 95) endorses "cultivating imagination." (Greene employs "releasing," a term that implies intra-subjective intervention.) Kieran Egan (1992) also privileges the imagination, a faculty for which I have both respect and fear, given its historic roles in racism and sexism. Implying the primacy of ethics (as do Greene and Egan), Nussbaum (2010, 95) emphasizes the role of narrative in imagination, the cultivation of which requires empathy. Relying on Saidiya Hartman, I have questioned empathy across racial difference, as it has so often dissolved into projective misidentification. It takes the intellectual and psychological discipline of academic study or, in Nussbaum's formulation, serious "play" (2010, 97), to begin to cultivate empathy. As curriculum theorists have long known (see Macdonald 1995, 55), to cultivate such disciplined "play," the arts and humanities are prerequisite (Nussbaum 2010, 96),

As I acknowledged in the First Edition (Pinar 2004, 58), psychoanalytic theory enables us to theorize the subjective reconstruction the cultivation of empathy implies. (So do German conceptions of *Bildung*, if hampered by that concept's historic predilection toward fusion with the *Volk* and the authoritarian state, as we saw in chapter 3.) Like Deborah Britzman, Peter Taubman, and Madeleine Grumet, Nussbaum (2010, 97) too invokes psychoanalytic theory, specifically that of Donald Winnicott (1896–1971), the British pediatrician and psychoanalyst. The notion of "transitional object"—also referenced in the First Edition (2004, 248) and retained here (later in this chapter)—helps us understand how "play" permits us to express, through intellectual "objects," our inner experience into relational and specifically public terms. When ideas, informed by academic knowledge and lived experience, become "transitional objects" they accord meaning, both private and, when explained, public meaning. Ideas as transitional objects become conduits of self-expression and social communication while retaining their utter alterity as separate and distinct, grounded in disciplinary knowledge, as illustrated (for instance) by the concepts I cited from the scholarship on the Weimar Republic. In allegories-of-the-present, such ideas can be studied on their own terms *and* for their significance for us alive today.

The central curriculum question—*what knowledge is of most worth?*—invokes in its answering subjectivity, society, and the historical moment, as it directs us to ideas and knowledge (such as the Cold War) that encourage us to articulate what is at stake not only for us as teachers and students, but as persons struggling to understand what we experience. Through intellectual play—like jazz (see Aoki 2005 [1990], 367), a deeply disciplined and creative undertaking—we can thread our lived experience through what we study, and vice versa. Such self-exploratory and self-expressive play becomes the communication of what Pasolini termed free indirect subjectivity. To the extent it restructures the provinciality of locality (or of nationality, as Pasolini's preference for the Fruilian dialect testifies), such play provides opportunities for the worldliness a cosmopolitan education invites.

The example of transitional object that Nussbaum (2010, 98) provides—Linus' security blanket in Charles Schultz's *Peanuts*—is too simple and even misleading, as it obscures the communicative potential of transitional objects by emphasizing their self-referential function. Yes, transitional objects are "dear" to us and represent intimate extensions of inner psychic life. But they are also objects in themselves (distinct from our engagement with them) as well as efforts to communicate with others. Moreover, their self-expressive function doubles back on the self, reconstructing subjectivity, as such self-expression reconfigures inner life through public dialogue (and vice versa). This subjective engagement in social discourse requires us to remain intellectually open, as Nussbaum (2010, 100) knows, "further develop[ing] the capacity to endow the forms of others, in imagination, with inner life."

Nussbaum seems less interested in the role of free indirect subjectivity in social reconstruction (although it is explicit in the epigraph opening this section) than she is in making a curricular point. Invoking Winnicott again, Nussbaum (2010, 101) reminds—as it is imperative to do, given school deform's demands for the sciences and mathematics (as Barack Oabama uncritically reasserts: Chang 2009, 1)—that "key" in the cultivation of intellectually and emotionally rich play are the arts. For Winnicott, Nussbaum (2010, 101) reminds, the:

> primary function of art in all human cultures is to preserve and enhance the cultivation of the "play space," and he saw the role of the arts in human life as, above all, that of nourishing and extending the capacity for empathy. In the sophisticated response to a complex work of art, he saw a continuation of the baby's delight in games and role-playing.

Informed by existentialism rather than by psychoanalysis, Maxine Greene (2001) has emphasized this point. In talks to teachers made over two decades at the Lincoln Center in New York as well as in several important books composed while a distinguished professor at Teachers College, Columbia University, Greene articulated the social significance of aesthetic education. Nussbaum's work would have been strengthened by studying Greene's, even if the scholarly expertise of the two philosophers (ancient Greek philosophy in Nussbaum's case, existential phenomenology in Greene's) is at odds with each other.

For Nussbaum, the visual arts are necessarily primary in the education of sensibility; she also acknowledges the primacy of poetry, as has, for instance, Pier Paolo Pasolini, whose emphasis on montage—as social homology—promises much for curriculum design (as I hope this book suggests). Nussbaum provides instead important historical examples, among them the 19th-century American Bronson Alcott, whose Socratic pedagogy at the Temple School she describes in her chapter 4 (2010, 62). Nussbaum also references the legendary 20th-century Indian poet, playwright, short-story writer, and painter Rabindranath Tagore, winner of the Nobel Prize for Literature in 1913. Also an educator, Tagore met and corresponded with Maria Montessori and may have influenced John Dewey (see 2010, 69). For Tagore, Nussbaum (2010, 104) reports, the arts "promote both inner cultivation and responsiveness to others." As I trust is clear by now, such "inner cultivation" and "responsiveness to others" structure curriculum as complicated conversation. As Nussbaum would no doubt agree, Ravitch (2010, 226) now appreciates:

> Without a comprehensive liberal arts education, our students will not be prepared for the responsibilities of citizenships in a democracy,

nor will they be equipped to make decisions based on knowledge, thoughtful debate, and reason.

Within the broad and variegated academic field of education, only curriculum theory embraces this insight. Other specializations obsess over "what works," micromanaging learning and teaching and administration, often uncritical collaborators with politicians' deform *du jour*. School deform proceeds only in ignorance of the compelling scholarship not only of Nussbaum, but of curriculum theorists as well. Given our systematic silencing by politicians determined to destroy what was once a public school system that was the envy of the world, the critique of Martha Nussbaum—one of the great public intellectuals of our day—is required reading for us all.

II Reactivating the Past

[E]very subject finds herself obligated to search for the future in the past.

—Kaja Silverman (2000, 49)

Not only the field of education is reluctant to abandon social engineering. Contemporary scholars and intellectuals generally, James Carey (1992, 137), points out, have "themselves internalized the technical psychosis," thereby contributing to the "cults of engineering, mobility, and fashion at the expense of roots, tradition, and political organization" (1992, 138). The accelerating disintegration of American civic culture can be countered only by "deliberately reducing the influence of modern technics and by cultivating the realms of art, ethics, and politics" (1992, 138), as Martha Nussbaum knows. School deform emphasizes only the technical, and not just through the privileging of mathematics, science, and computers in the curriculum, but by de-emphasizing, when not outright closing, arts programs. In pedagogy, deformed by the New York State Commissioner of Education to tennis serves (see chapter 1), the obsession with finding "what works" intensifies. If only we can find the right technique, the right modification of classroom organization (small groups, collaborative learning, dialogue) or teach in the right way (not teach at all but, rather, "facilitate learning"), if only we have students self-reflect or if only we install "standards" or, simply, focus on "excellence," then students will learn what we teach them.

Tying the public school curriculum to test scores and, then, requiring teachers to do whatever is necessary to raise students' test scores: this political manipulation performs for the right wing the institutionalization of cultural authoritarianism in the name of "accountability" while duping gullible liberals that all is being done on behalf of "underserved" populations. In this sphere of "displaced and deferred action," the right wing forces teachers to do their political "dirty work," deflecting public attention from their own policy failures. And it does so by the compulsive repetition of commonsense categories such as "accountability." As Michael Moriarty (1991, 36) has noted (if in a different context): "Coercion is camouflaged as the statement of the obvious."

Social engineering had its genesis, in part, in American pragmatism, in William James' construal of the significance of thought as its "effects" on situations (see Simpson 2002, 98–99). After psychoanalysis, it is clear that accompanying, indeed informing, the attunement of thought to reality (which cannot be limited to thought's "effect" on "practical" situations) is an ongoing effort at understanding. "Understanding" reconstructs how we discern a situation, and both we and the situation—because they are organically connected—are reconstructed.

The American preoccupations with business and religion tend to be anti-intellectual, as Richard Hofstadter has documented. The "business-minded" are determined to design "effects" on situations that can be predicted and made profitable. In this sense, social engineering is the complement of capitalism. The "religiously minded" mangle the present by disavowing it ("the best is yet to come") or by employing religious rituals (such as prayer) to try to manipulate present circumstances. In this sense, Protestantism and capitalism are intertwined, as Weber knew.

The promise of social engineering—of "what works"—rings repeatedly in the politics of education as well as in much research and teaching in the broad field of education, including teacher education, now focused especially on "learning technologies" such as the computer. The hypertextuality of the Internet contributes to the insubstantial and "fantastic" character of the public sphere. Like those "fantastic mass-produced images that shape our perceptions of the world"—the contemporary version of Kracauer's "mass ornament"—hypertext may "not only encourage a defensive contraction of the self but blur the boundaries between the self and its surroundings" (Lasch 1984, 19). Narcissism and presentism intensify each other.

The future we face in cyberspace may exacerbate the cultural crisis—subjective disintegration in service of authoritarianism, enforced by instrumentalism—that not only imperils the project of public education but threatens the very sustainability of the planet. Technological progress substitutes for social progress (see Lasch 1984, 42). Moreover, "technology undermines the self-reliance and autonomy of both workers and consumers" (Lasch 1984, 43), not to mention of teachers and students. While the curriculum as "complicated conversation" can occur in cyberspace, through computer technologies, the dissolution of subjectivity in cyberculture can just as easily diminish as make more thoughtful such dialogical encounter. The mutability, immateriality and anonymity of cyberspace mirror a public sphere reduced to a shopping mall where "niche shopping" means "niche sociability," where the only meaning of "citizen" is as "consumer." Without a (especially natural) world in which we are grounded existentially and to which we are committed politically, we dissolve as individuals and disappear as citizens. As Lasch (1984, 32–33) understood:

> [T]he collapse of our common life has impoverished private life as well. It has freed the imagination from external constraints but exposed it more directly than before to the tyranny of inner compulsions and anxieties. Fantasy ceases to be liberating when it frees itself from the check imposed by practical experience of the world. Instead it gives rise to hallucinations.

"Complicated conversation" is not a series of solipsistic soliloquies, cryptic (too often not proofread) monosyllabic email messages, although it can occur in cyberspace and can be furthered by judicious and thoughtful use of "intellectual technologies," as, for instance, John Willinsky's (2006) public knowledge project demonstrates. But engaging in complicated conversation is complicated; it makes no promises about raising test scores. As Deborah Britzman, Peter Taubman, and Alice Pitt have demonstrated, communication is riddled with intrapsychic and intersubjective crosscurrents and social contradictions; it is an aspiration, not an empirical fact. It cannot be measured.

While undistorted and unconstrained speech may not be possible, communication through understanding is. As Carey (1992, 25) realized: "reality is brought into existence, is produced, by communication—by, in short, the construction, apprehension, and utilization of symbolic forms." The reconstruction of reality is, in short, intellectual labor. It is not solving cognitive puzzles, guessing items on multiple-choice tests. It occurs in solitude and with others. We cannot know what intellectual labor will bring; like the future, serious and creative thought is often enigmatic, sometimes contradictory, even incalculable. While curriculum as complicated conversation in the service of social and self-reflective understanding *will* transform the present, it will not do so in predictable ways, certainly not according to politicians' self-interested and ideology-laden agendas. As Martha Grace Duncan (1996, 187) has observed: "[I] believe, as Socrates did, that there is no voluntary evil, only ignorance. It follows that understanding automatically leads to change; more exactly, understanding, in itself, *is* change." Without understanding, there is only spectacle, fascism in our time.

Curriculum theory and the complicated conversation it supports seek the truth of the present, not its manipulation for profiteering. Profiteering may prove to be an important curricular topic, but it becomes so in the name of understanding and critique, not entrepreneurship. Intellectual agency is preferable to entrepeneurship. Erudition, a discipline-informed interdisciplinarity, intellectuality, self-reflexivity: curriculum as complicated conversation invites students to encounter themselves and the world they inhabit (and that inhabits them) through academic study, through academic knowledge, popular culture, all threaded through their own lived experience. One powerful historical example—glimpsed in the First Edition (Pinar 2004, 46)—is how African American autobiographical practices constituted "a *public* rather than a *private* gesture, [in which] *me-ism* gives way to *our-ism* and superficial concerns about *individual subject* usually give way to the *collective subjection* of the group" (Cudjoe 1984, 9; quoted in Fox-Genovese 1988, 70). Subjective and social reconstruction were, in African American autobiography, co-extensive and reciprocally related.

With the inauguration of national curriculum reform during the early 1960s, what remained of the progressive dream—education for democratization, that is, schooling for psychosocial as well as intellectual development—was past. We whose interest was the *educational* significance of the curriculum awoke in the aftermath of the 1960s national curriculum reform movement to find that we were "invited" to be, in a word, bureaucrats. Our job was not to study the complex relations among schooling, society, and subjectivity, but, rather, to accept the vocationalistic conflations of school curriculum with the academic disciplines (one must learn to think like a mathematician) and the marketplace (job skills future employers require) to ensure that students "learn" what others—politicians, policymakers, profiteers—declared to be worth learning. Vocationalism, academic and economic, ruled the day. As Joseph Schwab (1978, 302, 303) acknowledged:

> Of the five substantial high school science curriculums [making up 1960s national curriculum reform], four of them—PSSC, BSCS, CHEMS, and CBA— were instituted and managed by subject matter specialists; the contribution of educators was small and that of curriculum specialists near the vanishing point. ... Educators contribute expertise only in the area of test construction and evaluation, with a contribution here and there by a psychologist.

Even Project English and other humanities curriculum projects of the period were conducted under the direction of subject-matter academicians (see Clifford and Guthrie 1988, 176).

Directed by disciplinary specialists, the 1960s national curriculum reform movement was animated, as Jerome Bruner (1977 [1960], 1) acknowledges, by "what is almost certain to be a long-range crisis in national security, a crisis whose resolution will depend upon a well-educated citizenry." Why this "resolution" did not depend also—primarily—upon the savvy of politicians and military personnel already in place is now, I trust, clear to you. After their failures, marked by the Soviet launching of the Sputnik satellite, politicians searched for a scapegoat, what their precedessors in post-World War I Germany vividly called "the stab in the back." As Bruner (1997 [1960], 1) observed: "One of the places in which this renewal of concern [for national security] has expressed itself is in curriculum planning for the elementary and secondary schools." In fact the crisis in national security was *displaced* into curriculum planning, in effect, the stipulation and control of what is taught and learned in school. Scientific and military failure was relocated as the failure of public education in America.

The preparation of thoughtful and informed teachers cannot occur in such convoluted circumstances. Nor will it occur if stipulated as a form of social engineering, figuring out how to get students to score higher on standardized tests. The professional preparation of teachers *is* the project of academic understanding. It must be kept free of the authoritarian regimen of the school-as-business, disfigured today as cram school. The professional preparation of teachers requires understanding curriculum as interdisciplinary, threaded through self-formation and attuned to the historical moment. In the professional preparation of teachers, then, converge multiple projects of intellectual understanding, including understanding the essential *antagonism* between "business thinking" and the process of education.

Just as graduate study in business schools cannot guarantee wealth or medical training ensure public health, professional teacher education cannot guarantee success, certainly not when success is as misconstrued as student performance on standardized examinations. Just as well-trained physicians cannot save every patient or shrewd attorneys win every case, even a well-prepared—knowledgeable, intellectually engaging and socially committed—teacher may not perform well in certain settings, with certain students, at certain schools. As any teacher (and parent) knows, much depends on the situation, including the character of the children (which changes dramatically over time) and the (also changing) circumstances in which they live and study. Despite teachers' and parents' best efforts, children do not always—even when we force them—do what we know is best for them. While influenced in important ways by teaching, student learning is fundamentally a function of study. Teachers offer opportunities, but they—like parents, physicians, attorneys, economists, and preachers—cannot guarantee success. Only the teaching profession gets singled out for "accountability." It is an empty, pernicious, *stupid* slogan, a covert gendered and racialized demand that disables teachers from the thoughtful performance of their profession.

Try as they may, teachers will not "reach" all students, especially students who do not study (or who cannot study, due, for instance, to conditions at home), who decline to listen and participate (or, due to their psychological or physiological states, cannot listen and participate) in class. Intelligence plays no small part, of course, although the exact ratio of "nature" to "nurture" remains unresolved. We cannot change genetics, but teachers can conduct ourselves as if "nurture" were the primary determinant in educational accomplishment. Teachers are responsible for being well-informed, socially engaged, and self-aware, for being pedagogically spirited and adaptable and ethically committed, for making every effort to engage students intellectually and psychosocially. *But it is sheer nonsense to assert that teachers are accountable for students' learning.* Even students (and, secondarily, their parents and caregivers) are not solely responsible for their educational accomplishment.

Traditionally, when curriculum had been conceived as a conversation, the concept connoted "conversing" with those great, usually white male minds of Western civilization whose ideas presumably transcended the temporal and cultural locales of their origin. That patriarchal and Eurocentric concept is no longer in fashion, and for good reason. European high culture is no longer the center of American or Western civilization, especially as that is codified and theorized in academic scholarship and inquiry. But the political decentering of European knowledges and knowing hardly means that curriculum is no longer students' and teachers' conversations with ideas, including European ones, as these are recorded in primary source material, textbooks, and other curricular artifacts and technologies.

Curriculum remains pre-eminently that conversation, but it is also a conversation among the participants, one which supports and explores the possibilities of unpredicted and novel events, unplanned destinations, conversation which incorporates life history and politics and popular culture as well as official, institutional, academic knowledge. While hardly turning away from the problems of the everyday classroom and the practical pedagogue, to understand curriculum today requires acknowledging the limits of teaching. Curriculum conceived as a "complicated conversation" cannot be framed as another technique that will somehow get the American educational engine humming smoothly again. Education is, of course, no mechanical affair, and yet, astonishingly, politicians still proceed on the false assumption that if we only make the appropriate adjustments—in the curriculum, teaching, learning, administration, counseling, the establishment of "standards"—then those test scores will soar. It is a mad, mostly male, fantasy.

The school curriculum (especially the secondary school curriculum) is a political settlement of what Herbert Kliebard (1986) has characterized as the struggle for the American curriculum. As we saw in chapter 4, we educators lost that struggle; politicians and businessmen (often intersecting categories) won. The children lost. With its emphasis on the bottom line, the school is now a business, no longer a factory perhaps, now not even a corporation (Fiske 1991), but definitely a cram school. "Freedom schools" are history; we are living in Weimar times. What could happen next should make us shudder.

What we have today—still, unbelievably—is 19th-century faculty psychology, contemporary versions of that presumably long-ago discredited idea that the mind is a muscle which must be exercised by all the basic weights (once the academic disciplines, now "cognitive skills") if it is to bulge. Once bulging, clearly visible by high test scores, America will remain rich and powerful. Poverty and crime will disappear and the G.N.P. will seek the sky. This is a masculinized fantasy which conflates "mind" with "muscles" and test scores with national supremacy and economic productivity. Despite this stacked deck, the overwhelming odds, the great gamble—the American dream of democratization and self-realization, inextricably intertwined as each depends upon and extends the other—must again be waged by those of us committed to the project of public education. Those children in our classrooms compel us to continue to converse, privately and in public, inspired by those who have gone before us, committed to those who are yet to come.

III Understanding the Present

> We have educational establishments without consequences, working frantically to hand on an education that leads nowhere and has come from nothing.
> —Bertolt Brecht ([1932], in Kaes, Jay, and Dimendberg 1995, 616)

Not only is the school the place where parents send their children when they send them away from home, it is where, politicians proclaim, the fate of the nation is formed, as they ascribe to schools salvational expectations—the elimination of poverty for instance—not even the church, presumably with God on its side, has managed to fulfill. Add to these exorbitant expectations the memory of schools as the primary sites of the social revolutions of the 1950s and 1960s, accented by the Supreme Court-mandated end to racial segregation in schools and students' (especially university students') participation in civil rights struggles and anti-Vietnam War protests. For a decade American society seemed to be unraveling. In 1957 the Russians launched the satellite Sputnik, shocking Americans into the realization that the U.S. had fallen behind the Soviet Union in the "space race." Neither the Eisenhower administration nor American scientists were blamed for this setback. In a stunning sleight of hand that would be repeated again and again during the decades to come, *schools* were blamed. Through school *reform* American national—in the 1950s military, in the 1980s and afterward economic—superiority would be restored. Through *school reform* the "excesses" of democracy—epitomized in conservatives' minds by millions of protesting students—could be contained and redirected. Emphasizing science and mathematics (and, later, technology) would institutionalize military, scientific, and economic priorities. It would also institutionalize historical amnesia. Aligning the school curriculum with standardized tests replaces academic knowledge with so-called cognitive skills. "The fundamental issue goes unnoticed," Christopher Lasch (1995, 177) reminds, "the abandonment of the historic mission of American education, the democratization of liberal culture."

In converting public schools to cram schools, school *reform* is, as you now realize, school *deform*. It accomplishes the destruction of these historic and quintessentially American institutions dedicated to the education of the public. Teaching to the test stops the democratization of culture that can only be enacted through complicated conversation informed by academic knowledge. No longer educating "individual speakers fully in control of their reactions and respected as individuals," school deform reduces "citizens to abstractions, whose reactions are measured statistically" (Chun 2006, 167). Why have students been replaced with test scores? Why have the public schools—established to prepare the young for life in a social democracy—been destroyed?

Because schools were associated with scientific failure (in the 1950s), social upheaval (in the 1960s) then (in the late 1970s and early 1980s) with economic failure, and because they substitute for the authority over the young that parents fear they have lost, schools are symbolic sites associated with a series of traumatizing historical events. As symbolic sites, schools became scapegoated as the alleged cause for scientific and economic setbacks and ongoing cultural and economic crises. Moreover, the school became the one site where all of these trauma could presumably be *corrected*. Like no other public institution, the school has been singled out as an Archimedean lever for economic growth, social justice, and national superiority. Like no other educational institution, the public school curriculum has been—continues to be—subject to political manipulation (McKinley 2010, March 10).

This bizarre state of affairs becomes intelligible when we reflect on the dynamics of traumatic experience, which is what the "60s" were for many (and not only conservative) Americans. Studies of traumatized individuals, Cathy Caruth (1996, 63) reports, reveal "nothing other than the determined repetition of the event of destruction." From concentration camp survivors to shell-shocked veterans of the Vietnam War, the traumatized suffer a high suicide rate. Significantly, survivors kill themselves only after they have reached safety (1996, 63). Is not this same series of events—trauma followed by self-destruction—discernible in the deform of America's public schools? During the Cold War (not limited to the 1950s, but especially intense during that decade, culminating in the threat of total annihilation in the Cuban Missile Crisis), during the 1960s (protests and street violence threatening social dissolution), during the late 1970s and early 1980s (economic crises accented by the oil embargo and ballooning federal budget deficits), and during the decade just past (terrorism and the economic crisis), America has undergone a series of trauma. Rather than "working through" each of these crises, including through the school curriculum—by studying each, situating these events historically and understanding them—politicians have relocated (as if in an effort to confine) to schools the anxiety associated with these trauma. Defensively, in "over-determined" fashion, politicians demand that the school curriculum be bleached of controversy, "return" to the "basics," ensure student learning. In short, schools are to set things right.

As you might imagine, accompanying each of these traumatic events was an acute sense of being tested. Now that the Cold War was been won, now that racial politics have shifted (from the street violence of the 1960s to violent rhetoric on right-wing radio talk shows), now that even the latest round of irrational and senseless wars (Iraq and Afghanistan) are (presumably) ending, now that economic recovery (however fragile) seems under way, the subjective sense of the nation being tested remains, apparently unabated. Now, however, the threat is not only military (protecting American lives from terrorists) or economic (deficits, structural unemployment, China's economic ascendancy); the threat is, as it was during the 1950s, domestic, a "stab in the back." The threat still gets projected onto the nation's teachers, aided and abetted by the nation's education professors. The nation's anxiety over trauma past and present is projected onto our children and those charged with educating them. Because the nation is felt to be at risk, no child must be left behind in the "race" to the "top."

Because the stakes are so high—the fate of the nation is at hand— "we-the-people" must, politicians proclaim, ensure student success. Because teachers are responsible for student failure, only forceful, extensive, and detailed regulation of teachers' daily conduct can correct our course. Indeed, there must be consequences for school failure, as politicians pretend there are in business. Indeed, schools should *become* businesses: test scores are the same as profits; test scores, not erudition or understanding, are the bottom line. Tests are the *only* measure of success or failure. No profit, no business: schools should close, teachers should be fired. Never mind that not all businesses close when profits plummet, as the 2008 financial bailouts made crystal clear. Nor are all employees fired. In fact, many receive bonuses, funded by public monies. Never mind that educational "outcomes"—that reductionistic distortion of the concept of "consequences"—cannot be quantified. Never mind that the consequences of academic study are rarely short term, and cannot be traced through quantified cause–effect chains. And recall that it is *only* schools that have been subjected to such simplistic and sadistic scrutiny.

Let's dwell on that last point. Do politicians speak, for instance, of closing law firms if their rates of successful case outcomes do not improve each year? Do politicians initiate investigations of law schools, demanding statistical demonstrations of the effectiveness of law-school classes on the numbers of cases their students, now attorneys, win? How often do politicians pontificate about the tens of thousands of patients who die each year in U.S. hospitals due to medical mistakes? Do politicians express outrage over "failing hospitals"? Was there a commission formed during the Reagan administration (as there was concerning education, alleging that schools had placed *A Nation at Risk*) upon discovering that almost *half* of the drugs approved by the Food and Drug Administration (FDA) during 1976–1985 had caused "serious post-approval adverse reactions, including permanent disabilities and deaths" (LaCapra 2009, 160)? Does the continued existence of "sin" stimulate politicians' cries concerning "failing churches"?

School deform is not only abusive to children and unjust to teachers, it is disastrous for democracy. While John Dewey's idea of the classroom as the laboratory for democracy was always aspirational, the idea nonetheless acknowledges that what children learn there is not entirely irrelevant to the social lives they live later. This idea surfaced again in *Brown v. Board of Education*, Jonathan Zimmerman points out, wherein the Supreme Court ruled that compulsory school attendance laws and public expenditures for public education demonstrate the nation's "recognition of the importance of education to our democratic society" (quoted in Zimmerman 2010, 31). What classroom experience teaches children, Zimmerman (2010, 31) specifies, is nothing less than the "habits of democracy: reason, deliberation, tolerance, fairness, compromise, and more." These are habits, he points out, especially germane in a multicultural society and, I would add, in a shrinking global village. They are habits that become intelligent only as they are informed by academic knowledge.

School deform is based on two false assumptions, one regarding the relation between teaching and learning, and the second regarding the relation between school and society. First, teachers have never been, are not now, will never be, responsible for student learning. Every teacher, and parent, knows this. While we parents like to take credit for our children's successes, we know that finally the credit goes to them. We may have loved, fed, and encouraged them, but without their willingness to work there can be no success, not in school, not anywhere. We may reflect on our responsibility when our children fail, but whatever our failings we parents are painfully aware we cannot control our children's every move, even with the latest tracking devices. If parents—whose genetic material their offspring often carry—are not responsible for their children's educational (under)achievement, how on earth can teachers be held responsible? Second, school deform is based on an obviously false assumption regarding the relation between school and society. Schools have never, cannot now, and will never be able to correct the legacies of past injustice and injury, however indispensable they can be to understanding them. Insisting, as school deform zealots do, that schools can accomplish what government, business, the family, and the church have not, evidently cannot accomplish, and that we can know that schools are performing these miracles by assessing standardized test score results is simply stupid.

As can be the case for survivors of trauma, school deform can also end in violence and suicide. In May 2010 the principal of New York City Public School 20 in Fort Greene, Brooklyn, Sean Keaton, was arrested, accused of assaulting a teachers' union representative during a meeting. While students of P.S. 20 were enjoying their last full day of school, Mr. Keaton was arraigned in court on assault charges. The reporter decodes the event as a culture clash (Newman 2009, 1), but I do not see how we can eliminate from consideration the increased pressure high-stakes testing creates for all educators, especially administrators. In Japan, the national obsession with test scores led to student suicides. In the United States it has led to cheating and occasional violence, and not only directed toward representatives of demonized teachers' unions.

In August 2010 *The Los Angeles Times* published a database of what in school deform jargon gets called "value-added analysis." The newspaper listed the name of every teacher in the Los Angeles Unified School District who had been rated "less effective than average" (quoted in Lovett 2010, A21), meaning that his or her students had failed to perform adequately on standardized tests. Among those listed was Rigoberto Ruelas, described by his colleagues as a "devoted" teacher, one who tutored students before school, stayed with them after the school day had ended and, on weekends, took students from his South Los Angeles elementary school to the beach (Lovett 2010, A21). After his name appeared in the newspaper last August, Ruelas became "noticeably depressed," and, in early September, he committed suicide (Lovett 2010, A21).

The suicide school deform performs is not only individual; it is national. By scripting the school curriculum and aligning it with standardized tests, politicians silence the complicated conversation that is the curriculum, the very core of education in a social democracy. The public school curriculum is where expert knowledge gets explained to those without (even skeptical about) expertise. The public school curriculum is where the significance of expert knowledge for everyday life and for our civic ideals is explained, discussed, and debated. The curriculum is the site where national history and culture are explained, worked through, and recreated. It is where academic knowledge gets rearticulated through students' and teachers' lived experience, reconstructing it so that it becomes *educational experience*. Because the academic curriculum is a complicated conversation and not a business meeting or military drill, its enactment requires intellectually independent teachers whose professional acumen is informed first and foremost by their erudition, secondarily by their savvy, always by their ethical commitment to children. This academically informed acumen becomes personified in the subjectivity and specifically the speech of the individual teacher who is then professionally obligated to exercise her or his intellectual judgment in choosing *what knowledge is of most worth*. This is what we call academic freedom, and we take for granted its importance at the university level. Without academic—intellectual—freedom, we cannot teach. Disciplines cannot advance. Students cannot discover who they can be.

By emphasizing standardized test score outcomes, politicians ignore—indeed censor—what teachers and students know and can discover. In schools deformed by standardized testing regimes, the curriculum is aligned with tests, a form of ideological control. Without the originality and creativity an intellectually independent teacher enacts through complicated conversation, it really doesn't matter who teaches the children. It could be retired businessmen, or military personnel, or the *noblesse oblige* graduates of elite institutions who imagine they are "teaching for America." It doesn't matter because all politicians demand is "results," that is, test scores. Not only is that, in the phrase of one infamous "reformer," a "crappy education" (quoted in Dillon 2010, October 14, A19), it is not education at all. And because education and democracy are reciprocally related, school deform is a defeat for democracy in America.

So you see that my word play—school reform decoded as school deform—while accurate, actually understates the catastrophe we now witness. After achieving safety, the survivor of traumatic experience sometimes suicides. By disabling teachers from the subjectively structured expression of their academic expertise, ethical judgment and intellectual passions, by discrediting classroom deliberation (dialogical encounter disappears, replaced by the calculation of correct test responses), and by coercing students into mindless compliance by never-ending threats of future unemployment and national annihilation (or conversely, by bribes such as cellphone minutes), school deform "corrects" for the "excesses" of democracy by ending democracy. Without ethically informed, subjectivity-situated, historically attuned intelligence informed by academic knowledge, Americans will suffer intensifying economic inequality, social injustice, and political polarization. The Weimar Republic is America's own cautionary tale.

How does *quantifying* educational experience *end* educational experience? Even private "thought is predominately public and social," James W. Carey (1992, 28) reminds. Standardized tests destroy those lived links between the *spoken word* (the classroom is by definition a public square) and the *inner conversation* (carried on in rooms of one's own). When guided by a thoughtful, imaginative, and knowledgeable teacher (these are not specifiable behaviors!), connecting the two spheres—inner and public speech—supports subjective and social reconstruction. Why are these reciprocally related processes central to the education of the public? "Reality," Carey (1992, 30) explains:

> must be repaired for it consistently breaks down: people get lost physically and spiritually, experiments fail, evidence counter to the representation is produced, mental derangement sets in—all threats to our models of and for reality that lead to intense repair work.

School deform is not repair work. By silencing subjectivity and ensuring standardization of behavior, the standardized test-making industry and the politicians who fund it stop communication and enforce mimicry, ending reconstruction. The spontaneity of conversation disappears in the replication of memorized answers and the application of "cognitive skills" to solve conceptual puzzles unrelated to either inner experience or public life. Censored is that self-reflexivity dialogical encounter invites.

From Toronto, the great Canadian political economist and communications theorist Harold Innis saw it coming, even though he died in 1952, two years before *Brown v. Board of Education*, five years before Sputnik, and almost a decade before all hell broke loose in the 1960s. Today Innis is often remembered as the intellectual source for the waterfall that was the ingenious output of Marshall McLuhan, theorist of the global village where the medium is the message. Quoting Oscar Wilde watching Niagara Falls but thinking of the Innis–McLuhan sequence, Carey (1992, 142) quips: "It would be more impressive if it ran the other way." Carey (1992, 142) continues: "Despite its maddeningly obscure, opaque and elliptical character," Innis' work is the "great achievement in communications on this continent." Moving from research on political economy to communications theory enabled Innis to discern the historically shifting relations among the economy, culture, and communications. Even from within such interdisciplinary complexity Innis tried to warn us. His research on the new information technologies revealed, in his biographer's phrasing, a "historical drift away from living (or oral) communication and massively towards passive acceptance of mechanical messages" (Watson 2007, 412). This is nothing less than a shift away from "critical thinking and towards following orders on a mass scale" (Watson 2007, 412). So framed, the regime enforcing standardized test-taking can only be decoded as a forceful form of authoritarianism, of what we have customarily characterized as fascism. What Harold Innis understood was that orality, sociality, and introspection are reciprocally related, indeed mutually constitutive, as orality is not limited to speech acts but includes that contemplation, meditation, and inner speech that public dialogue reconstructs (Watson 2007, 254). School and university classrooms are the last remaining physical sites of such dialogue. Of course school "reformers" want instruction moved online!

In our time technological development substitutes for moral improvement and social democracy. Social democracy and moral improvement (themselves reciprocally related) rest on and follow from some form of subjective coherence. Without a "self" (however contingent, dispersed, and culturally variable), self-reflection, understanding, and agency disappear. It appears, as we saw in chapter 5, that technology—and, specifically, life online—erodes subjective coherence. Through the ongoing "stress of super-stimulation" (Kroker 1984, 76), subjectivity dissolves into a series of sensory experiences, always accented by their immediacy, installing a presentism that blurs boundaries not only between past and future but between self and other. Alterity fades as the world becomes an extension of what is familiar. The canonical curriculum question—*what knowledge is of most worth?*—devolves into "what's in it for me?"

Despite initial affirmations of the Internet as inevitably democratizing, as the site of creative freedom, it now seems for many it has become a site of subjective dissolution. Although not formally controlled by the state, technology is controlled commercially. The distinction—between state and commercial control—may prove to be slight, as it is this "control over the speed, dissemination, and implanting of new technologies by the corporate command centers of North America which subverts the very possibility of an age of 'creative freedom'" (Kroker 1984, 82). Freedom requires academic knowledge, critical thinking, and subjective agency. Instead we have exhibitionism, voyeurism, and narcissism, punctuated by surveillance and assault. Among school-age children, such assault takes the pernicious form of bullying. "Without the education of perspective or, for that matter, in the absence of a 'multidimensional perspective' on technique," Arthur Kroker (1984, 77) observed, "it will surely be the human destiny to be imprinted by the structural imperatives, the silent grammar, of the new world information order." Here Kroker is discussing Marshall McLuhan, a McLuhan whose celebration of the "global village" and a "new," that is, "tribal" and "organic," individual was tempered by a sober realization that the metastasizing global "technostructure" could be less a vibrant village than a soulless labyrinth through which we wander without aim or destination (Kroker 1984, 64). A school deformed *is* a soulless labyrinth.

IV Finding the Future

> We do not create the world, but we are the site of its realization.
> —Kaja Silverman (2009, 153)

By the 1940s, Harold Innis realized that "myopia" was the cultural crisis of the West, and that it was interrelated with the West's obsession with technological development (Watson 2007, 188, 302). Not thirty years later across Lake Ontario in Rochester, New York, Christopher Lasch (1978) elaborated the historically specific association of presentism with narcissism. By the 1970s, Lasch knew, narcissism had come to characterize contemporary American life. A culture of narcissism had been intensified by the imagistic and transitory character of mass advertising, the press of fashion in the culture industry, all haunted by "radical evil." For Lasch (1984) that radical evil had been Nazi Germany and the Holocaust, a historical fact, he argued, unassimilable by a rational mass consciousness. The unassimilability and unintelligibility of mass extermination coupled with an unstable public sphere constructed by the culture industry and threatened by nuclear war had resulted in a presentistic, solipsistic, narcissistic self (Lasch 1984).

Under such circumstances, the curricular task becomes the recovery of memory and history in ways that psychologically allow individuals to re-enter politically the public sphere in privately meaningful and ethically committed ways. The public sphere becomes the "commons," not another place to plunder for profit. How to substitute reconstruction for exploitation in a historical moment consumed by the latter? It is not obvious (let alone easy), of course, but in studying the past students can begin to free themselves from the present. Pasolini (quoted in Rumble 1996, 58, emphasis added) understood:

> Now I prefer to move through the past, precisely because I believe that *the past is the only force to contest the present*; it is an aberrant form, but all the values that were the values which formed us—with all that made them atrocious, with their negative aspects—are the ones that are capable of putting the present into crisis.

Subjective reconstruction requires reactivating the past in the present, rendering the present past. Such intellectual labor is not only intrasubjective, of course, as it requires as it precipitates social engagement. Such complicated conversation within oneself and with others reinvigorates "the oral tradition, with its emphasis on dialogue and dialectic, values and philosophical speculation, as the countervailing culture to the technological culture of sensation and mobility" (Carey 1992, 135). Part of the project of *currere* is to contradict presentism by self-consciously cultivating the temporality of subjectivity, insisting on the distinctiveness *and* simultaneity of past, present, and future, a temporal complexity in which difference does not dissolve onto a flattened never-ending "now," but is stretched as it is spoken, reconstructing the present as temporally and spatially differentiated. Presentism, then, not only erases time but space, as place becomes nowhere in particular, cyberspace (Chun 2006, 43). In the midst of such a cultural calamity, the education of the American public requires, above all, the cultivation of historicity. Historical consciousness structures as it can reinvigorate self-reflexive intellectuality through academic study.

Contra Diane Ravitch, such education cannot take a single or uniform curricular form, as it relies on the individual teacher's self-critical creativity and academic knowledge that enable her or him to speak to the specificity of her students and their situations as they articulate them. Uniformity and standardization destroy orality, memory, and history. While a point made in a different context, Kaja Silverman's (2000, 62) sense of the significance of the past underlines our aspiration for education:

> [T]he subject ... does not seek to bury, forget, or transcend the past. Rather, this subject holds himself always open to new possibilities for the deployment of that signifying constellation which most profoundly individualizes him. He is receptive to the resurfacing in the present and future of what has been—not as an exercise in narcissistic solipsism, but rather as the extension in ever new directions of his capacity to care.

In this temporal and ethical sense, curriculum as complicated conversation—inevitably variable in theme and form—portends subjective and social reconstruction.

Our professional calling is nothing less than the subjective reconstruction of the public sphere through complicated conversation, a resuscitation of the progressive project in which we understand that self-realization and democratization are inextricably intertwined. That is, in addition to providing competent individuals for the workplace and for further study in higher education, we must renew our commitment to the democratization of American society, a communicative process that requires the psychosocial and intellectual education of the self-reflexive individual. That means that academic knowledge as well as popular culture must be studied in novel and changing—indeed, self-expressive—curricular forms so that individual students and groups are provoked to explore in academic terms their lived experience. Such academic study can be supported, if deepened and widened, when guided by self-reflexive educators whose own intellectual interests remain alive and present in the tutelage of their students. The curriculum—animated by an ongoing intimacy with the academic disciplines as they are practiced at the university—provides the intellectual and social concepts by means of which the individual comes to form. Speaking of Robert Musil, Jonsson (2000, 140–141) points out:

> The social order provides the forms that enable an individual to *be*, in the most elementary sense of the word. These forms determine the nature and meaning of all human expressions. Only by using and thus realizing these forms can the human being emerge as a subject for itself and in itself.

That last sentence is key. Social forms structure subjectivity, but they need not determine it, that is if the individual reconstructs these forms, subjectively and socially. "Revelation," Stéphane Mosès (2009 [1992], 37) reminds us, "is the event in which man awakens to his original reality of a personal subject."

The curriculum driven by standardized tests depersonalizes students and teachers as it splits off the curriculum from subjective attachments. This is a catastrophic, fascistic, event. Once again the psychoanalytic notion of "transitional objects" can help us understand how the curriculum as complicated conversation functions as a bridge between the social and subjective. Lasch points out that children outgrow the need for transitional objects, but only because—like Nussbaum, Lasch (in 1984, 194) quotes Winnicott to make the point—the "transitional phenomena have become diffused, have become spread out over the whole intermediate territory between 'inner psychic reality' and the 'external world as perceived by two persons in common,' that is to say, over the whole cultural field."

It is not, of course, with the "whole cultural field" that the individual becomes engaged, but only those elements of it which "speak" (however indirectly) to the self in its situation. That is why student and faculty concerns and interests must animate academic study. Without subjective interest structuring the curriculum, students become split off, alienated, only self-absorbed, learning either to "do school" for "good grades" or performing their lack of "motivation" in a variety of, including violent (bullying), ways, requiring, perhaps, "special" or "correctional" education. The educational point of the curriculum is to draw students out of themselves into unknown (to them) terrains of the "cultural field," enabling them to engage with the world with insight, passion, and competence while never breaking the bridges of psychic attachment that makes the process of education subjectively and socially meaningful. It is "the symbolism of transitional objects," Lasch (1984, 194) appreciated, that "occupies the borderland between subjectivity and objectivity."

As the totalitarian temptation of our time, school deform relies on punishment, not pleasure. As Kaja Silverman (2000, 46) points out, "it is through the practice of desire rather than through its renunciation that humans approach what has traditionally been called virtue. Indeed, it is the relinquishing of desire that, for Lacan, represents 'sin'." To emphasize the point Silverman quotes from Lacan's Seminar VII: "The only thing of which one can [finally] be guilty is of having given ground relative to one's desire" (in Silverman 2000, 47). The point of public education is not self-abandonment nor that suspension, until adulthood, of satisfaction too many—including "successful"—schools stipulate as scores on standardized tests (see Pope 2001). The point of public education is not to become "accountable," forced into positions of "gracious submission" to self-promoting politicians and profit-seeking businessmen plundering public budgets. The point of public education is to become an individual, a citizen, a human subject engaged with intelligence and passion in the problems and pleasures of his or her life, problems and pleasures bound up with the problems and pleasures of everyone else in the nation, everyone on this planet.

To focus on the educational significance of schooling for the culture at large means associating academic knowledge with the individual himor herself, teaching not only what is, for instance, historical knowledge, but also suggesting its possible consequences for the individual's selfformation in the historical present, allowing that knowledge to shape the individual's coming to social form. Doing so is an elusive threading of subjectivity through the social forms and intellectual constructs we discover through study, reanimating original passions through acting in the world. "What we do in school in the classroom," Alan Block (2009, 73) suggests, "is to forever pursue lost objects," and "this pursuit and effort is both an personal and a communal obligation." In fact, he adds, addressing teachers directly, "until we find our own lost articles and establish our relationships to self, until we activate our own potential, we ought not to undertake assisting others" (2009, 77).

Conversation, then, takes place both intersubjectively *and* intrasubjectively, in public squares and in rooms of our own. In privacy we turn away from the maelstrom of everyday life, and in solitude and silence we might hear ourselves, undistracted by the onslaught of empty information. We can look for what we've lost. That we only do offline. Carey (1992, 140) calls on us to:

> dismantle the fetishes of communication for the sake of communication, and decentralization and participation without reference

to content or context [that] citizens now suffer in many areas from overloads of communication and overdoses of participation. We should address ourselves directly to the overriding problems: the uprooting of people from meaningful communities and the failure to organize politically around authentic issues.

Working from within, in complicated conversation with others, we can re-experience the oral tradition, in which intrasubjective and intersubjective dialogical encounter permits possibilities for "meaningful communities" (including classrooms), creating social bonds that can reconstitute themselves around "authentic issues," such as climate change and school deform.

"Conversation and silence," Mary Elizabeth Moore (2002, 225) observes, "naturally lead to culmination and new beginnings." Passage is what William E. Doll, Jr. (2002, 49) has in mind when he points out that "conversation" derives from the Latin *conversare*, meaning "to turn oneself about." Conversation, Doll points out, derives from the same Proto-Indo-European root as does the word *converge*, meaning "to approach the same point from different directions ... to tend toward a common conclusion" (*American Heritage Dictionary*; quoted in Doll 2002, 49). "Thus," Doll (2002, 49) concludes, "there is a historical binding between conversation and convergence—through personal conversation we turn ourselves about and converge or come together. In conversation lie our hopes for both convergence and transformation." "Conversation is," he notes (quoting Gadamer), "a process of coming to an understanding" (Gadamer 1993 [1960], 385; quoted in Doll 2002, 49). In studying ourselves, in elaborating and recasting our relationships with ourselves, we are reminded of the inextricability of the social and the subjective.

The ethical imperative that informs our professional labor as educators and scholars is no simple "application" of an abstract ideal. There can be no application of theory into practice: such social engineering is inevitably authoritarian. Ewa Plonowska Ziarek's (2001, 1) neologism "dissensus" underscores that understanding occurs through conflict and uncertainty. Such an ethics refers to what she deems an "irreducible dilemma of freedom and obligation," what she terms an "ethos of becoming" and an "ethos of alterity," one that structures a "non-appropriative relation to the Other" (Ziarek 2001, 2). So conceived, the educational project is nothing less than the composition of "new modes of life" (2001, 2). "New" means that all faculty need not necessary "share" the same "vision," that we allow, while we commit to work through, conflict, disagreement, and uncertainty. We find the future through difference, including the differences between its historical particularity and its mythological universality. "Wisdom," Block (2009, 88) says simply, "is the joining of past and present." Allegory enables such "joining."

To engage in allegory, academic—intellectual—freedom must be our primary professional possession. That is no opportunity for self-indulgence but a demand for discipline. Only through the rigorous reconstruction of private passion into public service can we honor our calling as educators. That calling requires that we never coincide with ourselves, that we are always reaching out to engage difference and otherness, as the concept of allegory reminds. "[A]llegory pleasures otherness," Ronell (2003, 108) emphasizes; "to the extent that it organizes itself around difference and absence, it never comes back to itself." As non-coincident with itself, allegory enacts subjective and social reconstruction, as it stages the educational experience of juxtaposing the present with the past, subjectivity with society. To exercise the intellectual independence allegory requires, we educators must face the anti-intellectualism embedded in our profession and enforced by politicians. Too often we educators have mistaken busywork for academic work, authoritarianism for authority, indifference for professional dignity. To reaffirm our intellectual authority as teachers means ongoing humility and self-criticism. It means remaining students, always studying across the disciplines, as well as reading in depth and over time in at least one. Probably teachers should be enrolled in universities each term, and not only in education departments or in the academic subject they teach, although study in these fields is self-evidently important. Teachers must also study fields outside their immediate expertise and interest; they will benefit from the study of interdisciplinary fields, especially, given the gendered and racial history of our present situation, African American studies, and Women's and Gender Studies. When teachers come to us education professors, we must not (only) commiserate with them, we must provide provocative intellectual challenges.

Our professional commitment is to the academic—intellectual—understanding of self and society in the historical moment toward the democratization of American culture. Such a commitment means we value the "life of the mind" as it is embodied in the concrete lives of our students, as persons and as citizens. Of course, we teach "cognitive skills" and "core knowledge," but always in lived relation to those with whom we work. We must abandon infantilized positions from which we pretend helplessness, demanding to know "what works," the authoritarianism of instrumental rationality. Courage, not force, is the coin of our realm. "To be a teacher," Block (2009, 115) reminds us, "is to be brave." Intellectual courage requires psychological courage, working in every way ethically possible to encourage our students to take advantage of the opportunities we offer them. Students deserve praise when they succeed, and they—and, secondarily, their parents—must take responsibility when they decline (or are unable) to learn.

If we are to teach during this totalitarian time probably we will want to join with others in reducing the political influence of business and (especially fundamentalist) religion, those twin and intersecting forces of anti-intellectualism in American culture that Richard Hofstadter identified so cogently. This is not to endorse either socialism or secularism. But it is to insist that rhetoric of business be restricted to business, not forced onto the profession of education where it has no business. It is to insist that spirituality remain a private (if shared) experience, not politicized and recoded as educational policy, where it too often has meant the imposition of intellectual constraints if not outright censorship (see Zimmerman 2002).

We cannot get "there" from "here" and "now." The entrance to the future is located in the past. "A denial of the past," Lasch (1978, xviii) points out, "superficially progressive and optimistic, proves on closer analysis to embody the despair of a society that cannot face the future." As the method of *currere* aspires to support temporality in the character structure of the individual, curriculum theory insists that the education of the public is necessarily and profoundly historical. Not segregated in courses so labeled (characteristic of the system of academic vocationalism), historicity infuses all subjects, however interdisciplinary and interest-driven.

Such a project breathes life into a progressive project currently on display only in museums. It is to reformulate the Deweyan commitment to democracy and education in light of our situation, our time, our lives, and the lives of our and others' children, all children. I claim the progressive tradition while disavowing its excesses, including its past racialization and its tendencies to bifurcate education into social reform *or* child-centeredness, as well as its naive confidence in organizational restructuring, and its suspicion of academic study for its own sake. In the present historical moment, to be progressive is to endorse academic study as valuable for its own sake, not for its "cash value" in the market, not for its capacity to correct the historical injuries and present injustices right-wing politicians have deflected onto schools.

In our time, progressivism is the intellectual and political tradition that emphasizes the potential of academic knowledge for subjective and social reconstruction. Such a view of knowledge is congruent with the understanding of curriculum as a "complicated conversation," disclosing, as that phrase does, the relational character of ideas, in relation not only one to the other, but pointing as well to their embodiment and personification in individual lives, their origin and expression in social movements and trends, their rootedness in the historical past, their foreshadowing of our individual and national futures, and our future as a species as well. It is a view of academic knowledge as allegory.

"To teach," Alan Block (2009, 117) knows, "is to be a prophet in a degraded world." Despite our gracious submission, despite the anti-intellectualism around us and within us, let us recommit ourselves to our profession, committed to erudition and understanding, personified in interdisciplinary forms of *praxis* requiring regression, progression, analysis, and synthesis. Subjective and social reconstruction characterizes the *educational* experience of academic knowledge in schools that serve the species, not only the economy. Such a fundamental reaffirmation of the American public education is not, however, utopian. "Schooling," Christopher Lasch (1995, 160) rightly emphasizes, is not "a cure-all for everything that ails us."

As did the founder of public schools in the United States, Horace Mann, too many Americans today still believe that good schools can eradicate crime, eliminate poverty, construct committed citizens out of "abandoned and outcast children," and serve as the "great equalizer" between rich and poor (Mann, quoted in Lasch 1995, 160). We might have done better, Lasch concludes, had we started out less ambitiously. "If there is one lesson we might have been expected to learn in the 150 years since Horace Mann took charge of the schools of Massachusetts," Lasch (1995, 160) writes, "it is that the schools can't save society." He notes crime and poverty have not disappeared and the gap between rich and poor only widens. "Maybe," he suggests, "the time has come—if it hasn't already passed—to start all over again" (1995, 160).

Lasch is right. While scapegoating teachers, the last five decades of school "reform" are aimed at making the present system "work." Politicians understand that authoritarianism is the only way to force children to excel at tasks in which they have little interest. Test-driven curriculum is the means to install authoritarianism, all the while deflecting attention away from its intensely political motives and anti-educational effects. As Lasch (1995, 162) himself acknowledges, "[p]eople readily acquire such knowledge as they can put to good use." Especially after Sputnik, schools are not permitted to provide opportunities for students to put academic knowledge "to good use." Like a pyramid scheme, academic vocationalism justifies the acquisition of academic knowledge because it leads to more knowledge, presumably resulting in a credential enabling upward mobility. Cram schools are even worse; at least academic vocationalism is academic. Cram schools are focused on intellectually vacuous "skills." Neither, however, connects academic knowledge to self-formation and the historical moment, what Christopher Lasch himself—as one of the nation's greatest public intellectuals—so powerfully did.

"What democracy requires," Lasch (1995, 162) understood, "is vigorous public debate not information." The notion of "complicated conversation" includes "vigorous public debate" but it is broader, supporting solitary study and intellectual adventure in rooms of one's own as well as in classrooms as civic squares. Complaining about the surfeit of information, Lasch (1995, 162–163) acknowledged that democracy "needs information too, but the kind of information it needs can be generated only by debate." While in agreement with him, I insist on expanding Lasch's conception as a curriculum theory, including, perhaps even emphasizing debate, but supporting a broad range of intellectual pursuits, some of which will be conducted in solitude and might not always result in public discussion. Acknowledging that subjective interest is the prerequisite for erudition (but thinking still only of public debate), Lasch (1995, 163) points out:

> We do not know what we need to know until we ask the right questions, and we can identify the right questions only by subjecting our own ideas about the world to the test of public controversy. Information, usually seen as the precondition of debate, is better understood as its byproduct. When we get into arguments that focus and fully engage our attention, we become avid seekers of relevant information. Otherwise we take in information passively—if we take it in at all.

Except for his exclusive focus on the concept of "debate," this is a succinct statement of curriculum as "complicated conversation."

Lasch is thinking not of the public school but of journalism, reporting that political debate began to decline at the beginning of the 20th century, at about the same time when the press was becoming more "responsible," more "professional," more "objective." In the early 19th century, Lasch (1995, 163) reports, the press had been "fiercely partisan." It was Walter Lippmann, he continues, who articulated most forcefully the view that the role of the press was to "circulate information, not to encourage argument" (Lasch 1995, 170). "Lippmann had forgotten," Lasch (170) surmises:

> that our search for reliable information is itself guided by the questions that arise during arguments about a given course of action. It is only by subjecting our preference and projects to the test of debate that we come to understand what we know and what we still need to learn.

I would supplement the word "debate" with "public scrutiny and intellectual judgment," but the educational point is well taken: curriculum as complicated conversation must be linked to subjective investment and public deliberation. "In short," Lasch (1995, 170) summarizes, expressing what every teacher knows, "we come to know our own minds only by explaining ourselves to others." While teaching includes debate and argument, curriculum is a broader concept than either.

"If we insist on argument [especially understood as 'teaching,' as in explaining ourselves to others, which he suggests above] as the essence of education," Lasch (1995, 171) writes, sounding for the moment just like a curriculum theorist:

we will defend democracy not as the most efficient but as the most educational form of government, one that extends the circle of debate as widely as possible and thus forces all citizens to articulate their views [in the civic square that is the classroom], to put their views at risk, and to cultivate the virtues of eloquence, clarity of thought and expression, and sound judgement.

Directly confronting the structuring of education for the production of specialized elites (Conant's aristocracy of talent), Lasch (1995, 171) insists that "direct democracy" must be "re-create[d] ... on a large scale." While he is thinking of the press, not the school, the concept upon which he fastens— the town meeting—expresses well the concept of the classroom as civic square. While reductive as a model for all educational activity, it expresses succinctly what it means to reconstruct the public sphere in curriculum and teaching. If we supplement it by including opportunities for individual exploration and discovery, sometimes in solitude, we have the rudiments of what it means to reconstruct the subjective and social spheres in curriculum and teaching.

None of this is exactly new, as it is, Lasch notes, what Dewey argued in *The Public and Its Problems* (1927), a book written in reply to Lippmann, whose 1922 *Public Opinion* is the "founding book in American media studies" (Carey 1992, 75). Anticipating the "auditory turn" in which the hegemony of visuality is contested, and in curriculum theory specifically (see Aoki 2005 [1990]), and referencing James Carey (1992, 77), Lasch points out that Dewey's concept of communication emphasized the ear rather than the eye (see 1995, 172). Lasch quotes Dewey (in 1995, 172):

Conversation has a vital import lacking in the fixed and frozen words of written speech. ... The connections of the ear with vital and outgoing thought and emotion are immensely closer and more varied than those of the eye. Vision is a spectator; hearing is a participator.

In endorsing the auditory over the ocular, Carey (1992, 79) points out, Dewey is arguing that language is not only a system of representations but a series of activities, and that "speech captures this action better than the more static images of the printed page." As taken up by Harold Innis and Marshall McLuhan in the decades that followed (as Carey acknowledges) this insight reasserts the primacy of the oral tradition in communication, a tradition (as Nussbaum and others remind) that honors the argument, allows the conversation to go where it must given those who are present. Debate and dispute structure discussion, as Lasch reminds, but it is open-ended thought that characterizes the curriculum as complicated conversation.

"The divorce of truth from discourse and action," Carey (1992, 84) continues, and the "instrumentalization of communication have not merely increased the incidence of propaganda; it has disrupted the very notion of truth, and therefore the sense by which we take our bearings in the world is destroyed." Ocularcentrism has not yielded the transparent truth but, rather, its obfuscation. It intensifies the ahistorical presentism and political polarization of the contemporary culture of narcissism. Without the lived, that is, subjectively structured temporality the method of *currere* encourages, we are consigned to the social surface, to the never-ending present, and what we see is what we get. When we listen to the past we become attuned to the future. From the past we can understand the present, which we *can* reconstruct. Subjective and social reconstruction is our professional obligation as educators in this fascistic moment of anti-intellectualism, public vilification, and political subjugation.

As is the case in every profession, there must be less than adequate teachers. After forty years of school deform, there may well be many. I have never known one, however. During the thirteen years I taught at the University of Rochester (1972–1985), I supervised student teachers of English each autumn, more than two hundred altogether I suppose. Several were stunning, many were astute, but even among the least impressive not one came close to "incompetent." A public school student for twelve years (from 1953 to 1965, first in Huntington, West Virginia, then in Pittsburgh, Pennsylvania, concluding in Columbus, Ohio), taking five to seven subjects during the secondary years (grades 7–12), even the one teacher I'd name as the weakest of them all—yes he was an assistant football coach teaching American history—conducted himself with dignity and competence. Each day he repeated in class the outline he had copied onto the blackboard. Perhaps he lacked the knowledge to engage us in discussion; perhaps he knew we didn't know enough to engage in discussion. Whatever Mr. Shade's motive, each day he repeated the outline and each day we copied it into our notebooks. Not my ideal classroom experience, but I acquired a sound (if sketchy) knowledge of the main events of U.S. political history. (My inspiring twelfth-grade government teacher—Mrs. Ott—taught me to interpret them.) True, I grew up in a (more or less) stable middle-class family; my parents were supportive (if not demanding); I had a desk on which to do homework. It never occurred to me or to any of my classmates that it was our teachers' obligation to make us learn, or that we studied what we did for the sake of some standardized test. Of course grades mattered, but knowledge mattered more. Education—in whatever form it took in the classroom—was an opportunity. And my parents made sure that I appreciated that it was my obligation to take advantage of it.

Reminding children and their parents that it is *their* responsibility to take advantage of the opportunities teachers offer them will win few elections. More profitable—not only for politicians, but for the education-related businesses which donate to their campaigns and which now plunder public budgets—is blaming teachers for students who, for whatever reasons, decline or are unable to take advantage of the profound opportunity education is. *Teachers are not responsible for student learning: students are.* Until that fundamental, perhaps unfortunate, but definitely unchanging fact is acknowledged in public discussions of education, we will continue to deform our public schools, degrading ourselves and our children by deluding everyone that standardized test scores are meaningful. Unless devised by classroom teachers to reference their specific assignments and actual classroom conversations, tests are only self-referential. Teachers may be forced to play along, but we don't have to fall for the ruse. Indeed, the sadistic stupidity of school deform deserves only our cold contempt. As Franz Rosenzweig reminds us from the past: "vocation is more primeval than condition" (Mosès 2009 [1992], 29). To exercise loyalty to the vocation and contest the conditions of its contemporary practice, teachers might invoke an ethics of intransigence.

From 1930 to 1934, Kurt von Hammerstein served as the Chief of Army Command, the highest-ranking officer in the *Reichswehr*, as Germany's army was known during the Weimar Republic. He was also, Adam Kirsch (2010, 52) tells us, an "undisguised opponent" of Adolf Hitler and the Nazis. While not prominent in the military or political history of the period—like, Kirsch notes, Kurt von Schleicher (see chapter 3), Hammerstein's friend and political ally, who served as the last Chancellor of the Weimar Republic before Hitler, and who was killed during Hitler's "Night of the Long Knives" in 1934—von Hammerstein was involved in the conspiracy to assassinate Hitler. By the time—July 20, 1944—the plot had failed, Hammerstein had been dead for more than a year. At his funeral, Kirsch continues, his family declined the usual military honors, refusing to allow the swastika flag to be draped on his coffin.

Reviewing a book recently published on Hammerstein (Enzensberger 2009), Kirsch (2010, 52) raises the question of the ethics of "intransigence," that admixture of "principle, arrogance, and willfulness" that fueled Hammerstein's refusal of Nazism. While not heroism, Kirsch (2010, 52) allows, intransigence is "more attainable," more realistic. True, intransigence can't be dissociated from selfishness; it is no instance of "moral greatness": still, intransigence might "stave off moral collapse" (2010, 52). In the First Edition of this book (Pinar 2004, 43–44), I invoked the African American concept of "sass" to inspire teachers' refusal of school deform. Perhaps sass in an Age of Authoritarianism is asking too much. Perhaps "intransigence" is more appropriate during this Weimar time in which the right rules the (school) house. True, intransigence is not, as Kirsch (2010, 54) makes clear, a "strong enough lever with which to move the world." He suggests a utopian vision might be, but I am not persuaded, as it is precisely such a utopian dream (however animated by political opportunism, liberal guilt, and right-wing revenge) that has metamorphosed into school deform. Enzensberger entitles one section of his book "The Horrors of the Weimar Republic," concluding that "we should be grateful that we weren't there" (quoted in 2010, 52). Kirsch agrees, then quotes (in 2010, 52) Bertolt Brecht's "To Those Born Later":

> You who will emerge from the
> flood
> In which we have gone under
> Remember
> When you speak of our failings
> The dark time too
> Which you have escaped.

Slandered and silenced, we teachers watched as politicians and profiteers plundered public education, replacing educational institutions with cram schools. Once there were *freedom schools* in America. Remember!

References

Addams, Jane (2002 [1902]). *Democracy and social ethics*. [Introduction by Charlene Haddock Seigfried.] Urbana: University of Illinois Press.

Adorno, Theodor W., Frenkel-Brunswick, E., Levinson, D., and Sanford, N. (1950). *The authoritarian personality*. New York: Harper & Row.

Agamben, Giorgio (2005). *State of exception*. [Translated by Kevin Attell.] Chicago: University of Chicago Press.

Aoki, Ted T. (2005 [1983]). Curriculum implementation as instrumental action and as situational praxis. In William F. Pinar and Rita L. Irwin (Eds.), *Curriculum in a new key: The collected works of Ted T. Aoki* (111–123). Mahwah, NJ: Lawrence Erlbaum.

Aoki, Ted T. (2005 [1984]). Competence in teaching as instrumental and practical action. In William F. Pinar and Rita L. Irwin (Eds.), *Curriculum in a new key: The collected works of Ted T. Aoki* (125–135). Mahwah, NJ: Lawrence Erlbaum.

Aoki, Ted T. (2005 [1985/1991]). Signs of vitality in curriculum scholarship. In William F. Pinar and Rita L. Irwin (Eds.), *Curriculum in a new key: The collected works of Ted T. Aoki* (229–233). Mahwah, NJ: Lawrence Erlbaum.

Aoki, Ted (2005 [1986/1991]). Teaching as indwelling between two curriculum worlds. In William F. Pinar and Rita L. Irwin (Eds.), *Curriculum in a new key: The collected works of Ted T. Aoki* (159–165). Mahwah, NJ: Lawrence Erlbaum.

Aoki, Ted (2005 [1987]). Inspiriting the curriculum. In William F. Pinar and Rita L. Irwin (Eds.), *Curriculum in a new key: The collected works of Ted T. Aoki* (357–365). Mahwah, NJ: Lawrence Erlbaum.

Aoki, Ted (2005 [1990]). Sonare and videre: A story, three echoes and a linger note. In William F. Pinar and Rita L. Irwin (Eds.), *Curriculum in a new key: The collected works of Ted T. Aoki* (367–376). Mahwah, NJ: Lawrence Erlbaum.

Aoki, Ted T. (2005 [1991]). Layered understandings of orientations in social studies program evaluation. In William F. Pinar and Rita L. Irwin (Eds.), *Curriculum in a new key: The collected works of Ted T. Aoki* (167–186). Mahwah, NJ: Lawrence Erlbaum.

Appiah, Kwame Anthony (2006). *Cosmopolitanism: Ethics in a world of strangers*. New York: Norton.

Applebee, Arthur N. (1996). *Curriculum as conversation: Transforming traditions of teaching and learning.* Chicago: University of Chicago Press.

Applebome, Peter (2010, September 27). In politics, just how far is too far? *The New York Times* CLIX (55,176), A16.

Asante, Molefi (1987). *The Afrocentric idea.* Philadephia, PA: Temple University Press.

Asante, Molefi (1992, December/January). Afrocentric curriculum. *Educational Leadership* 49 (4), 28–31.

Asanuma, Shigeru (2003). Japanese educational reform for the twenty-first century: The impact of the new course of study toward the postmodern era in Japan. In William F. Pinar (Ed.), *International handbook of curriculum research* (435–442). Mahwah, NJ: Lawrence Erlbaum.

Associated Press (2010, June 11). Anti-bullying law takes effect. *The Bellingham Herald,* A3.

Awkward, Michael (1995). *Negotiating difference: Race, gender, and the politics of positionality.* Chicago: University of Chicago Press.

Baker, Bernadette M. (2001). *In perpetual motion: Theories of power, educational history, and the child.* New York: Peter Lang.

Baker, Bernadette (Ed.) (2009). *New curriculum history.* Rotterdam/Boston/Tapei: Sense Publishers.

Barrow, Robin (1984). *Giving teaching back to teachers: A critical introduction to curriculum theory.* Totowa, NJ: Barnes & Noble.

Barthes, Roland (1981). *Camera lucida: Reflections on photography.* [Translated by Richard Howard.] New York: Hill and Wang.

Bauman, Zygmunt (1978). *Hermeneutics and social science.* New York: Columbia University Press.

Bederman, Gail (1995). *Manliness and civilization: A cultural history of gender and race in the United States, 1880–1917.* Chicago: University of Chicago Press.

Berliner, David C. and Biddle, Bruce J. (1996). *The manufactured crisis: Myths, fraud and the assault on America's public schools.* Cambridge, MA: Perseus.

Bestor, Arthur (1953). *Educational wastelands: The retreat from learning in our public schools.* Urbana: University of Illinois Press.

Black, Earl and Black, Merle (1992). *The vital South: How presidents are elected.* Cambridge, MA: Harvard University Press.

Blankinship, Donna Gordon (2010, November 21). Economists argue against bonus pay for teachers with masters. *The Bellingham Herald,* A1, A9.

Block, Alan A. (2009). *Ethics and teaching: A religious perspective on revitalizing education.* New York: Palgrave Macmillan.

Bobbitt, Franklin (1918). *The curriculum.* Boston, MA: Houghton Mifflin.

Boler, Megan (1999). *Feeling power: Emotions and education.* New York: Routledge.

Bosman, Julie (2010, July 29). E-books fly beyond mere text. *The New York Times* CLIX (55,116), C1.

Bowers, C. A. (1995). *Educating for an ecologically sustainable culture.* Albany: State University of New York Press.

Bowers, C. A. (2000). *Let them eat data: How computers affect education, cultural diversity and the prospects of ecological sustainability.* Athens: University of Georgia Press.

Braxton, Joanne M. (1989). *Black women writing autobiography: A tradition within a tradition.* Philadelphia, PA: Temple University Press.

Brennan, Teresa and Jay, Martin (Eds.) (1996). *Vision in context: Historical and contemporary perspectives on sight.* New York: Routledge.

Brick, Michael (2010 May 21). Texas school board set to vote textbook revisions. *The New York Times* CLIX (55,047), A17.

Britzman, Deborah P. (1998). *Lost subjects, contested objects: Toward a psychoanalytic inquiry of learning.* Albany: State University of New York Press.

Britzman, Deborah P. (2003 [1991]). *Practice makes practice.* [Revised edition.] Albany: State University of New York Press.

Britzman, Deborah P. (2009). *The very thought of education: Psychoanalysis and the impossible professions.* Albany: State University of New York Press.

Brooks, David (2010, July 9). The medium is the medium. *The New York Times* CLIX (55,096), A17.

Brown, Norman O. (1959). *Life against death: The psychoanalytical meaning of history.* Middletown, CT: Wesleyan University Press.

Bruner, Jerome S. (1977). Preface to reissued *The process of education.* Cambridge, MA: Harvard University Press.

Bruner, Jerome S. (1977 [1960]). *The process of education.* Cambridge, MA: Harvard University Press.

Bruner, Jerome S. (1996). *The culture of education.* Cambridge, MA: Harvard University Press.

Brynjolfsson, Erik and Saunders, Adam (2010). *Wired for information: How information technology is reshaping the economy.* Cambridge, MA: The MIT Press.

Bryson, Mary (2004). When Jill jacks in: Queer women and the net. *Feminist Media Studies* 4 (3), 239–254.

Buck-Morss, Susan (1993). Dream world of mass culture: Walter Benjamin's theory of modernity and the dialectics of seeing. In David Michael Levin (Ed.), *Modernity and the hegemony of vision* (309–338). Berkeley: University of California Press.

Butler, Judith (1990). *Gender trouble.* New York: Routledge.

Butler, Judith (1993). *Bodies that matter: On the discursive limits of "sex."* New York and London: Routledge.

Butler, Judith (1997). *The psychic life of power: Theories in subjection.* Stanford, CA: Stanford University Press.

Cannella, Gaile S. (1998). Early childhood education: A call for the construction of revolutionary images. In William F. Pinar (Ed.), *Curriculum: Toward new identities* (157–184). New York: Garland.

Carby, Hazel V. (1998). *Race men.* Cambridge, MA: Harvard University Press.

Carey, James W. (1992). *Communication as culture: Essays on media and society.* New York: Routledge.

Carlson, Dennis (1998). Who am I? Gay identity and a democratic politics of self. In William F. Pinar (Ed.) *Queer theory in education* (107–119). Mahwah, NJ: Lawrence Erlbaum.

Carnes, Mark C. and Griffen, Clyde (Eds.) (1990). *Meanings for manhood: Constructions of masculinity in Victorian America.* Chicago: University of Chicago Press.

Carson, Clayborne (1981). *In struggle: SNCC and the black awakening of the 1960s.* Cambridge, MA: Harvard University Press.

Carter, Dan T. (1979 [1969]). *Scottsboro: A tragedy of the American South.* [Revised edition.] Baton Rouge: Louisiana State University Press.

Caruth, Cathy (1996). *Unclaimed experience: Trauma, narrative, and history.* Baltimore, MD: The Johns Hopkins University Press.

Castenell, Jr., Louis A. and Pinar, William F. (Eds.) (1993). *Understanding curriculum as racial text: Representations of identity and difference in education.* Albany: State University of New York Press.

Chang, Kenneth (2009, November 23). White House begins campaign to promote science and math education. *The New York Times* online: www.nytimes.com/2009/11/24/science/24educ.html?emc=eta1 Accessed on February 28, 2011.

Chodorow, Nancy J. (1978). *The reproduction of mothering.* Berkeley: University of California Press.

Christian, Barbara (1985). *Black feminist criticism: Perspectives on black women writers.* New York: Pergamon Press.

Chun, Wendy Hui Kyong (2006). *Control and freedom: Power and paranoia in the age of fiber optics.* Cambridge, MA: The MIT Press.

Churchill, Ward and Wall, Jim Vander (1988). *Agents of repression: The FBI's secret wars against the Black Panther Party and the American Indian Movement.* Boston, MA: South End Press.

Clifford, Geraldine Joncich and Guthrie, James W. (1988). *Ed school: A brief for professional education.* Chicago: University of Chicago Press.

Cohen, Patricia (2010, August 24). Scholars test web alternative to the venerable peer review. *The New York Times* CLIX (55,142), A1, A3.

Collins, Gail (2010, May 1). Teachers always show up. *The New York Times* CLIX (55,027), A17.

Connelly, Marjorie (2010, June 7). More Americans sense a downside to an always plugged-in existence. *The New York Times* CLIX (55,064), A12.

Cowie, Jefferson (2010, September 6). That 70s feeling. *The New York Times* CLIX (55,155), A17.

Cox, Kira M. (2010, November 18). Documentaries examine education system from different perspectives. *The Bellingham Herald*, A2.

Crary, Jonathan (1990). *Techniques of the observer: On vision and modernity in the nineteenth century.* Cambridge, MA: MIT Press.

Crary, Jonathan (2002). *Suspensions of perception: Attention, spectacle, and modern culture.* Cambridge, MA: MIT Press/an October Book.

Cremin, Lawrence A. (1961). *The transformation of the school: Progressivism in American education, 1876–1957.* New York: Alfred A. Knopf.

Cudjoe, Selwyn R. (1984). Maya Angelou and the autobiographical statement. In Mari Evans (Ed.), *Black women writers* (6–24). Garden City, NY: Anchor Books.

Cusset, François (2008). *French theory: How Foucault, Derrida, Deleuze, &*

Co. *transformed the intellectual life of the United States*. [Translated by Jeff Fort.] Minneapolis: University of Minnesota Press.

De Castell, Suzanne (1999). On finding one's place in the text: Literacy as a technology of self-formation. In William F. Pinar (Ed.), *Contemporary curriculum discourses: Twenty years of* JCT (398–411). New York: Peter Lang.

Deleuze, Gilles (1986). *Foucault*. [Foreword by Paul A. Bové. Translated and edited by Sean Hand.] Minneapolis: University of Minnesota Press.

Deleuze, Gilles (1993). *The fold: Leibniz and the Baroque*. [Foreword and translation by T. Conley.] Minneapolis and London: University of Minnesota Press.

Dewan, Shaila (2010, February 13). Experts say schools need to screen for cheating. *The New York Times* online: www.nytimes.com/2010/02/13/education/13erase.html Accessed on February 28, 2011.

Dewey, John (1916). *Democracy and education*. New York: Macmillan.

Dewey, John (1920). *Reconstruction in philosophy*. New York: Henry Holt and Company.

Dewey, John (1938). *Experience and education*. New York: Macmillan.

Dillon, Sam (2007, August 27). With turnover high, schools fight for teachers. *The New York Times* online: www.nytimes.com/2007/08/27/education/27teacher.html?ex=1188878400&en=cb3359c4ba74f3c3&ei=5070&emc=eta1 Accessed on February 28, 2011.

Dillon, Sam (2008, November 13). A school chief takes on tenure, stirring a fight. *The New York Times* online: www.nytmes.com/2008/11/13/education/13tenure.html Accessed on March 7, 2011.

Dillon, Sam (2009, August 17). Dangling money, Obama pushes education shift. *The New York Times* online: www.nytimes.com/2009/08/17/education/17educ.html?emc=eta1 Accessed on February 28, 2011.

Dillon, Sam (2009, November 19). Gateses give $290 million for education. *The New York Times* online: www.nytimes.com/2009/11/20/education/20educ.html?emc=eta1 Accessed on February 28, 2011.

Dillon, Sam (2010, March 16). Administration seeks converts to education plan. *The New York Times* online: www.nytimes.com/2010/03/17/education/17educ.html Accessed on February 28, 2011.

Dillon, Sam (2010, April 7). A tentative contract deal for Washington teachers. *The New York Times* online: www.nytimes.com/2010/04/08/education/08schools.html Accessed on March 7, 2011.

Dillon, Sam (2010, September 3). U.S. asks educators to reinvent student tests, and how they are given. *The New York Times* CLIX (55,152), A11.

Dillon, Sam (2010, October 14). Washington chancellor's departure isn't expected to slow public school change. *The New York Times* CLIX (55,193), A10.

Disch, Lisa and Kane, Mary Jo (1996). When a looker is really a bitch: Lisa Olson, sport, and the heterosexual matrix. In Ruth-Ellen B. Joeres and Barbara Laslett (Eds.), *The second signs reader: Feminist scholarship* (326–356). Chicago: University of Chicago Press.

Doll, Mary Aswell (2000). *Like letters in running water: A mythopoetics of curriculum*. Mahwah, NJ: Lawrence Erlbaum.

Doll, Jr., William E. (1993). *A post-modern perspective on curriculum*. New York: Teachers College Press.

Doll, Jr., William E. (2002). Ghosts and the curriculum. In William E. Doll, Jr. and Noel Gough (Eds.), *Curriculum visions* (23–70). New York: Peter Lang.

Du Bois, Ellen Carol (1987). The radicalism of the woman suffrage movement: Notes toward the reconstruction of nineteenth-century feminism. In Anne Phillips (Ed.), *Feminism and equality* (127–138). New York: New York University Press.

Duncan, Martha Grace (1996). *Romantic outlaws, beloved prisons: The unconscious meanings of crime and punishment*. New York: New York University Press.

Easterly, William (2009, October 8). The anarchy of success. *The New York Review of Books* LVI (15), 28–30.

Editorial (2010, October 15). Protecting school reform in D.C. *The New York Times* CLIX (55,158), A22.

Egan, Kieran (1992). *Imagination in teaching and learning*. Chicago: University of Chicago Press. [Published in Canada by the Althouse Press, London, Ontario. The reference is to this edition.]

Egan, Kieran (2002). *Getting it wrong from the beginning: Our progressivist inheritance from Herbert Spencer, John Dewey, and Jean Piaget*. New Haven, CT: Yale University Press.

Eisner, Elliot W. (1979). *The educational imagination: On the design and evaluation of school programs*. New York: Macmillan.

Elmore, Richard (1993). School decentralization: Who gains? who loses? In J. Hannaway and M. Carnoy (Eds.), *Decentralization and school improvement: Can we fulfill the promise?* (33–55). San Francisco, CA: Jossey-Bass.

Engel, Susan and Sandstrom, Marlene (2010, July 23). There's only one way to stop a bully. *The New York Times* CLIX (55,110), A19.

Enzensberger, Hans Magnus (2009). *The silences of Hammerstein: A German story*. New York: Seagull.

Epstein, Jason (2010, March 11). Publishing: The revolutionary future. *The New York Review of Books* LVII (4), 4, 6.

Erlin, Matt (2009). Tradition as intellectual montage: F. W. Murnau's *Faust* (1926). In Noah Isenberg (Ed.), *Weimar cinema* (155–172). New York: Columbia University Press.

Ewing, Jack (2010, November 8). German army honors Jews who fought in World War I. *The New York Times* CLIX (55,218), A8.

Fabbri, Paolo (1994). Free/indirect/discourse. In Patrick Rumble and Bart Testa (Eds.), *Pier Paolo Pasolini: Contemporary perspectives* (78–87). Toronto: University of Toronto Press.

Fabre, Michel (1991). *From Harlem to Paris: Black American writers in France, 1840–1980*. Urbana: University of Illinois Press.

Filene, Peter G. (1998). *Him/her/self*. [Third edition; first edition published in 1974 by Harcourt, Brace, Jovanovich.] Baltimore, MD: The Johns Hopkins University Press.

Filler, Martin (2010, June 24). The powerhouse of the new. *The New York Review of Books* LVII (11), 24–27.

Fish, Stanley (2008, April 6, April 20). French theory in America. *The New York Times* online: http://opinionator.blogs.nytimes.com/2008/04/06/french-theory-in-america/ Accessed on February 28, 2011.

Fiske, E. (1991). *Smart schools, smart kids.* New York: Simon & Schuster.

Flannery, Tim (2009, November 19). A great jump to disaster. *The New York Review of Books* LVI (18), 56–58.

Flichy, Patrice (2007). *The internet imaginaire.* [Translated by Liz Carey-Libbrecht.] Cambridge, MA: The MIT Press.

Foderaro, Lisa W. (2010, April 19). Alternate path for teachers gains ground. *The New York Times* CLIX (55,015), A1, A19.

Fox-Genovese, Elizabeth (1988). *Within the plantation household: Black and white women of the old South.* Chapel Hill: University of North Carolina Press.

Fram, Lan and Tompson, Trevor (2010, October 8). Poll: Technology connects, stresses college students. *The Bellingham Herald,* A4.

Frankfurt, Harry G. (2005). *On bullshit.* Princeton, NJ: Princeton University Press.

Freire, Paulo (1968). *Pedagogy of the oppressed.* New York: Seabury.

Friedrich, Otto (1995 [1972]). *Before the deluge: A portrait of Berlin in the 1920s.* New York: HarperPerennial.

Furchgott, Roy (2010, September 15). A professor's review of online cheat sheets. *The New York Times* online: www.nytimes.com/2010/09/16/technology/personaltech/16basics.html Accessed on March 7, 2011.

Gabriel, Trip (2010, June 11). Pressed to show progress, educators tamper with test scores. *The New York Times* CLIX (55,068), A1, A10.

Gabriel, Trip (2010, August 2). For students in internet age, no shame in copy and paste. *The New York Times* CLIX (55,120), A1, A10.

Gabriel, Trip (2010, September 2). A celebratory road trip for education secretary. *The New York Times* CLIX (55,151), A18.

Gadamer, H.-G. (1993 [1960]). *Truth and method.* [Translated by C. J. Weinsheimer and D. G. Marshall.] New York: Continuum.

Gardner, Howard (1983). *Frames of mind: The theory of multiple intelligences.* New York: Basic Books.

Gates, Jr., Henry Louis (1996). *Colored people: A memoir.* New York: Alfred A. Knopf.

Gay, Peter (1978). *Freud, Jews, and other Germans: Masters and victims in modernist culture.* Oxford: Oxford University Press.

Gay, Peter (2001 [1968]). *Weimar culture: The outsider as insider.* New York: Norton.

Gerassi, John (1966). *The boys of Boise: Furor, vice, and folly in an American city.* New York: Macmillan.

Gillerman, Sharon (2009). *Germans into Jews: Remaking the Jewish social body in the Weimar Republic.* Stanford, CA: Stanford University Press.

Gilmore, David D. (1990). *Manhood in the making.* New Haven, CT: Yale University Press.

Gilmore, David D. (2001). *Misogyny: The male malady.* Philadelphia: University of Pennsylvania Press.

Gootman, Elissa (2009, June 4). Next test: Value of $125,000-a-year teachers. *The New York Times* online: www.nytimes.com/2009/06/05/education/05charter.html?emc=eta1 Accessed on February 28, 2011.

Gootman, Elissa and Gebeloff, Robert (2009, August 3). Gains on tests in New York schools don't silence critics. *The New York Times* online: www.nytimes.com/2009/08/04/nyregion/04scores.html Accessed on February 28, 2011.

Gordon, Lewis R. (1995). *Bad faith and antiblack racism.* Atlantic Highlands, NJ: Humanities Press.

Gough, Annette (1998). Beyond Eurocentrism in science education: Promises and problematics from a feminist poststructuralist perspective. In William F. Pinar (Ed.), *Curriculum: Toward new identities* (185–209). New York: Garl.

Grady, Denise (2010, November 25). Hospitals make no headway in curbing errors, study says. *The New York Times* CLIX (55,235), A1, A26.

Graff, Gerald (1992). *Beyond the culture wars: How teaching the conflicts can revitalize American education.* New York: Norton.

Grant, George P. (1966). Introduction to *Philosophy in the Mass Age* (iii–ix). Toronto: Copp Clark Publishing.

Grant, George (2005 [1965]). *Lament for a nation.* [40th anniversary edition.] Montreal and Kingston: McGill-Queen's University Press.

Green, Bill and Reid, Jo-Anne (2008). Method(s) in our madness: Poststructuralism, pedagogy and teacher education. In Anne Phelan and Jennifer Sumsion (Eds). *Critical readings in teacher education* (17–31). Rotterdam: Sense.

Greene, Maxine (1973). *Teacher as stranger.* Belmont, CA: Wadsworth.

Greene, Maxine (1995). *Releasing the imagination.* San Francisco: Jossey-Bass.

Greene, Maxine (2001). *Variations on a blue guitar: The Lincoln Center Institute Lectures on aesthetic education.* New York: Teachers College Press.

Greene, Naomi (1990). *Pier Paolo Pasolini: Cinema as heresy.* Princeton, NJ: Princeton University Press.

Greenhouse, Steven and Dillon, Sam (2010, March 6). School's shake-up is embraced by the President. *The New York Times* online: www.nytimes.com/2010/03/07/education/07educ.html Accessed on February 28, 2011.

Grice, H. (1975). Logic and conversation. In P. Cole and J. L. Morgan (Eds.), *Syntax and semantics* (41–58). [Vol. 3.] New York: Seminar Press.

Griswold, Robert L. (1998). The "flabby American," the body, and the cold war. In Laura McCall and Donald Yacovone (Eds.), *A shared experience: Men, women, and the history of gender* (323–348). New York: New York University Press.

Grumet, Madeleine R. (1978). Songs and situations. In George Willis (Ed.), *Qualitative evaluation* (274–315), Berkeley, CA: McCutchan.

Grumet, Madeleine R. (1988). *Bitter milk: Women and teaching.* Amherst: University of Massachusetts Press.

Hacker, Andrew (2009, April 30). Can we make America smarter? *The New York Review of Books* LVI (7), 37–40.

Hall, Sara F. (2009). Inflation and devaluation: Gender, space, and economics in G. W. Pabst's *The Joyless Street* (1925). In Noah Isenberg (Ed.), *Weimar cinema* (135–154). New York: Columbia University Press.

Halpern, Sue (2010, June 10). The iPad revolution. *The New York Review of Books* LVII (10), 22–26.

Hannaford, Ivan (1996). *Race: The history of an idea in the west.* [Foreword by Bernard Crick.] Baltimore, MD: The Johns Hopkins University Press.

Hardt, Michael and Negri, Antonio (2000). *Empire.* Cambridge, MA: Harvard University Press.

Harper, Phillip Brian (1996). *Are we not men? Masculine anxiety and the problem of African-American identity.* New York: Oxford University Press.

Harris, Scott Duke (2010, August 2). Survey measures depth of Web "time suck." *The Bellingham Herald,* A1.

Hartocollis, Anemona (2010, September 3). In medical school, seeing patients on day 1 to put a face on disease. *The New York Times* CLIX (55,152), A15–A16.

Hasebe-Ludt, Erika and Hurren, Wanda (Eds.) (2003). *Curriculum intertext: Place, language, pedagogy.* New York: Peter Lang.

Hastings, Max (2009, August 13). A very chilly victory. *The New York Review of Books* LVI (13), 53–56.

Haynes, Carolyn, A. (1998). *Divine destiny: Gender and race in nineteenth-century Protestantism.* Jackson: University Press of Mississippi.

Haynes, Stephen R. (2002). *Noah's curse: The biblical justification of American slavery.* New York: Oxford University Press.

Herf, Jeffrey (1984). *Reactionary modernism: Technology, culture, and politics in Weimar and the Third Reich.* Cambridge: Cambridge University Press.

Hernandez, Javier C. (2008, September 25). New effort aims to test theories of education. *The New York Times* online: www.nytimes.com/2008/09/25/education/25educ.html?fta=y Accessed on February 28, 2011.

Herzog, Todd (2009). Fitz Lang's M (1931). In Noah Isenberg (Ed.), *Weimar cinema* (291–309). New York: Columbia University Press.

Hetherington, Marc J. and Weiler, Jonathan D. (2009). *Authoritarianism and polarization in American politics.* Cambridge: Cambridge University Press.

Higginbotham, Evelyn Brooks (1996). African-American women's history and the metalanguage of race. In Ruth-Ellen B. Joeres and Barbara Laslett (Eds.), *The second signs reader* (3–26). Chicago: University of Chicago Press.

Hirsch, Jr., E. D. (2010, May 13). How to save the schools. *The New York Review of Books* LVII (8), 16–19.

Hoffman, Jan (2010, June 28). Online bullies pull schools into the fray: Principals struggle with policing off-campus meanness. *The New York Times* CLIX (55,085), A1, A12–A13.

Hofstadter, Richard (1962). *Anti-intellectualism in American life.* New York: Vintage.

Hofstadter, Richard (1996 [1965]). *The paranoid style in American politics and other essays.* Cambridge, MA: Harvard University Press.

Howard, John (1999). *Men like that: A southern queer history.* Chicago: University of Chicago Press.

Howe, Kenneth R. (2009). Positivist dogmas, rhetoric, and the education science question. *Educational Researcher* 38 (6), 428–440.

Huebner, Dwayne E. (1999). *The lure of the transcendent.* Mahwah, NJ: Lawrence Erlbaum.

Isenberg, Noah (2009). Introduction to *Weimar Cinema* (1–12). New York: Columbia University Press.

Izenberg, Gerald N. (2000). *Modernism and masculinity: Mann, Wedekind, Kandinsky through World War I*. Chicago: University of Chicago Press.

Jay, Martin (1993a). *Force fields: Between intellectual history and cultural critique*. New York: Routledge.

Jay, Martin (1993b). *Downcast eyes: The denigration of vision in twentieth-century French thought*. Berkeley: University of California Press.

Jay, Martin (2005). *Songs of experience: Modern American and European variations on a universal theme*. Berkeley: University of California Press.

Johnson, Dale D., Johnson, Bonnie, Farenga, Stephen J., and Ness, Daniel (2005). *Trivializing teacher education: The accreditation squeeze*. Lanham, MD: Rowman & Littlefield.

Johnson, David W. and Johnson, Roger T. (2009). An educational psychology success story: Social interdependence theory and cooperative learning. *Educational Researcher* 38 (5), 365–379.

Jonsson, Stefan (2000). *Subject without nation: Robert Musil and the history of modern identity*. Durham, NC: Duke University Press.

Judt, Tony (2010, March 25). Crossings. *The New York Review of Books* LVII (5), 14–15.

Judt, Tony (2010, April 29). Ill fares the land. *The New York Review of Books* LVII (7), 17–19.

Judt, Tony (2010, May 13). On being austere and being Jewish. *The New York Review of Books* LVII (8), 20–22.

Kaes, Anton (2009). *Metropolis* (1927): City, cinema, modernity. In Noah Isenberg (Ed.), *Weimar cinema* (173–191). New York: Columbia University Press.

Kaes, Anton, Jay, Martin, and Dimendberg, Edward (Eds.) (1995). *The Weimar sourcebook*. Berkeley: University of California Press.

Kennedy, Liam (1995). *Susan Sontag: Mind as passion*. Manchester and New York: Manchester University Press.

Kimmel, Michael S. (1990). Baseball and the reconstitution of American masculinity, 1880–1920. In Michael A. Messner and Don Sabo (Eds.), *Sport, men, and the gender order* (55–65). Champaign, IL: Human Kinetics.

Kimmel, Michael S. (1994). Consuming manhood: The feminization of American culture and the recreation of the male body, 1832–1920. In Laurence Goldstein (Ed.), *The male body* (12–41). Ann Arbor: University of Michigan Press.

Kimmel, Michael S. (1996). *Manhood in America: A cultural history*. New York: Free Press.

Kirsch, Adam (2008, October 23). The torch of Karl Kraus. *The New York Review of Books* LV (16), 64–66.

Kirsch, Adam (2010, June 10). Can we judge General von Hammerstein? *The New York Review of Books* LVII (10), 52–55.

Kliebard, Herbert M. (1970). Persistent issues in historical perspective. *Educational Comment*, 31–41.

Kliebard, Herbert, M. (1986). *The struggle for the American curriculum 1893–1958*. Boston: Routledge.

Knight, Louise W. (2005). *Citizen: Jane Addams and the struggle for democracy*. Chicago: University of Chicago Press.

Kracauer, Siegfried (1995). *The mass ornament: Weimar essays.* [Translated, edited, and with an introduction by Thomas Y. Levin.] Cambridge, MA: Harvard University Press.

Kristof, Nicholas D. (2010, November 18). A hedge fund republic? *The New York Times* CLIX (55,228), A31.

Kroker, Arthur (1984). *Technology and the Canadian mind: Innis/McLuhan/ Grant.* Montreal: New World Perspectives.

Kuhn, Thomas (1962). *The structure of scientific revolutions.* Chicago: University of Chicago Press.

LaCapra, Dominick (2004). *History in transit: Experience, identity, critical theory.* Ithaca, NY: Cornell University Press.

LaCapra, Dominick (2009). *History and its limits: Human, animal, violence.* Ithaca, NY: Cornell University Press.

Lasch, Christopher (1978). *The culture of narcissism: American life in an age of diminishing expectations.* New York: Norton.

Lasch, Christopher (1984). *The minimal self: Psychic survival in troubled times.* New York: Norton.

Lasch, Christopher (1995). *The revolt of the elites and the betrayal of democracy.* New York: Norton.

Lather, Patti (2007). *Getting lost: Feminist efforts toward a double(d) science.* Albany: State University of New York Press.

Lazarus, Neil (1999). Disavowing decolonization: Fanon, nationalism, and the question of representation in postcolonial theory. In Anthony C. Alessandrini (Ed.), *Frantz Fanon: Critical perspectives* (161–194). London: Routledge.

Ledbetter, Mark (1996). *Victims and the postmodern narrative or doing violence to the body: An ethic of reading and writing.* New York: St. Martin's Press.

Leiner, Marvin (1994). *Sexual politics in Cuba: Machismo, homosexuality, and AIDS.* Boulder, CO: Westview Press.

Lemert, Charles and Bhan, Esure (Eds.) (1998). *The voice of Anna Julia Cooper.* Lanham, MD: Rowman & Littlefield.

Lesko, Nancy (2000). Preparing to coach: Tracking the gendered relations of dominance on and off the football field. In Nancy Lesko (Ed.), *Masculinities at school* (187–212). Thousand Oaks, CA: Sage.

Lesko, Nancy (2001). *Act your age! A cultural construction of adolescence.* New York: Routledge/Falmer.

Levin, David Michael (Ed.) (1993). *Modernity and the hegemony of vision.* Berkeley: University of California Press.

Levin, Thomas Y. (1995). Introduction to Siegfried Kracauer's *The mass ornament: Weimar essays* (1–30). Cambridge, MA: Harvard University Press.

Lévy, Pierre (2001). *Cyberculture.* [Translated by Robert Bononno.] Minneapolis: University of Minnesota Press.

Lewin, Tamar (2009, August 8). In a digital future, textbooks are history. *The New York Times* online: www.nytimes.com/2009/08/09/education/09textbook. html Accessed on February 28, 2011

Lewin, Tamar (2010, July 21). States embrace core standards for the schools. Unusually fast action. U.S. offers yearly goals, and a deadline for a share of $3 billion. *The New York Times* CLIX (55,108), A1, A3.

Lilla, Mark (2010, May 27). The Tea Party Jacobins. *The New York Review of Books* LVII (9), 53–56.

Ling, Rich (2008). *New tech, new ties: How mobile communication is reshaping social cohesion.* Cambridge, MA: The MIT Press.

Lomotey, Kofi and Rivers, Shariba (1998). Models of excellence: Independent African-centered schools. In William F. Pinar (Ed.), *Curriculum: Toward new identities* (343–353). New York: Garland.

Lorde, Audre (1982). *Afterimages.* In *Chosen poems old and new.* New York: Norton & Co.

Lovett, Ian (2010, November 10). Teacher's death exposes tensions in Los Angeles. *The New York Times* CLIX (55,220), A21.

Luft, David S. (2003). *Eros and inwardness in Vienna: Weininger, Musil, Doderer.* Chicago: University of Chicago Press.

Luo, Michael (2010, September 1). In recession, new jobs often mean lower wages. *The New York Times* CLIX (55,150), A12.

Lyotard, Jean-Francois (1993). *The postmodern explained.* [Afterword by Wlad Godzich.] Minneapolis: University of Minnesota Press.

Macdonald, James B. (1995). *Theory as a prayerful act: Collected essays.* [Edited by Bradley Macdonald; introduced by William F. Pinar.] New York: Peter Lang.

Mailer, Norman (1957). *The white negro.* San Francisco: City Lights.

Malewski, Erik (Ed.) (2009). *Curriculum studies handbook: The next moment.* New York: Routledge.

Mantel, Hilary (2009, October 22). Dreams and duels of England. *The New York Review of Books* LVI (16), 8–12.

Massing, Michael (2009, August 13). The news about the Internet. *The New York Review of Books* LVI (13), 29–32.

McBride, Patrizia C. (2006). *The void of ethics: Robert Musil and the experience of modernity.* Evanston, IL: Northwestern University Press.

McCarthy, Margaret (2009). Surface sheen and charged bodies: Louise Brooks as Lulu in *Pandora's Box* (1929). In Noah Isenberg (Ed.), *Weimar cinema* (217–236). New York: Columbia University Press.

McCormick, Richard W. (2009). Coming out of the uniform: Political and sexual emancipation in Leontine Sagan's *Mädchen in Uniform* (1931). In Noah Isenberg (Ed.), *Weimar cinema* (271–289). New York: Columbia University Press.

McKibben, Bill (2010, November 11). All programs considered. *The New York Review of Books* LVII (17), 44–46.

McKinley, Jr., James C. (2010, March 10). Texas conservatives seek deeper stamp on texts. *The New York Times* online: www.nytimes.com/2010/03/11/us/politics/11texas.html Accessed on February 28, 2011.

McKinley, Jesse (2010, October 4). Several recent suicides put light on pressures facing gay teenagers. *The New York Times* CLIX (55,183), A9.

McNeil, Linda M. (2000). *Contradictions of school reform: Educational costs of standardized testing.* New York: Routledge.

Medina, Jennifer (2010, July 29). Students' passing rates plummet in New York. *The New York Times* CLIX (55,116), A21.

Medina, Jennifer (2010, October 11). Warning signs long ignored on New York's school tests. *The New York Times* CLIX (55,190), A1, A18–A19.

Mendelsohn, Daniel (2010, March 25). The wizard. *The New York Review of Books* LVII (5), 10–13.

Merleau-Ponty, Maurice (1966). *Phenomenology of perception*. London: Routledge and Kegan Paul.

Messner, Michael A. (1992). *Power at play: Sports and problem of masculinity*. Boston: Beacon Press.

Miller, James E. (1993). *The passion of Michel Foucault*. New York: Simon & Schuster.

Miller, Janet L. (1990). *Creating spaces and finding voices: Teachers collaborating for empowerment*. Albany: State University of New York Press.

Miller, Janet L. (2005). *The sound of silence breaking and other essays: Working the tension in curriculum theory*. New York: Peter Lang.

Mitchell, W. J. T. (1994). *Picture theory: Essays on verbal and visual representation*. Chicago: University of Chicago Press.

Molnar, Alex (2002). The commercialization of America's schools. In William E. Doll, Jr. and Noel Gough (Eds.), *Curriculum visions* (203–212). New York: Peter Lang.

Moore, Mary Elizabeth Mullino (2002). Curriculum: A journey through complexity, community, conversation, culmination. In William E. Doll, Jr. and Noel Gough (Eds.), *Curriculum visions* (219–227). New York: Peter Lang.

Morgenson, Gretchen (2010, September 27). Raters ignored proof of unsafe loans in securities, panel is told. *The New York Times* CLIX (55,176), B1, B2.

Moriarty, Michael (1991). *Roland Barthes*. Stanford, CA: Stanford University Press.

Morris, Marla (2001). *Holocaust and curriculum*. Mahwah, NJ: Lawrence Erlbaum.

Morris, Marla (2002). Curriculum theory as academic responsibility: The call for reading Heidegger contextually. In Marla Morris and John A. Weaver (Eds.), *Difficult memories* (227–247). New York: Peter Lang.

Moses, Daniel Noah (1999, Spring). Distinguishing a university from a shopping mall. *The NEA Higher Education Journal* 15 (1), 85–96.

Mosès, Stéphane (2009 [1992]). *The angel of history: Rosenzweig, Benjamin, Scholem*. [Translated by Barbara Harshav.] Stanford, CA: Stanford University Press.

Mosse, George L. (1985). *Nationalism and sexuality: Respectability and abnormal sexuality in modern Europe*. New York: Howard Fertig.

Moynihan, Daniel P. (1965). *The Negro family: The case for national action*. Office of Policy, Planning and Research, Department of Labor. Washington, DC: Government Printing Office.

Munoz, José Esteban (1996). Famous and dandy like B. 'n' Andy: Race, pop, and Basquiat. In Jennifer Doyle, Jonathan Flatley, and José Esteban Munoz (Eds.), *Pop out: Queer Warhol* (144–179). Durham, NC: Duke University Press.

Musil, Robert (1955 [1905]). *Young Torless*. [Preface by Alan Pryce-Jones.] New York: Pantheon Books.

Musil, Robert (1990). *Precision and soul: Essays and addresses.* [Edited and translated by Burton Pike and David S. Luft.] Chicago and London: University of Chicago Press.

Musil, Robert (1995 [1979]). *The man without qualities.* [Translated by Sophie Perkins and Burton Pike.] New York: Knopf. [The 1979 edition quoted in the introduction was published in London by Secker and Warburg. Foreword by Elithne Wilkins. Translated by Ernst Kaiser.]

National Commission on Excellence in Education (1983). *A nation at risk: The imperative for educational reform.* Washington, DC: United States Department of Education.

Newman, Andy (2009, June 27). As cultures clash, Brooklyn principal faces assault charges. *The New York Times* online: www.nytimes.com/2009/06/27/nyregion/27principal.html Accessed on February 28, 2011.

Nietzsche, Friedrich (1983a). On the uses and disadvantages of history for life (Essay 2, foreword). In *Untimely meditations* (translated by R. J. Hollingdale). New York and London: Cambridge University Press.

Nietzsche, Friedrich (1983b). Schopenhauer as education (Essay 3, sections 7 and 8). In *Untimely meditations* (trans. R. J. Hollingdale). New York and London: Cambridge University Press.

Nussbaum, Martha C. (2010). *Not for profit: Why democracy* needs *the humanities.* Princeton, NJ: Princeton University Press.

Oakeshott, Michael (1959). *The voice of poetry in the conversation of mankind.* London: Bowes & Bowes.

O'Shaughnessy, Lynn (2009, July 20). The other side of "test optional." *The New York Times* online: www.nytimes.com/2009/07/26/education/edlife/26guidance-t.html Accessed on February 28, 2011.

Otterman, Sharon (2010, October 13). Despite money and attention, it's not all A's at 2 Harlem schools. *The New York Times* CLIX (55,192), A18–A19.

Otterman, Sharon (2010, November 10). Schools leader in New York City ends 8-year run. *The New York Times* CLIX (55,220), A1, A28.

Pasolini, Pier Paolo (2005 [1972]). *Heretical empiricism.* [Translated by Ben Lawton and Louise K. Barnett.] Washington, DC: New Academic Publishing, LLC. [First published in 1972 by Aldo Garzanti Editore; first English edition in 1988 by Indiana University Press.]

Patton, Paul (2000). *Deleuze and the political.* London: Routledge.

Peters, Jeremy W. (2010, September 6). Some newsrooms shift coverage based on what is popular online. *The New York Times* CLIX (55,155), B1.

Peukert, Detlev J. K. (1992). *The Weimar Republic: The crisis of classical modernity.* [Translated by Richard Deveson.] New York: Hill and Wang.

Phelan, Anne and Sumsion, Jennifer (Eds.) (2008). *Critical readings in teacher education.* Rotterdam: Sense.

Pinar, William F. (2004). *What is curriculum theory?* [First edition.] Mahwah, NJ: Lawrence Erlbaum.

Pine, Richard (1995). *The thief of reason: Oscar Wilde and modern Ireland.* New York: St. Martin's Press.

Pinker, Steven (2010, June 11). Mind over mass media. *The New York Times* CLIX (55,068), A27.

Polanyi, Michael (1958). *Personal knowledge.* London: Routledge and Kegan Paul.

Pope, Denise Clark (2001). *Doing school: How we are creating a generation of stressed out, materialistic, and miseducated students.* New Haven, CT: Yale University Press.

Pope, Tara Parker (2010, June 7). An ugly toll of technology: Impatience and forgetfulness. *The New York Times* CLIX (55,064), A13.

Posnock, Ross (1998). *Color and culture: Black writers and the making of the modern intellectual.* Cambridge, MA: Harvard University Press.

Pronger, Brian (1990). *The arena of masculinity: Sports, homosexuality and the meaning of sex.* New York: St. Martin's Press.

Rauch, Angelika (2000). *The hieroglyph of tradition: Freud, Benjamin, Gadamer, Novalis, Kant.* Madison, NJ: Fairleigh Dickinson University Press.

Ravitch, Diane (2000). *Left back: A century of battles over school reform.* New York: Simon and Schuster.

Ravitch, Diane (2010). *The death and life of the great American school system: How testing and choice are undermining education.* New York: Basic Books.

Ravitch, Diane (2010, November 11). The myth of charter schools. *The New York Review of Books* LVII (17), 22–24.

Raywid, Mary Anne and Schmerler, Gill (2003). *Not so easy going: The policy environments of small urban schools and schools-within-schools.* Charleston, WV: ERIC.

Reich, Robert B. (2010, September 3). How to end the Great Recession. *The New York Times* CLIX (55,152), A19.

Rhodes, Frank H. T. (2001, September 14). A battle plan for professors to recapture the curriculum. *Chronicle of Higher Education,* B7–B10.

Rhodes, John David (2007). *Stupendous miserable city: Pasolini's Rome.* Minneapolis: University of Minnesota Press.

Richtel, Matt (2010, August 16). Outdoors and out of reach, studying the brain. *The New York Times* CLIX (55,134), A1, A10.

Richtel, Matt (2010, August 25). No time for downtime: At work or play, plugged in to fill every little moment. *The New York Times* CLIX (55,143), B1, B7.

Rickover, H. (1959). *Education and freedom.* New York: E. Dutton.

Rickover, H. (1963). *American education—A national failure: The problem of our schools and what we can learn from England.* New York: E. Dutton.

Ripley, Amanda (2010, January/February). What makes a great teacher? *Harper's Magazine,* 58–66.

Roberts, David D. (1995). *Nothing but history: Reconstruction and extremity after metaphysics.* Berkeley and Los Angeles: University of California Press.

Rogowski, Christian (2009). Movies, money, and mystique: Joe May's early Weimar blockbuster, *The Indian Tomb* (1921). In Noah Isenberg (Ed.), *Weimar cinema* (55–77). New York: Columbia University Press.

Ronell, Avital (1992a). *Crack wars.* Lincoln: University of Nebraska Press.

Ronell, Avital (1992b). Video/television/Rodney King: Twelve steps beyond the pleasure principle. *Differences* 4 (2), 1–15.

Ronell, Avital (2003). *Stupidity*. Urbana and Chicago: University of Illinois Press.

Root, E. Merrill (1958). *Brainwashing in the high schools: An examination of American history textbooks*. New York: Devin-Adair.

Rorty, Richard (1991). *Essays on Heidegger and others. Philosophical papers. Volume 2*. Cambridge and New York: Cambridge University Press.

Rosen, Jeffrey (2000). *The unwanted gaze: The destruction of privacy in America*. New York: Random House.

Rothstein, Richard, Jacobsen, Rebecca, and Wilder, Tamara (2008). *Grading education: Getting accountability right*. Washington, DC: Economic Policy Institute and New York: Teachers College Press.

Rugg, Harold (1963). *Imagination*. New York: Harper & Row.

Rumble, Patrick (1996). *Allegories of contamination: Pier Paolo Pasolini's* Trilogy of Life. Toronto: University of Toronto Press.

Sandlin, Jennifer A., Schultz, Brian D., and Burdick, Jake (Eds.) (2010). *Handbook of public pedagogy: Education and learning beyond schooling*. New York: Routledge.

Sang-Hun, Choe (2010, May 29). As Internet swallows adults, South Korea expands addiction aid. *The New York Times* CLIX (55,055), A4.

Santner, Eric L. (2006). *On creaturely life: Rilke, Benjamin, Sebald*. Chicago: University of Chicago Press.

Sartre, Jean-Paul (1981). *The family idiot: Gustave Flaubert 1821–1857*. [Translated by Carol Cosman.] Chicago and London: University of Chicago Press.

Sarup, Madan (1992). *Jacques Lacan*. Toronto: University of Toronto Press.

Savran, David (1998). *Taking it a like a man: White masculinity, masochism, and contemporary American culture*. Princeton, NJ: Princeton University Press.

Schrag, Peter (2007, September). Schoolhouse crock: Fifty years of blaming America's educational system for our stupidity. *Harper's Magazine*, 36–44.

Schwab, Joseph (1978). *Science, curriculum and liberal education: Selected essays, Joseph J. Schwab*. [Edited by I. Westbury and N. Wilkof.] Chicago: University of Chicago Press.

Seigfried, Charlene Haddock (1996). *Pragmatism and feminism*. Chicago: University of Chicago Press.

Seixas, Peter (Ed.) (2004). *Theorizing historical consciousness*. Toronto: University of Toronto Press.

Sekyi-Otu, Ato (1996). *Fanon's dialectic of experience*. Cambridge, MA: Harvard University Press.

Shapin, Steven (2010). *Never pure: Historical studies of science as if it was produced by people with bodies, situated in time, space, culture, and society, struggling for credibility and authority*. Baltimore, MD: The Johns Hopkins University Press.

Shipps, Dorothy (2000). Echoes of corporate influence: Managing away urban school troubles. In Larry Cuban and Dorothy Shipps (Eds.), *Reconstructing the common good in education: Coping with intractable dilemmas* (82–105). Stanford, CA: Stanford University Press.

Shirley, Dennis (1992). *The politics of progressive education: The Odenwaldschule in Nazi Germany*. Cambridge, MA: Harvard University Press.

Silberman, Charles (1970). *Crisis in the classroom: The remaking of American education*. New York: Random House.

Silverman, Kaja (1992). *Male subjectivity at the margins*. New York and London: Routledge.

Silverman, Kaja (2000). *World spectators*. Stanford, CA: Stanford University Press.

Silverman, Kaja (2009). *Flesh of my flesh*. Stanford, CA: Stanford University Press.

Simpson, David (2002). *Situatedness, or, why we keep saying where we're coming from*. Durham, NC: Duke University Press.

Simpson, Mark (1994). *Male impersonators: Men performing masculinity*. [Foreword by Alan Sinfield.] New York: Routledge.

Sizer, Ted (1984). *Horace's compromise: The dilemma of the American high school*. Boston, MA: Houghton Mifflin.

Slavin, Robert E. (2008). What works? Issues in synthesizing education program evaluations. *Educational Researcher* 37 (1), 5–14.

Soros, George (2010, August 19). The Euro and the crisis. *The New York Review of Books* LVII (13), 28–30.

Spivak, Gayatri Chakravorty (2003). *Death of a discipline*. New York: Columbia University Press.

Spring, Joel (1976). *The sorting machine*. New York: David McKay.

Spring, Joel (2007). *A new paradigm for global school systems: Education for a long and happy life*. Mahwah, NJ: Lawrence Erlbaum.

Steiner, George (1998). Introduction to Walter Benjamin's *The origin of German tragic opera* (7–24). London: Verso.

Strike, Kenneth A. (2008). Confessions of a sublimated cleric. In Leonard J. Waks (Ed.) *Leaders in philosophy of education: Intellectual self-portraits* (241–249). [With a Foreword by Israel Scheffler.] Rotterdam and Tapei: Sense Publishers.

Taubman, Peter M. (2009). *Teaching by numbers: Deconstructing the discourse of standards and accountability in education*. New York: Routledge.

Taubman, Peter M. (in press). *Disavowed knowledge: Psychoanalysis, education, and teaching*. Albany: State University of New York Press.

Taylor, Mark C. (1980). *Journeys to selfhood: Hegel and Kierkegaard*. Berkeley: University of California Press.

Tomkins, George S. (2008 [1986]). *A common countenance: Stability and change in the Canadian curriculum*. Vancouver: Pacific Educational Press.

Torres, Sasha (1996). The caped crusader of camp: Pop, camp, and the *Batman* television series. In Jennifer Doyle, Jonathan Flatley, and José Esteban Munoz (Eds.), *Pop out: Queer Warhol* (238–255). Durham, NC: Duke University Press.

Townsend, Kim (1996). *Manhood at Harvard: William James and others*. New York: Norton.

Trelease, Allen W. (1971). *White terror: The Ku Klux Klan conspiracy and the southern reconstruction*. Baton Rouge: Louisiana State University Press.

Tröhler, Daniel (2003). The discourse of German *Geisteswissenschaftliche Padagogik*—A contextual reconstruction. *Paedagogica Historica* 39 (6), 759–778.

Tröhler, Daniel (2006). The "Kingdom of God on Earth" and early Chicago pragmatism. *Educational Theory* 56 (1), 89–105.

Tyack, David and Hansot, Elizabeth (1990). *Learning together: A history of coeducation in American schools.* New Haven, CT: Yale University Press.

Tyler, Ralph (1949). *Basic principles of curriculum and instruction.* Chicago: University of Chicago Press.

Urbina, Ian (2009, August 7). Beyond beltway, health debate turns hostile. *The New York Times* online: www.nytimes.com/2009/08/08/us/politics/08townhall.html Accessed on February 28, 2011.

Urbina, Ian (2010, September 15). Washington mayor's loss may imperil school reform. *The New York Times* online: www.nytimes.com/2010/09/16/us/16fenty.html?_r=1&ref=ianurbina Accessed on March 7, 2011.

Vega, Tanzina (2010, October 11). Web code offers new ways to see what users do online. *The New York Times* CLIX (55,190), A1, A3.

Viano, Maurizio (1993). *A certain realism: Making use of Pasolini's film theory and practice.* Berkeley: University of California Press.

Wallace, Michele (1978/1979). *Black macho and the myth of the superwoman.* New York: The Dial Press. [Published in London in 1979 by John Calder.]

Wang, Hongyu (2004). *The call from the stranger on a journey home: Curriculum in a third space.* New York: Peter Lang.

Wapner, Paul (2010). *Living through the end of nature: The future of American environmentalism.* Cambridge, MA: The MIT Press.

Ware, Vron (1992). *Beyond the pale: White women, racism and history.* London: Verso.

Watson, Alexander John (2007). *Marginal man: The dark vision of Harold Innis.* Toronto: University of Toronto Press.

Weaver, John A., Appelbaum, Peter M., and Morris, Marla (Eds.) (2001). *(Post) modern science (education): Propositions and alternative paths.* New York: Peter Lang.

Webber, Julie A. (2003). *Failure to hold: Politics, proto-citizenship and school violence.* Lanham, MD: Rowman & Littlefield.

Weitz, Eric D. (2007). *Weimar Germany: Promise and tragedy.* Princeton, NJ: Princeton University Press.

Wertham, Fredric (1953/1954). *Seduction of the innocent.* New York: Rinehart and Co.

Westbrook, Robert (1991). *John Dewey and American philosophy.* Ithaca, NY: Cornell University Press.

Williamson, Joel (1984). *The crucible of race: Black-white relations in the American South since emancipation.* New York: Oxford University Press.

Willinsky, John (2006). *The access principle.* Cambridge, MA: MIT Press.

Wraga, William (2002, August–September). Recovering curriculum practice: Continuing the conversation. *Educational Researcher* (31) 6, 17–19.

Young-Bruehl, Elisabeth (1996). *The anatomy of prejudices.* Cambridge, MA: Harvard University Press.

Zaretsky, Eli (2004). *Secrets of the soul: A social and cultural history of psychoanalysis.* New York: Alfred A. Knopf.

Zeleny, Jeff (2009, March 10). Obama calls for overhaul of education system. *The New York Times* online: http://thecaucus.blogs.nytimes.com/2009/03/10/obama-calls-for-overhaul-of-education-system/ Accessed on February 28, 2009.

Ziarek, Ewa Plonowska (2001). *An ethics of dissensus: Postmodernity, feminism, and the politics of radical democracy*. Stanford, CA: Stanford University Press.

Zimmerman, Jonathan (2002). *Whose America? Culture wars in the public schools*. Cambridge, MA: Harvard University Press.

Zimmerman, Jonathan (2010, October 14). What are schools for? *The New York Review of Books* LVII (15), 29–31.

Zinn, Howard (1965, November 23). Schools in context: The Mississippi idea. *The Nation*, 10.

Index